Creating Paint Shop Pro
Web Graphics

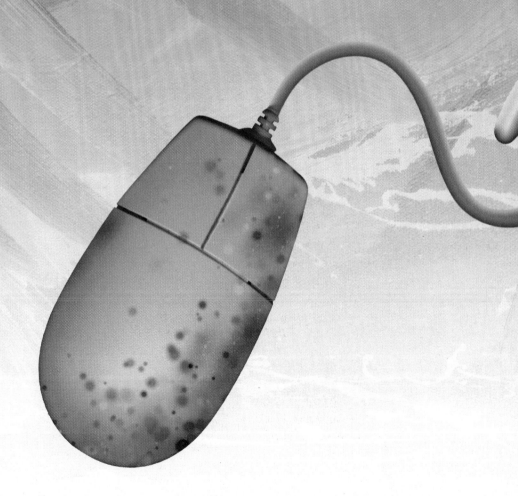

Written by

Andy Shafran

with

Brad Castle
Lori Davis
Pat Kalbaugh
Robin Kirkey
Dick Oliver

Creating Paint Shop Pro Web Graphics Second Edition

Library of Congress Catalog Card Number: 98-65980

ISBN: 0-9662889-0

5   4   3   2   1

Educational facilities, companies, and organizations interested in multiple copies of this book should contact the publisher for quantity discount information. Training manuals, CD-ROMs, electronic versions, and portions of this book are also available individually or can be tailored for specific needs.

MUSKA LIPMAN

Muska & Lipman Publishing
9525 Kenwood Road, Suite 16-372
Cincinnati, Ohio 45242
www.muskalipman.com
publisher@muskalipman.com

This book composed in Melior, Columbia, Helvetica, and Courier typefaces using QuarkXpress 4.0.
Printed in Cincinnati, Ohio in the United States of America

Credits

Publishing Manager
Andy Shafran

Operations Manager
Elizabeth Shafran

Editor
Ruth Younger

Technical Editors
Jasc Software Inc.

Book Designers
Dave Abney &
Cathie Tibbetts

Cover Designer
Dave Abney

Project Manager
Cathie Tibbetts

Art Director
Dave Abney

Production Team
DOV Graphics
Dave Abney
Dottie Decker
Michelle Frey
Tammy Norton
Cathie Tibbetts
Linda Worthington

Contents Editor
Tammy Norton

Indexer
Dottie Decker

Printer
C.J. Krehbiel Co.

About the Authors

Andy Shafran

andy@shafran.com
http://www.shafran.com

Andy Shafran is a computer professional who has been writing books, developing Web pages, and consulting for years. With over 250,000 books in print, Andy has written or contributed to nearly 20 books on topics ranging from Paint Shop Pro to Microsoft FrontPage and HTML.

Andy lives in Cincinnati, home of the Reds and Skyline chili. An avid Reds fan, Andy can often be found at baseball games at home and when traveling.

Acknowledgements

There are *many* people I would like to thank for helping me on this project. First and foremost is my wife. Thanks, Liz, for all your help, support, and cajoling to make this project a reality.

Next I'd like to thank all the authors who contributed to this book. Your friendship and expertise helped make this the best book I have ever worked on. Thanks also to my colleagues and students at ZDU (Ziff-Davis University) who have worked tirelessly to bring Paint Shop Pro to the masses and run the best set of classes on the Internet.

The production of this book was a huge project. Thanks to Cathie Tibbetts, Dave Abney, and the rest of the crew at DOV Graphics for designing the interior and cover of this book. Thanks also to Pat Latham for patiently educating me on how printers print books and for being a great individual with whom to work. Ruth Younger was marvelous in crossing my I's and dotting my t's.

Finally, I'd like to thank the individuals at Jasc Software. Chris Anderson has helped me on this project from the very beginning. A special thanks to Eric Pogue and Todd Matzke, my technical eyes and ears. Jon Ort and Joe Fromm always answered incessant technical questions as well. They kept me close to Jasc's inner workings while making sure I accurately described all the new features in PSP 5.

Lori Davis

(Chapters 7 and 11)
http://www.geocities.com/SiliconValley/Way/3306/

An artsy sort nearly all her life, and a Net fanatic since the early 1980s, Lori Davis found that Web graphics provided a wonderful melding of two of her longtime interests. She started out with Paint Shop Pro, and even though she's since used many other graphics programs as well, Lori still finds PSP the ideal tool for creating Web graphics. You can see this at her PSP tutorial Web site, Lori's Web Graphics.

Acknowledgements

Thanks to my husband, Larry, for his good-natured tolerance of my long hours at the computer and for his helpful and amusing comments on the example projects I developed for this book. I'd also like to acknowledge two people who were very important early in my life in encouraging me to let my artistic urges run wild: my kindergarten teacher, Miss Feldman, and my high school art teacher, Sr. Jeanne LaFreniere. My thanks to them for putting up with—and even smiling on—my rambunctiousness.

Pat Kalbaugh

(Chapter 14 and Appendix B)
http://www.ptialaska.net/~pkalbaug/

A professional Web graphic artist and site designer, Pat Kalbaugh resides in Juneau, Alaska. She began exploring the World Wide Web in 1995 and was immediately fascinated with Web graphics and design. In 1996 she started her own Web design business, Sirius Web Craft (siriusweb.com). Pat is also on Andy's Paint Shop Pro teaching staff at ZDU and enjoys helping students develop their creativity and talent for Web graphics. In her free time Pat enjoys traveling, golfing, and training her dogs for obedience trial competitions.

Acknowledgements

Thanks to my husband, Karl, for his patience, understanding, and support while I worked on this project during our vacation. Also, thanks to my dogs, Beamer and Fanny, for giving up their precious lap time to my laptop.

Robin Kirkey

(Chapter 5)

http://www.charm.net/~kirkey

Robin Kirkey is a self-taught graphic artist. She's grown through the stages of ascii-art and ansi-art as the field of online art began to expand. She was sysop of her own bbs for many years before entering the realms of the Internet and Web graphics & design. Paint Shop Pro has been her primary graphics editor for many years.

Acknowledgements

Mom, this one's for you: Thanks for providing me with the educational tools and moral support throughout my life that helped me realize a dream! Derek, Andrew, and Kari, my beloved children: See, all those hours I spent "blowing up the computer" finally paid off. Thank you for your patience! David, my husband: You've provided me with love and support, the computer tools and education I wanted, and you've always believed I'd find my way. Thank you for enhancing my life. Friends: You know who you are. Thanks for your care and concern.

Brad Castle

(Chapter 16)

http://www.castleen.com

Brad Castle has been part of the Paint Shop Pro classes staff at ZDU since early 1997. He currently operates the Odds N Ends Web site that caters to users of Paint Shop Pro with tutorials and tips. Brad is also the owner of Castle Enterprises, his own consulting and Web design/hosting business. He and his wife Rebecca live in Ashland, Ohio, and have four children who constantly compete with them for computer time.

Acknowledgements

I wish to thank my wife Becky, who tolerates the time I spend on the computer, and the kids, who would prefer that I go to bed earlier so they can use my machine to play games. Thanks also to my fellow teaching assistants in the ZDU Paint Shop Pro classes who helped me find answers when I was stumped, and to the students in those classes who shared their incredible imaginations and creativity, giving us all ideas to work from in our own endeavors. Last, but most certainly not least, I wish to thank my mother-in-law, whom many know simply as Mag. She administered the push that got me back into computers after a long time away from them.

Foreword

The world is changing at a neck-breaking pace. Familiar places have evolved into cyber-locations, bars and coffee shops are being replaced by chat rooms, and resumes and Christmas letters are often augmented and sometimes completely replaced by Web sites and e-mail.

Previously words on paper were enough, but communication has quickly evolved to digital text, accompanied by pictures, sounds, and animations. As methods change and technology becomes more accessible, our messages become increasingly more powerful.

In the early years of computing, the world of digital graphics and imaging was inhabited by professionals and computer "geeks." They entranced observers with a digital universe of wonder and surprise, bound only by the fertile imaginations of the innovators and beholders. In recent years, computing power has plummeted in cost while usability has soared, making the digital imaging technology accessible to the masses.

As early pioneers in graphics software and precursors to the Web and Internet, Jasc Software continues to ride the wave of new technology, carrying users worldwide along the crest of the graphics adventure. We've raised the cyber-ceiling by developing applications that epitomize our slogan: "The Power to Create." Indeed, we bring software to computer imaging enthusiasts at a new level, empowering all levels of computer users to create great graphics. This latest version of Paint Shop Pro continues our tradition of providing feature-rich software via an easy-to-use interface that vastly expands the graphical capabilities of users.

With Paint Shop Pro 5, Jasc Software carries on the graphics revolution, placing layers, Picture Tubes, and digital cameras in your graphics arsenal. We are confident that you will enjoy the product of our latest labor of love and benefit from Paint Shop Pro 5, the culmination of over a year's intensive development.

This book is the ideal companion to Paint Shop Pro 5. Reading it will put you on an enchanted path through the magical features PSP offers. Written by some of the world's leading experts in Paint Shop Pro, this innovative guide has literally thousands of hours of professional experience and Web Graphic creation compressed within the covers.

Enjoy Paint Shop Pro 5, and enjoy this book. Together, they will prepare you to excel in the dynamic realm of computer graphics.

Chris Anderson
chrisa@jasc.com
Vice-President of Marketing, Jasc Software, Inc.

Contents in Brief

Contents

Part III Advanced Image Techniques

Part IV Practical Use of Images on Your Web Pages

Introduction

Welcome to the new and improved *Creating Paint Shop Pro Web Graphics, Second Edition!* This is the best—and only—book you'll need for creating great-looking graphics for your Web site. Using Paint Shop Pro 5, I've completely revised this book from cover to cover, bringing together all the creative techniques that let you build eye-catching graphics in little time.

Graphics are the heart and soul of the World Wide Web. Nearly every page you visit, every site you bookmark, and every hour you spend browsing focuses on Web sites built around exciting and innovative Web graphics.

This 384 page, full-color book leads you through all of the ins and outs of learning how to use the most effective graphics program out there: Paint Shop Pro. In the next sixteen chapters, you'll learn how to painlessly build images from scratch, edit and scan photos, work with digital cameras, and build cohesive sets of graphics for an entire Web site.

By reading this Introduction, you can learn many of the important assumptions and conventions that are prevalent throughout the book before you start Chapter 1. I'll explain how the book will teach everything you need to know about Paint Shop Pro 5 and Web Graphics and why it is vital to your WWW library. You will also learn what level of Web proficiency I assumed you, the reader, would have when I wrote this book. Finally, I provide a summary of each chapter for quick reference. You will discover why this is the most useful—and only—book about Web Graphics you'll ever need! Read on and enjoy *Creating Paint Shop Pro Web Graphics, Second Edition.*

What You'll Learn in This Book

This book teaches you how to effectively master Paint Shop Pro 5, one of the world's leading graphics packages. You'll learn how to use impressive tools and techniques to create great graphics for your Web sites with Paint Shop Pro. This award-winning software is all you'll need to create graphics from scratch. Every image presented, every example used, and every graphic on this book's companion Web site has been created and edited within Paint Shop Pro. I not only *explain* how to use this excellent product, but I *show* you as well.

Below, I've listed several important concepts that you will learn. Keep these concepts in mind as you read; they were the guiding principles I had in mind when writing.

▶ **Graphics can make, or break, a decent Web page.**

▶ **Paint Shop Pro 5 has all the necessary tools built in to create great Web Graphics.**

▶ **Expert-looking graphics can come from non-graphics experts who have the right knowledge of Paint Shop Pro.**

▶ **Creating Web Graphics is all about optimizing colors, shapes, and photos so they look good and download fast when placed on Web pages.**

Readable and Friendly Text

As you read this book, you'll find I don't gloss over difficult subjects nor do I assume you understand all sorts of new terminology. Instead, I give you complete explanations, step-by-step techniques, and comprehensive coverage of the features found within Paint Shop Pro.

I'm not going to waste your time by talking about obscure issues such as hue saturation, or by worrying about all 16.7 million colors with which you can paint. Instead, I'm going to provide you with a practical guide to making Web graphics. You'll find help in achieving all your image-related goals in these easy-to-understand and fun-to-read chapters. You'll enjoy seeing entertaining examples and building graphics that can complement a variety of different Web pages.

Who Is This Book For?

This book is geared toward all levels of Paint Shop Pro (PSP) and World Wide Web (WWW) users. Paint Shop Pro 4 users will find it a comprehensive guide to all the new and critical pieces of functionality, while new PSP users will see it as a guide to start with simple and progress to advanced techniques. I've specifically included topics for users of varied levels so this can be the only book you'll ever need to learn how to effectively use Paint Shop Pro.

That said, I suggest several prerequisites that would make your life much easier when you actually begin building and integrating Web graphics into your site. Below are a few assumptions I made about you and your skill level while I organized and wrote this book. Keeping these assumptions in mind, I tried to avoid boring you with pointless details so the book would be as useful as possible.

▶ **You're a Web User**—You should already be connected to the WWW at home, work, or school, and understand how to use Netscape or Internet Explorer to comfortably surf from one site to another.

▶ **You Can Build Web Pages**—This book focuses on creating and using graphics on a Web page and only glosses over some HTML techniques that specifically pertain to using graphics effectively. If you don't know anything about HTML or building simple Web pages, go to your local bookstore and grab a solid reference on the subject. I recommend *Creating Your Own Web Pages, Second Edition* or *Teach Yourself HTML 4 in 24 Hours*.

▶ **You Want to Learn**—This book has been carefully planned and laid out to be most useful and efficient for those learning Web graphics. Working with graphics can sometimes be challenging—particularly when working with advanced options and features. However, your desire to learn graphics will make understanding even the trickiest tasks a breeze.

▶ **You're Running Windows 95, 98, or NT 4, or above**—Paint Shop Pro 5 is only available for the PC platform. Other graphics software products are available for Mac users, but they are not covered here. Additionally, you should be familiar with installing and running programs on your own computer.

How This Book Helps You Create Web Graphics

In general, this book is intended to be read from beginning to end, as the easiest subjects tend to be presented first, with the hardest last. I start off with basic generalities that everyone should know when using graphics on the Web, then focus on specific advanced Paint Shop Pro subject areas.

Feel free, however, to use this book as a reference. Remember that some chapters do build on previous ones; but many subjects are self-contained and organized logically in the order that you're likely to need them.

For your convenience, I've split the book into four sections, each containing four chapters. Below I've listed the sections of the book, along with brief descriptions of the chapters they contain.

Part I: Web Graphics Basics

Part I introduces several concepts that are important to understanding Web graphics. Chapter 1, "A Web Crawler's Beginning," demonstrates how crucial graphics are to a Web page. In this chapter, I also describe the major graphical file types you will encounter and I review the basic HTML tags used when adding graphics and images to your Web page.

Chapter 2, "Using and Installing Paint Shop Pro 5," discusses the best software utility available for creating and working with graphics: Paint

Shop Pro 5. I'll show you how to download and install this software, then give you a quick tour of some basic Paint Shop Pro features you will use regularly.

Chapter 3, "Creating Simple Graphics," focuses on using the Paint Shop Pro drawing tools to make simple but useful graphics in both color and black and white. You will learn when to use many popular text and drawing tools within Paint Shop Pro and how to save your images into the different graphical formats.

Finally, Chapter 4, "Editing Images & Photos," tells you where you can find graphics that already exist and modify them to fit your needs rather than create your own from scratch. There are already millions upon millions of pictures, photographs, and drawings available for you to use on your Web page.

Part II: Making Great Images

Once you get your feet wet with Part I, we will start building and working with more advanced images in Part II. Chapter 5, "Images & Special Effects," uses the interactive deformations, filters, and other built-in techniques. This is one of the most enjoyable chapters in the book!

Next up is Chapter 6, "Picture Tubes and Web Graphics," where you learn how to make buttons, icons, bars, and titles that jazz up any Web page within moments. PSP Picture Tubes, a great new feature, are covered in this chapter.

Chapter 7, "Using PSP Layers," teaches you how to use the best new feature in PSP 5—Layers. A powerful technique, layering lets you build complex graphics in a structured and modular manner.

Finally, in Chapter 8, "The Black and White Alternative," I discuss in-depth the advantages and disadvantages of using black and white instead of color images on your Web pages. You will see how Paint Shop Pro facilitates the conversion of color graphics to black and white and vice versa. Also, you will find out how to use a little-known HTML keyword that allows you to create both color and black and white images on a single page to improve effective download time for visitors to a Web site.

Part III: Advanced Image Techniques

Part III builds on what you will learn in Parts I and II, and explains how to incorporate several advanced image techniques into a Web page to enhance your site's appearance and performance. Chapter 9, "Using Scanners and Digital Cameras," allows you to keep up on the latest digital imaging technology. You'll see how new image editing features let you take images directly from your scanner and digital camera into PSP.

Chapter 10, "Creating Transparent GIFs," explains a popular GIF feature that changes an image's appearance on a Web page. By making the background color of an image transparent, the image blends in harmoniously when placed on a page that uses many colors and background graphics. Paint Shop Pro makes GIF transparency easy.

Through Chapter 11, "Moving Graphics: Creating GIF Animation," you learn how to save multiple graphics into a single GIF file that loads and runs as a true animation in your Web Browser. GIF animation is a powerful technique that you'll have fun learning.

Last in this part is Chapter 12, "Making Your Graphics Lean." This chapter describes many different ways by which you can trim down your graphic's file size. Any one of the techniques described here will significantly improve performance for visitors who stop by your site. Because download time is the biggest adversary for creating a user-friendly Web page, you need to keep your graphics small, lean, and efficient.

Part IV: Practical Use of Images on Your Web Pages

Part IV, the last section of this book, demonstrates how to integrate all the concepts covered in the previous chapters. Chapter 13, "Web Graphics as Image Maps," will show you how to define different areas of an image to link to different HTML pages on the WWW. Called Image Maps, this powerful technique puts your best PSP graphics to work for you!

Chapter 14, "Background Graphics and Colors," discusses an extremely popular topic—using cool graphics in the background of a Web page. By remaining in the background, these graphics appear behind all the other images and text on your Web page. This allows you to change the style of any page by simply updating the background graphic. Paint Shop Pro lets you build thousands of different types of graphics and then optimize them to use in the background of Web pages.

Chapter 15, "HTML Tips for Web Images," is a collection of the most important techniques you can use when putting together your own Web site. Even with great graphics, you'll want to learn proper ways to design and optimize your pages to maximize your visitors' enjoyment.

Last but not least is Chapter 16, "Cool PSP Techniques," which ties the entire book together. This chapter is structured differently, showing you many different powerful step-by-step techniques for creating innovative Web Graphics.

Appendixes

At the back of this book are two Appendixes, which contain additional information you will find useful when building Web Graphics. Appendix

A, "Graphical Resources on the Web," lists dozens of important sites that you as a PSP user will find handy.

Finally, Appendix B, "Paint Shop Pro Tool Reference," provides an overview of all the major features found within PSP. This is the most-often requested section from the first edition, and we've delivered. Complete, comprehensive, and useful, you'll refer to this appendix frequently.

Conventions Used in This Book

As you read, you will find several different conventions that highlight specific types of information that you'll want to keep an eye out for:

▶ All HTML codes and tags will appear in `FULL MONOSPACE CAPS`. This will enable you to tell the difference between text that appears on-screen and text that tells your Web Browser what to do. Web Browsers don't care whether your HTML tags are in full caps.

▶ All URLs are displayed in **boldface.** You can type them into your browser window and go directly to the site referred to.

Besides the above textual conventions, I also use several different icons throughout this book, shown below.

TIP

Text formatted in this manner offers extra information related to the issue being discussed. You'll find personal anecdotes and experiences, specific design techniques, and general information extras in "Tip" boxes.

CAUTION

Actions and commands that could make irreversible changes to your files or potentially cause problems in the future are displayed in this manner, as "Caution" material. Make sure you read this text carefully as it could contain important information that directly affects enhancing your Web page.

NOTE

Notes present interesting or useful information that isn't necessarily essential to the discussion, but provides additional material that may help you avoid problems, or offers advice relating to the topic.

Keeping the Book's Content Current

You made a long-term investment when you purchased this book. To keep your investment paying off, I've developed a comprehensive companion Web site for you, the reader of this book. The site contains:

- ▶ Up-to-date information on the world of graphics
- ▶ Special offers on software and products just for readers
- ▶ Corrections or clarifications to the book's text and images
- ▶ New resources you can use to stay on the cutting edge
- ▶ URLs of readers like you who submit their Web site
- ▶ An interactive discussion to talk about Web Graphics
- ▶ Extra chapters and techniques that we couldn't cram in here
- ▶ Much More!

Essentially, this up-to-date Web site is your one-stop shop for everything about Paint Shop Pro and Web Graphics, so take advantage of it!

Stop by at:

http://www.muskalipman.com/graphics

Or, if you'd like to send e-mail to the book staff directly, we'd love to hear from you. Your input and comments are critical to making sure this book covers all the right information in an easy-to-use manner. Send e-mail to the book staff at:

graphics@muskalipman.com

Part I
Web Graphics Basics

1

A Web Crawler's Beginning

Approximately 120 years ago when the telephone was invented, nobody could imagine the concept of real time conversations with people from all over the city, let alone the world. People were still relying on the pony express and the telegraph to exchange communications with one another. Terms such as "telephone operator," "dial tone," and "cordless telephone" had yet to be coined.

Soon after its invention, the telephone literally revolutionized the communications industry—and the world. Today, a new type of burgeoning technology—the Internet—is introducing completely new communications concepts that are once again transforming the way we can communicate and visit with one another. Riding this wave of popularity is the World Wide Web (WWW), the Internet's graphical way to jump from site to site and visit any Web page across the world, right from your own personal computer. The key to the popularity of the Web can be summed up in a single word—*graphics*. Graphics are the most important feature that makes the WWW fun to browse, highly informative, and extremely popular among all age groups and nationalities.

This chapter introduces you to many important features of graphics and demonstrates how they can be used with the World Wide Web. I'll introduce you to all sorts of terms you'll come across and explain why graphics are the linchpin in the WWW's popularity.

▶ **Understand the Web's Popularity**
Graphics are only a part (a large part) of what makes the Web so popular. Understand how ease of use and availability has helped stoke the growing fire of this technology.

▶ **Define *Web Graphics***
Before we can start creating our own images, it's important to understand exactly what a *Web graphic* is and how to create one.

▶ **Decide What File Type to Use**
Web graphics come in multiple file types, each with its own
advantages and disadvantages in certain situations. Learn which file
type to use, when, and why.

▶ **Review Image Placement HTML Tags**
You'll want to review this section to remember how to use the
common image tags in HTML. It covers adding a simple image to a
Web page and formatting it to your own specifications.

Graphics Made the Web Explode in Popularity

The Internet has been around for many years. Originally it just connected
universities and government computers together, but now it encompasses
businesses, organizations, and individuals from all over the world.
Compared to the Internet's lengthy existence, the WWW has only been
around for a few years. Conceived in 1991, the first graphical Web
browser—Mosaic—was released in 1992. In 1994, the Netscape browser
was released. Since then the Internet's popularity has skyrocketed. The
Web's popularity grew because of the easy and attractive way Netscape
allowed people to visit the different Web sites around the world. No
longer did you have to rely on boring text-only Internet information.
Today, two popular browsers share the limelight—Netscape's Navigator
(Communicator) and Microsoft's Internet Explorer.

Anyone can display a logo, photograph, or video clip that millions of
people may experience when they stop by. Museums are able to display
their masterpieces, companies can show products for sale, and CNN
shows live footage—all from within a single piece of software—your Web
browser. Taking advantage of the power to share your images is what this
book is all about—learning how to use cool and advanced graphics on
your Web pages to make them more enjoyable to look at and more
attractive for Web users to visit.

Don't worry if you aren't a professional artist; even simple graphics can
drastically change the appearance of a Web page with little effort on your
part. Here's a simple example that will show you what I mean. Figure 1.1
shows a boring Web page for a fictional aquarium for which I'll build a
Web site periodically throughout this book. This text-only page is less
than exciting and probably doesn't pique your interest, even if you are a
fish fan.

Fig 1.1
This aquarium page is
boring to visit.

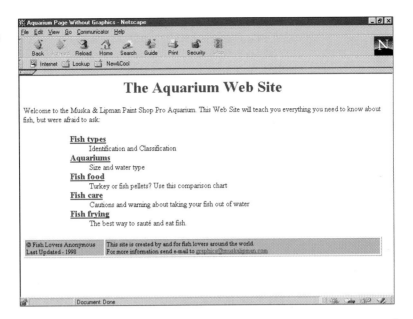

Now take a look at figure 1.2. This is the same page with a few simple
images created with a Paint Shop Pro feature called *Picture Tubes*.

Fig 1.2
Creating the images in
this example took
under five minutes.

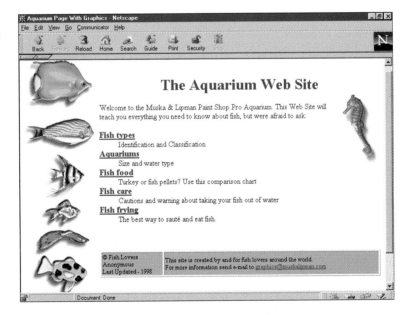

As you'll learn later in this book, the graphics in figure 1.2 were created using PSP *Picture Tubes*, which are extraordinarily usable and flexible. The important lesson to learn from this example is that even simple graphics can make a Web page truly worthwhile. These graphics took only a few minutes to create.

NOTE

Here's a brief lesson on how the Internet and WWW works on a technical level. Every time you want to explore the Web, you must use your computer to call into a local Internet provider. This phone connection (or direct line access from home, work, or school) lets your computer request individual Web pages from any site across the world. By typing in the URL (or unique address) for a specific page, the computers on the Internet know what text and graphics to send to your computer.

For example, if you visit http://www.muskalipman.com, you are actually requesting that an entire page of information be sent to your computer. After a few moments, your computer starts receiving the text and images from that Web page, which you can see as it downloads, or appears on your computer. Then you can read that first page, visit another site, or click on a different link from the page you are viewing.

In many ways, the World Wide Web is similar to Gopher, a text-only Internet application. Like the Web, Gopher allows computers on the Internet to communicate with each other, but it can only send text files back and forth. So, using a Gopher browser, you have a lot of information at your fingertips, but it's not pretty to look at, and it's not nearly as easy to use as the WWW.

Besides graphics, many WWW features make the Web popular and easy to use. Below is a list of reasons the Web's popularity continues to rise:

► **Web Pages Are Easy to Create**—Using just a few tools and the HyperText Markup Language (HTML), anyone can create fantastic-looking pages with little difficulty. HTML is a logical formatting language—meaning you tell your Web browser how you want text and graphics to appear and the browser follows your textual commands.

► **It's Easy to Get Online**—A few years ago, connecting to the Internet was a pain. You had to learn a whole new set of technical mumbo-jumbo just to turn your computer on, let alone connect your modem, install the correct software, and worry about talking to the Internet. Nowadays, Windows 95 and 98 has made getting online a comparative breeze! Companies such as America Online and Microsoft have built their entire business on this online environment.

▶ **Multimedia Is Finally Here**—Video, sound, text, and graphics are all part of the daily Web experience. While this book focuses on creating great graphics, many sites you visit and create will offer true multimedia to visitors.

▶ **A Lot of Information Is Available**—With over 100 million Web pages in existence (that number is constantly rising), there is literally a spot for everyone and every interest on the WWW. All hobbies, professions, sports, lifestyles, and issues have their own dedicated Web sites.

What Are Web Graphics?

Since this book is all about **Web Graphics** and Paint Shop Pro, it's important to get a handle on what Web Graphics actually are and how photos, images, and graphics can be created specifically for use on the Web. Simply put, Web Graphics are computer-saved images that are created and optimized specifically to work on a Web page. Working in conjunction with special HTML tags (which I'll talk about later in this chapter), graphics can be included on any Web page in a matter of moments. However, they have to be saved in a certain format to work properly with popular Web browsers such as Netscape and Internet Explorer.

This section introduces you to four major categories of graphics that you'll encounter when exploring the Web. Each has its own specific traits and purpose for being included on a Web page. You'll learn more about creating all these different types of graphics throughout this book.

Logos and Headlines

Almost every page you'll visit will have some sort of logo or headline graphic that makes the site attractive and enjoyable. Often, these graphic elements serve as a quick introduction to the page you are visiting. An example of how a logo/headline graphic is used can be found at the *Web Site Garage* **(http://www.websitegarage.com),** an online resource for honing up your Web site. Shown in figure 1.3, this site has a comprehensive set of images that load each time you visit it, which sets the theme for the entire site. You *know* this site is all about tuning things up just by looking at the main images.

Fig 1.3
These icons are
particularly distinctive
and useful to visitors
who stop by.

Many sites use their own logos and other headline graphics consistently
throughout their pages.

Icons

The most common graphics type you'll come across is the icon, a small
image used to represent another command or action. On the WWW, icons
are often used instead of regular text to connect Web pages to one
another. In general, icons fulfill a double duty: they enhance the
appearance of a Web site, and they guide visitors to different pages of
information. A great example of icons can be found at Yahoo
(http://www.yahoo.com), the most popular Web site in the world (shown
in figure 1.4). Yahoo carefully crafts and uses icons at the top of its main
page to represent other places to go within their site. Clicking on the
Newspaper icon takes you to the daily news while the baby icon shows
you what is new in Yahoo-land.

Part I Web Graphics Basics

Fig 1.4
These icons are particularly insightful and useful to visitors.

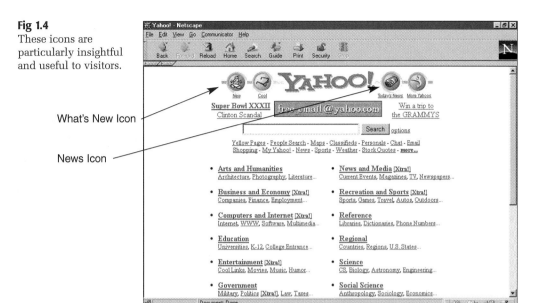

What's New Icon

News Icon

Photographs and Pictures

Most personal and professional Web pages usually have some sort of photograph or picture included on them. One site that always has photos is CNN. The CNN Web site relies on photographs to help visitors visualize a news story as it is published online, just like a newspaper does on paper. Figure 1.5 below shows the main CNN home page with several photos supporting important news items. This Web site just looks exciting, even before you've read the text!

Fig 1.5
This Web site, with all copyrights on text and photos reserved to CNN, relies on photos as an important component.

You'll probably use photos on your site by scanning them in and editing them with Paint Shop Pro. Using PSP, you can control the exact size of the picture, cut away extra parts of the photo (called cropping), and even change the colors!

Background Graphics

Another common way to use graphics on a Web page is to add them to the background, behind the text and information that normally appears on your site. The effect is like setting a place mat beneath your plate. You can see the full plate and only that part of the place mat that isn't covered by the plate.

Background graphics are common tools for adding real life to Web pages. You can create and use a variety of background graphics to depict different designs, colors, and styles for your Web site. Chapter 14, "Background Graphics and Colors," steps you through making your own images from scratch and shows you in more detail how they work. Figure 1.6 shows a personal Web page that uses an interesting background graphic (**http://www.shafran.com/personal/audrey.htm**). This graphic, built in a few minutes, consists of faded-out letters created in Paint Shop Pro.

Fig 1.6
This page uses background images, icons, and photos.

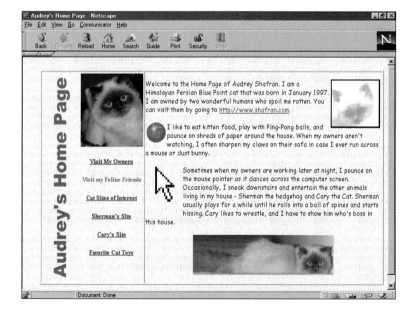

What Is Paint Shop Pro?

Now that you understand the different types of Web graphics, it's time to familiarize yourself with the next key ingredient: Paint Shop Pro. Paint Shop Pro is a top-notch graphics creation and editing software package created by Jasc Software Inc. **(http://www.jasc.com).** Often referred to as PSP for short, Paint Shop Pro is limited evaluation software, which means that you get the opportunity to test-drive the program before deciding whether or not you want to purchase it.

This book teaches you all about using Paint Shop Pro to create amazing-looking graphics from scratch. You'll learn everything from how to install and configure PSP on your computer to using advanced, professional caliber options that will impress all visitors to your site.

Paint Shop Pro has been around for years and has always had a strong following. It offers the power and flexibility that expensive graphics packages such as Adobe PhotoShop have, but at a fraction of the cost. Jasc Software succeeded in improving their high-quality software with their latest release: Paint Shop Pro 5.

NOTE

Many people have written e-mail comments and questions asking why *this book* focuses on Paint Shop Pro instead of other shareware and non-shareware graphics packages. The answer is easy, Paint Shop Pro is simply the finest product in its category. Many other graphics packages exist and can create good-looking images, but none offer the same degree of flexibility and power while letting let you test their product before you purchase it.

Understanding Different Web Image Types

Graphics are saved on your computer in a standard file format so they can be viewed and manipulated with all programs. As you can probably imagine, all images aren't necessarily saved in the same image format. Just as you can use different types of graphics on your Web page, you can also select from many graphic formats when creating images for your Web pages. Literally dozens of different standards dictate how graphics should be saved and stored on a computer disk. Most Web browsers, however, only recognize two standard graphical formats—GIF and JPEG.

In this section I'll talk about these two popular image formats, as well as two other important formats—PNG and PSP. All these formats are completely supported by Paint Shop Pro 5.

NOTE

Most differences in the graphical formats center around file compression. When a graphic is saved onto the computer, it is transformed into a whole bunch of 1's and 0's—binary format, the language in which computers communicate.

Some graphic formats simply write all of the 1's and 0's into a big file. This results in bigger files, but the computer doesn't have to work very hard to translate the binary numbers into your picture. Unfortunately, images of this type tend to have a very large file size, often taking hundreds of bytes on your computer for an image that appears very small on the computer screen. This increases the amount of time a visitor has to wait when stopping by your Web site.

Other formats use different methods for saving binary numbers, which result in smaller files. Using compression techniques, your computer might replace a repeating series of binary numbers with a single smaller number, resulting in a smaller file size. While you end up with smaller files, your computer tends to take a few extra moments to decompress your images before displaying them on the screen. Often you'll sacrifice image quality for improved file compression, forcing you to make a decision on what's most important for your images—quality or size.

Most of the different formats are some combination of performance, file size, and compression techniques. It's important, though, to realize that a single graphic can be saved in many different graphics formats and that each format will result in a different file size, or even altered quality of picture.

GIF

The most popular image type you'll run into on the WWW is the GIF (Graphical Interchange Format). Pronounced "*jif,*" this file type was pioneered by CompuServe to provide information in a standard graphical format for its customers. Sometimes known as the CompuServe Image Format, GIF set an image standard nearly ten years ago and was the first file type supported by the WWW.

The GIF image format uses a popular compression algorithm called Lempel-Ziv-Welsh, the easiest and most efficient way to compress files into the smallest possible size. The Lempel-Ziv-Welsh algorithm is equivalent to stuffing all your clothes into a suitcase and filling it to its limit. You are left with a reasonably sized file that is universally recognized on all computers and by almost every graphics program. By far, GIFs are the most popular image file type in the world. By compressing, and subsequently decompressing your file (unpacking your suitcase), you don't lose any detail. All colors remain the same, and your image never changes its appearance from its original look.

A few years ago, the developers of the GIF algorithm (CompuServe) discovered that they were using a patented formula for compression. Unisys, the patent owner, decided to enforce their ownership, causing professional graphics software developers to pay a royalty to support the GIF image type. This patent dispute brought two other image formats into the limelight—JPG and PNG. As a user of PSP, you don't have to worry about any of the patent dispute.

There are two significant limitations to using GIFs on your Web pages:

Photo Efficiency

Because of the way GIF compression and pictures work, the GIF format is typically very inefficient when working with scanned or digital photographs. If you scan a photograph into your computer and save it as a GIF, you'll be surprised how large your file might end up—particularly when compared to the other major WWW graphic standard: JPEG. GIFs are perfect for hand-drawn art (called line art in the publishing world), icons, logos, and headlines, but are not optimal for photos. You'll almost never use the GIF format to save pictures.

Only 256 Different Colors

Each GIF only lets you use 256 different colors within each image. Although that sounds like a lot, it isn't when you consider that many of the vivid and colorful graphics and photographs found on the Web today use thousands of colors.

JPEG

The other popular image type on the WWW, JPEG, makes up for many of the GIF deficiencies. A more recent development, JPEG stands for Joint Photographic Experts Group. Also commonly known as JPG, this format was developed to be significantly more efficient than GIFs in several circumstances, especially those involving larger images with many colors. JPEG uses a more advanced compression algorithm than the GIF format, and this algorithm shrinks most of your graphics into a smaller file when they use a lot of colors, such as you'll find in scanned photographs.

The JPEG compression algorithm works much differently than the GIF format but also has some drawbacks. GIFs take the original image and shrink it as tight as it can be shrunk. JPEGs use a "lossy" algorithm, which results in some loss of detail when images are saved and viewed in this format. It's the equivalent of having somebody take out a few items of clothing from your packed suitcase to make your suitcase smaller—you actually forfeit some items to get the smaller/lighter suitcase. As a result, JPEG files are sometimes not as detailed as GIF images, but can offer as much as a 35% improvement in file size and compression!

Part I   Web Graphics Basics

Don't worry too much about losing detail during compression, particularly when working with photographs. When saving your JPEG, you get the option of indicating how much detail the JPEG can lose. The higher the detail, the larger the file size. At the highest quality of detail, JPEGs are about equal to GIFs as far as file size goes. You'll learn how to control these characteristics in Chapter 3, "Creating Simple Graphics."

Additionally, since JPEGs were built to handle photographs, they are much more efficient at managing lots of colors and shades. This means that JPEG files tend to be smaller, look better, and, consequently, download more quickly for those browsing the WWW. This makes JPEG images more attractive to Web developers because visitors can see their images much more quickly. In addition, the JPG image format supports up to 16.7 million different colors—significantly more than GIF files.

Most Web browsers support both JPEG and GIF file formats interchangeably. Both can be optimized to be more efficient when using the Web. See Chapter 12, "Making Your Graphics Lean," for more detail on common performance enhancements.

PNG

Recently, a new type of image has gained popularity because of the legal issues and technical limitations that surround the use of GIFs. This image type is called Portable Network Graphics—PNG (pronounced *ping)*, and has finally become widely supported on the Web.

PNG graphics offer a compromise between the GIF and JPEG formats. PNGs offer enhanced compression among images and can handle multiple colors and larger pictures well, without using a "lossy" compression scheme. They represent a significant file size savings over the GIF format, though not quite as good as JPEG images. PNG graphics can perform all the same advanced tricks that you find in both JPEG and GIF file formats, making them ideal vehicles for displaying graphics on the Web.

Unfortunately, PNG images aren't a panacea either. Only recent versions of Netscape Communicator/Navigator and Microsoft Internet Explorer (versions 4 and above) support viewing the PNG images inside of a Web page, just like GIFs and JPGs. This means you have to be *very* careful using the PNG format, because if people stop by using an older Web browser, they won't be able to see your images—a real problem! Personally, I use only GIF and JPG images on my Web site, since I have no control over the browser my visitors use.

For more information on the PNG graphics type, visit my favorite PNG information center at **http://www.cdrom.com/pub/png/** (figure 1.7).

Fig 1.7
The home of the PNG
graphics format

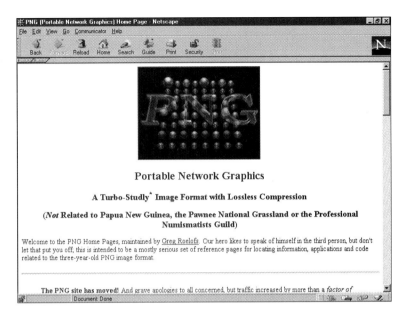

PSP

The PSP format is completely new and supported only by Paint Shop Pro version 5 (and above). Invented by Jasc Software, the PSP format was created to let you do all types of advanced image manipulation inside of Paint Shop Pro. Then, once you are finished editing your images, you can easily and quickly convert your PSP format images into GIF, JPG, PNG, or any of the other popular image formats you may need.

The PSP format is important because several Paint Shop Pro techniques require you to store your images in this format.

Graphics Format Comparison Chart

This section presented a lot of potentially confusing information on different image formats. Below, I've included a short chart that compares these four formats and helps you decide when you'll work with each of them.

Table 1.1
Image Format
Comparisons Chart

Format	# of colors	When to Use
PSP	16.7 million	Creating and editing advanced images within PSP, then you can convert them to another format
GIF	256	Creating Logos, icons, headlines, or small images
JPG	16.7 million	Working with Photographs or images based originally on photographs
PNG	16.7 million	When you know all your visitors have current Web browsers that support the PNG format.

TIP

Many other popular graphical formats are still commonly used for various applications. Don't despair if you have a set of images in another file format that you want to add to your Web pages. You have two options that will let you use virtually any image format imaginable on your Web page.

Using Paint Shop Pro, you can convert an image from nearly any imaginable type into the popular GIF or JPEG file types. In Chapter 3, "Creating Simple Graphics," I show you how to convert graphics back and forth between file types and formats (Don't worry—it's easy!). That way you can use the newly converted GIF or JPEG in your Web page as you normally would.

Or, you can use advanced Web browser technology that lets you include nonstandard images in your Web page. This technology, called plug-ins, works with all popular Web browsers. Using a special plug-in, you can add images of essentially any format to your Web page, without the worry of converting them from one format to another. Visit **http://www.inso.com/products/retail/qvp-retail/html/qvpretai.htm** to learn more about QuickView Plus, an exciting plug-in for browsers that lets you see all types of different file types.

Basic HTML Tags for Adding Images

Although this book doesn't focus on learning all the HTML tags required for building Web pages, several chapters will show you how to use special HTML options to increase your image's performance or appearance. Again, it's important that you have a general grasp of HTML before you start using this book; otherwise some tactics and techniques are likely to be confusing or difficult to understand.

CAUTION

This book is not meant to teach you everything about HTML, but merely to refresh your memory on the basics and to show you innovative ways to use some advanced tags.

Many books exist to help you learn HTML or make it easier to develop Web sites. If you want a more complete reference to HTML, check out *Creating Your Own Web Pages, Second Edition*, published by Que. Alternatively, many tools exist to make learning HTML a thing of the past. Among the best is Microsoft FrontPage 98, which can be purchased at nearly any local computer store.

To help you out, I've included a brief review of the HTML tags required to add images to your Web page. I'll show you how to place an image on your Web page and give you some general tips to remember.

Your first step is to obtain the image you want to use—in GIF or JPG format. Save your image in the same file subdirectory as your HTML file. Next, add the <u>IMG></u> tag to your HTML listing. If your image file name is <u>AIRPLANE.GIF</u>, then you add the following tag:

```
<IMG SRC="AIRPLANE.GIF">
```

Similarly, if you had a JPG file—<u>AIRPLANE.JPG</u>, you'd just use this alternative file name instead:

```
<IMG SRC="AIRPLANE.JPG">
```

Your Web Browser then adds the image to the Web page and displays it when you load that page. Figure 1.8 shows my browser displaying the airplane image. Make sure you use the complete path when adding your image with HTML. For example, if this image was found in a subdirectory named PICTURES, I'd use the following tag instead:

```
<IMG SRC="PICTURES\AIRPLANE.GIF">
```

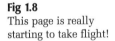

Fig 1.8
This page is really starting to take flight!

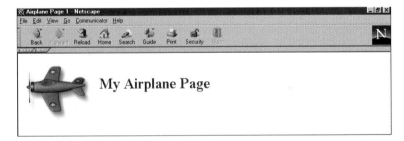

Setting Your Image Alignment

You have considerable control over how your image appears on-screen. One of the best ways to customize the appearance of your image is to set its alignment. You can have it line up on the left-hand side of the screen (the default setting), center it, or right-justify it—your choice.

All you have to do is add the <u>ALIGN=</u> keyword to your <u>IMG></u> tag. To align your image on the left-hand side of screen, use the following tag:

```
<IMG SRC="AIRPLANE.GIF" ALIGN=LEFT >
```

or on the right-hand side:

```
<IMG SRC="AIRPLANE.GIF" ALIGN=RIGHT >
```

To center your image, just add the <CENTER> and </CENTER> tags around your image:

```
<CENTER><IMG SRC="AIRPLANE.GIF"></CENTER>
```

To see how your browser would display each of the three alignment options, take a look at figure 1.9.

Fig 1.9
Many alignment options are at your fingertips.

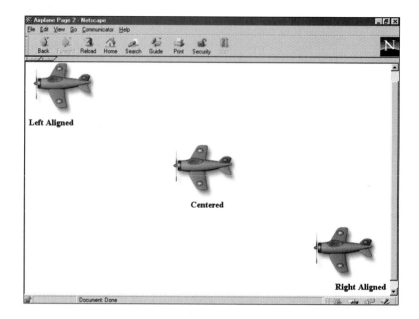

Providing Alternative Text

One of the most important enhancements you can make to your image is unlikely to often be seen. I'm talking about adding alternative text that appears whenever a visitor stops by who doesn't have the capability, or desire, to download and display the images you added to your Web page. This text also appears when visitors hover their mouse over an image that has already been loaded on a Web page.

Since downloading images can sometimes take quite a while, some people instruct their Web browser *not* to automatically download and display Web images when browsing. Instead, these users will see a short blurb of text describing the image they could be seeing. Additionally, some Web browsers might not support all popular image types. Although JPG and GIF are common standards, new formats such as PNG, or older non-graphical browsers, might not be able to recognize your image. In fact, some WWW browsers, like Lynx, don't support graphics at all, and designing a Web site that is accessible to these users, at least in some minimal fashion, isn't such a bad idea.

It's important to accommodate these alternative situations so that your Web page is accessible to everyone. Adding alternative text is easy: just add the <u>ALT</u> keyword to your image tag. So, to add a small phrase to my airplane image, I use the following tag:

```
<IMG SRC="AIRPLANE.GIF" ALT="airplane.gif (7058 bytes)">
```

The ALT text appears either when the image loads, or when the mouse pointer is set on top of the image.

One common practice employed when using alternative text is to add an exciting and informative phrase that makes visitors *want* to download your fully graphical page. Instead of the dull phrase I used above, try this tag instead:

```
<IMG SRC="AIRPLANE.GIF" ALT="A sizzling fighter jet! ">
```

Which description sounds more interesting?

In general, try to keep your alternative text short and to the point by eliminating extraneous words.

Using Images As Links

Many people choose to use images simply as decoration on their Web page—they just want to add more life and color to an otherwise uninteresting site. On the other hand, it is also common to link your Web images up to another HTML file on the Web. This allows visitors to see your image as usual, but when they click their mouse on it, they are taken to another site!

Linking Web pages together requires using the <u><A HREF></u> tag, which stands for Hypertext Reference. You add a hypertext link to another page on the WWW by specifying its unique address, or URL (Universal Resource Locator). All this does is specify your image as the link. So, to link the airplane image to **http://www.airplane.com**, I'd use the following text:

```
<A HREF="http://www.airplane.com">
<IMG SRC="AIRPLANE.GIF" ALT="A sizzling fighter jet! ">
</A>
```

The Web browser displays the image in a similar fashion, but now a blue border appears around the image, indicating that it is now "hot," or linked to another site. When your mouse moves over the image, the pointer turns into a miniature hand and the linked Web address appears in the status bar at the bottom of the screen. Notice also, that the ALT text appears next to your mouse pointer (figure 1.10).

Fig 1.10
This airplane is now linked to another Web site.

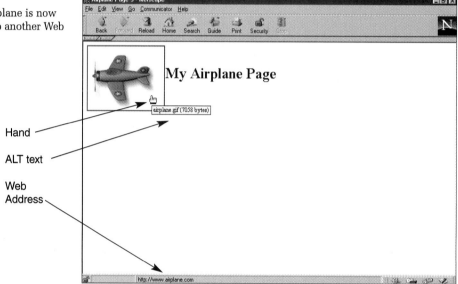

You'll often find yourself linking up graphics between two different Web pages.

Adding "clickable" images to Web pages is just the beginning. One advanced way you can use images is to link different parts of an image to different Web addresses. This technology, called "image maps," allows you to specify as many different areas of an image as you like. I'll step you through the whole process of creating image maps in Chapter 13, "Web Graphics As Image Maps." Figure 1.11 shows an example of the Cover Girl Web site **(http://www.covergirl.com)** using clickable image maps.

Fig 1.11
This interactive Web
site uses great images.

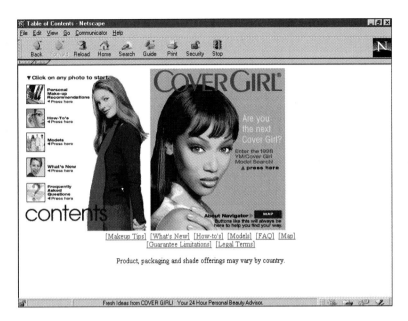

Creating Your Own Web Site

As I stated in the Book's Introduction, one of the pre-requisites to
creating cool Web graphics is having a Web page. Learning the basics to
HTML are of no help unless you have your own corner of the Internet to
place them on.

There are many different companies which provide you with Web space
for reasonable fees. These companies allow you full access to make
changes to your site, offer support, and much more. One of my favorites
is Site America (**http://www.siteamerica.com**), as shown in figure 1.12.

Fig 1.12
This interactive Web
site uses great images.

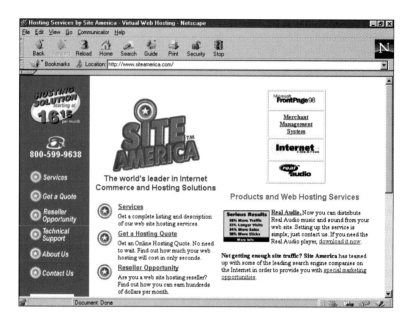

Home to thousands of different Web sites, Site America has world class service, toll-free support telephone numbers, affordable domain name hosting and registration services, FrontPage support, and more. On top of that, they have many different hosting plans which fit any budget.

In addition, there are several free spots on the Web which let you upload and create a handful of Web pages at no extra cost. In general, they are mainly geared for creating personal sites. Two of my favorites are:

http://xoom.xoom.com
Xoom.Xoom – Home to 1 Million Web pages

http://www.geocities.com
Geocities – the original spot on the Web for free space.

NOTE

In the interest of full disclosure, I use Forman Interactive (**http://www.forman.com**) to host my personal Web site. Forman is a sister company of Site America and focuses on helping small businesses publish great-looking web sites.

In addition, I also use Tango Development (**http://www.tangodevelopment.com**), a talented consulting company to create and maintain many sites, including the one for this book. Tango takes care of the development and page maintenance, so I don't have to.

2

Using and Installing Paint Shop Pro 5

When building a house, a construction worker uses a hammer, screwdrivers, and other building tools. When making dinner, a chef uses the oven, pots and pans, and mixing bowls. Similarly, when creating your own graphics, you'll want to get your hands on tools that optimize the drawing and manipulating of images.

Many different tools exist to help you create your own Web graphics, but one stands out from all the rest: Paint Shop Pro 5. Paint Shop Pro 5 is the best all-around computer program for everything that has to do with graphics. An award-winning piece of software, Paint Shop Pro gives you 30 days to test-drive the program before you need to decide whether to purchase it.

In this chapter, you will learn all about downloading, installing, and using Paint Shop Pro for yourself. I'll even take you on a quick tour of some of Paint Shop Pro's most useful and impressive features so you can quickly become a great graphics developer. You'll learn what's new with Paint Shop Pro 5 and how you can leverage these features to your advantage.

▶ **Understand Paint Shop Pro 5**
Paint Shop Pro 5 is a robust and impressive graphics package available for Windows users. Learn what its capabilities are for you, the Web graphic developer.

▶ **Install Paint Shop Pro**
Software is useful to you only when it's installed on your computer. I'll show you how to set up PSP quickly and without hassle.

▶ **Tour Common Features**
I'll lead you through a handful of commands and icons of which every Paint Shop Pro user should be aware.

▶ **Build a Set of Cool Images**
Following a step-by step method, you'll build several different Web images using some of the most exciting PSP features.

What Is PSP?

Paint Shop Pro (PSP) is a professional-caliber graphics program put together and released by Jasc Software Inc. Comparable to high-priced graphics programs, Paint Shop Pro 5 allows experts and novices to create graphics using advanced features such as image layering. You can develop, edit, re-size, warp, and convert over thirty different image formats into graphics perfect for Web or print pages.

NOTE

Jasc Software Inc. (**http://www.jasc.com**) is a software company located in Minneapolis, Minnesota. They specialize in producing powerful graphics and graphics management software for Windows-based computers. Founded in 1991, Jasc Software is the leader in graphics-file technology and has a corner on the personal graphics utility market, dubbed *prosumer.*

Originally a shareware-only company, Jasc Software has become one of the most respected software companies due to the value and quality of their products.

Paint Shop Pro gives you all the power and flexibility of a high-end graphics program, such as Adobe PhotoShop, but for a smaller price tag. As evaluation software, you can run PSP 5 for up to 30 days before you will be required to pay for and register the software so you can continue running it on your computer. You can use the full scope of functionality available in PSP during this 30-day trial period.

If you are an existing Paint Shop Pro customer and have already registered a previous version of the product, Jasc Software makes it easy for you to upgrade. You can pay a special upgrade price instead of buying the whole software package from scratch. PSP 5 is priced under $100. Check out **http://www.jasc.com** for current pricing and upgrade policies.

By encouraging visitors to download and try out their software, Jasc Software wants to convince you of their software value before you decide to purchase PSP.

Whether you want to scan and save a new image, create a set of buttons for your Web site, or simply change the colors on a single page banner, Paint Shop Pro will enable you to do virtually anything you want. In this chapter, I talk about Paint Shop Pro, version 5. Created especially for Windows 95 and Windows NT4 and above, Paint Shop Pro 5 is an efficient, well-designed tool that all Web developers should have at their fingertips. If you still use Windows 3.1, PSP 3.X is available for your use; but this earlier version doesn't have the flexibility you'll find in more recent releases. Unfortunately, a Macintosh version of PSP is not available.

NOTE

In this book, I use Paint Shop Pro 5 for Windows 95. Depending on the exact version of software you have (5.01 or 5.1, for example) and the Operating System you use (Windows 98 or NT 4, for example), your screens and dialog boxes may appear slightly different from those depicted here.

Obtaining Paint Shop Pro

You can obtain Paint Shop Pro for your own use in several ways. The easiest and quickest is to download the evaluation version of Paint Shop Pro directly from the Jasc Software Web site (see figure 2.1):

http://www.jasc.com

Fig. 2.1
The Jasc Software home page is the clearinghouse for everything pertaining to Paint Shop Pro.

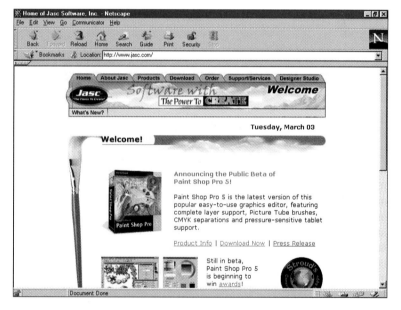

While there, you might want to check out some of Jasc Software's other graphics-related products. Jasc Software offers a wide variety of tools for managing and creating all sorts of graphics files.

Although downloading PSP initially may take a while, depending on the speed of your Internet connection, you only have to do it once. You'll always be able to find the latest version of Paint Shop Pro 5 on the Jasc Software Web site.

Installing Paint Shop Pro

Once you've downloaded or purchased PSP, installing it is a snap. Simply find the file you downloaded on your computer system with Windows Explorer, then double-click on it with your mouse.

Tell PSP where to install the program on your hard drive, and it will take care of all the rest. After you finish the installation, you can run Paint Shop Pro 5 immediately. From your Windows 95 Start menu, choose **P**rograms, Paint Shop Pro, Paint Shop Pro 5 to start the program. See figure 2.2 for a view of what Paint Shop Pro should look like when running. If you are using the limited evaluation version of PSP, you can now use Paint Shop Pro for 30 days before your time limit expires.

Fig. 2.2
Paint Shop Pro looks like your standard Windows application.

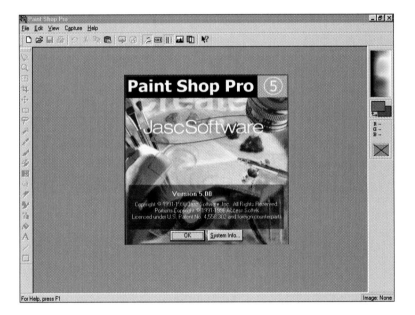

Registering Paint Shop Pro

At the time of this writing, Paint Shop Pro 5 cost under $100, and is a great value for anyone interested in creating and manipulating graphics. In comparison, Adobe PhotoShop costs $895 (street price is around $540). Paint Shop Pro is the most affordable graphics program available that offers sophisticated functionality, technical support, and ease of use.

The easiest way to register Paint Shop Pro is to order it on-line at **http://www.jasc.com/order.html**. With secure user encryption techniques, you can safely charge PSP to a major credit card in a matter of moments. The PSP on-line order page is shown in figure 2.3.

Fig. 2.3
Jasc Software makes it
easy for you to order
Paint Shop Pro.

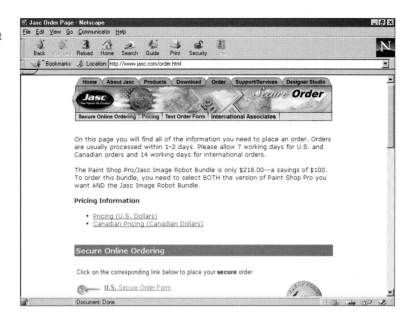

CAUTION

Sending your credit card information over the Internet is very secure if you
are using Netscape version 1.1 or higher, or Internet Explorer 2.0 or higher.
These encryption techniques provided by Netscape and Microsoft enable
complete data encryption so that prying eyes won't be able to see and filch
your credit card number for unsavory purposes.

Buying stuff on-line, such as books, software, and CD's is not only common
but safe—much safer than speaking your credit card number into a cordless
telephone, for example. That said, you can always call Jasc Software directly
if you still feel uncomfortable typing in your credit card on-line.

Besides purchasing Paint Shop Pro directly on-line at Jasc Software's Web
site, you can also buy it from your favorite computer store, such as
CompUSA or Microcenter. Purchasing Paint Shop Pro authorizes you to
use the software and entitles you to free technical support. You also
receive a complete user manual, many sample images on the PSP CD, and
a tutorial.

NOTE

If you prefer to order Paint Shop Pro the old-fashioned way (via telephone),
or you don't have a secure Web browser, call 1-800-622-2793 or 612-930-9800
and you can talk directly to a sales representative.

A Quick Tour of Paint Shop Pro

Now that you have Paint Shop Pro installed and running on your computer, let's start using it. If you are using the limited evaluation version, every time you start Paint Shop Pro, you will be reminded how much time you have left until your temporary license expires. Click on the **OK** button to continue, and you will see the main Paint Shop Pro 5 window.

As you'll quickly notice, most of the screen is blank—wide open for you to start building and creating your own Web graphics. You'll want to take notice of several toolbars and icon sets that line the top and sides of your screen. These icon sets, called toolbars (or palettes) in Paint Shop Pro, allow you to perform many common tasks at the click of your mouse button. In fact, several commands are only available through their respective icons. In this section, I'll show you each toolbar (or palette) and follow with an overview of what each is used for.

Note that many of these toolbars and palettes change, depending on what you are doing inside PSP. This feature, called Context-Sensitive functionality makes stepping you through every window you'll ever experience difficult in this quick tour, but you should get at least a flavor of the command types you can expect in each window.

The Tool Bar

Fig. 2.4
The Tool Bar

First off is the Tool Bar (figure 2.4), which is a set of miniature icons that represent common file commands you often use. Commands such as open, close, and view graphics are all accessible as an icon in the Tool Bar, as well as icons that toggle on and off the Control Palette, Color Palette, and Tool Palette (discussed below). If you aren't sure what each icon represents, let your mouse hover over it for a moment or two, and a small label will appear next to your mouse pointer.

You'll use this set of tools and icons often.

The Tool Palette

Fig. 2.5
The Tool Palette

The Tool Palette contains the main set of commands that you'll use to draw, paint, add new shapes and text, and generally edit your images. Shown in figure 2.5, this palette is covered in depth throughout this book. In the Tool Palette, you can select parts of your image, select a paint brush to use, touch up your graphic, or work with PSP Picture Tubes, flexible clip-art that comes in many shapes, sizes, and colors. You can even erase bits and pieces of your image with this palette.

The Control Palette

Fig. 2.6
The Control Palette

The set of selections in the Control Palette (see figure 2.6) dynamically changes, depending on which icon in the Tool Palette (figure 2.5) you select. Sometimes the Control Palette is a single set of options; other times you have multiple tabs of characteristics from which to choose. For example, when you click on the Paint Brushes icon from the Tool Palette, you can control your Brush Size and Paper texture.

Clicking on the Control Palette icon from the Tool Bar toggles this palette on and off.

TIP

Always keep your eye on the Control Palette to see what options are at your fingertips when you work with images. You will get additional flexibility with these dynamic options that determine how your Tool draws or makes changes to the graphic.

The Color Palette

Fig. 2.7
The Color Palette

Down the right-hand side of the screen, you'll notice the Color Palette (figure 2.7). From the Color Palette, you can choose the colors in which you are going to draw new shapes, text, or painting onto your image. Move your mouse over the vast array of colors at the top of the Color Palette. This section is called the Color Picker because you can click on any of the millions of different colors and shades to use when you draw or paint. The number of colors you can pick depends on the bit depth of the image.

Below the Color Picker is a set of two overlapping colors. These two colors represent the foreground and background painting colors that are currently active. The color on top (upper-left corner) is associated with your *left* mouse button while the color below (bottom-right corner) is associated with the *right* mouse button. You can set these colors by clicking the left or right mouse button anywhere in the Color Picker.

The Layer Palette

Fig. 2.8
The Layer Palette

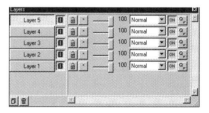

New to Paint Shop Pro 5 is the concept of layers. Layers let you separate your image into different levels so you can edit and modify pieces of a graphic at one time. The Layer Palette shown in figure 2.8 is the control center for creating, editing, and locking individual layers within your PSP images.

For much more information on how to use PSP Layers to their maximum potential, check out Chapter 7, "Using PSP Layers."

The Histogram Window

Fig. 2.9
The Histogram Window

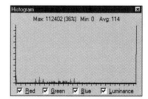

The Histogram Window is the final PSP toolbar to get familiar with. Used for advanced image creation by Web developers, the Histogram Window is a graphical representation of the color values used in your images. Many designers use it to check contrast and adjust their images to be optimized for printing. This feature is covered in Chapter 9, "Using Scanners and Digital Cameras."

Toggling the Toolbars

Each set of tools can be toggled on or off by clicking on its respective icon within the main PSP Tool Bar or by choosing **View**, **T**oolbars from the menu bar to bring up the Toolbars dialog box (figure 2.10).

Fig. 2.10
Toggle on and off the various Paint Shop Pro toolbars from here.

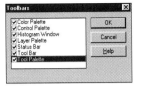

Select all the toolbars that you want to see from here, then click on the **OK** button to continue editing your images.

A Quick PSP Tutorial

Now that you're familiar with how to install Paint Shop Pro and you've taken your quick PSP tour, let's take a few moments to learn how to use some of the most important and useful features of Paint Shop Pro that you will use for creating web graphics.

This section gives you a broad overview of the types of features you can expect from Paint Shop Pro 5, each of which are covered later in this book. Besides bland features such as opening and saving your images, Paint Shop Pro allows you to crop part of an image, change colors instantly, and even deform your images to create interesting characteristics.

CAUTION

All of the topics covered in the next few pages are fully discussed later in this book. This section shows you the type of cool images available to you and how PSP lets you create them. Although the many steps listed may seem overwhelming, the process is very straightforward.

Let's get started by creating a new image from scratch. Choose **File**, **New** from the Paint Shop Pro menu bar to bring up the New Image dialog box shown in figure 2.11.

Fig. 2.11
Here's where all of your
new images start.

1. From the New Image dialog box, you can select the size of your new image in pixel coordinates or inches. Your computer screen's height and width is measured in pixels, not inches or centimeters. (I'll talk more about pixels and image size in the next chapter.) For now, simply enter 300 for both the height and width and make sure pixels (rather than inches) are selected. Then click the OK button and a medium-sized empty box should appear.

TIP

If your new image isn't simply white, it's probably because your current background color is set to something other than white. That's because the default PSP behavior is to make all new images whichever color is selected for your background (shown in the Color Palette).

2. Once your drawing space is ready to go, click on the Paint Brushes icon from the Tool Palette (see the icon in the margin at left).

3. From the Tool Controls tab in the Control Palette, pick a Paper Texture in which to work. (I selected Letters for this example.) Paper Textures let you paint with a cool texture instead of a solid thick coat of paint.

4. Click on the Brush Tip tab in the Control Palette and increase your brush size to something over 100 pixels. (I used a 124-pixel brush width for this example.)

5. Next, pick a light foreground color using the PSP Color Picker. I used a light shade of red (pinkish) for this example, but a light shade of any color would work nicely. Figure 2.12 shows all of the PSP settings outlined in the steps above, ready to build an image.

Fig. 2.12
Notice the 300 x 300 empty white box and all my Control Palette settings.

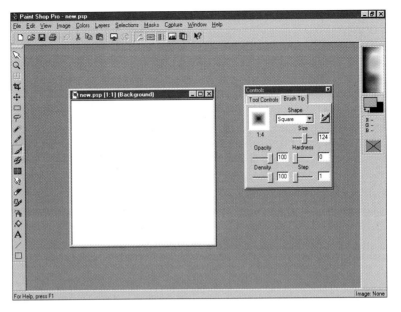

6. Here's where you get to be creative. Using your mouse, paint letters on the screen using Paint Shop Pro Paper Textures (covered in detail in the next chapter). Click and hold your left mouse button inside your white box, and you'll start drawing a lettered background on your image. Figure 2.13 shows my background with the letters included.

Fig. 2.13
Don't worry if your background of letters isn't perfect; we'll fix that in a few moments!

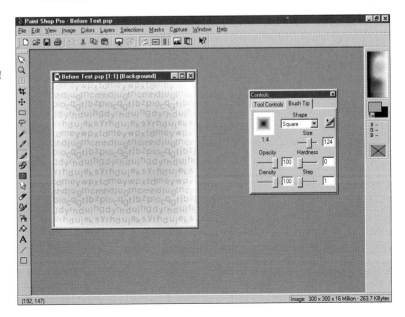

7. Now click on the Text icon from the Tool Palette. This tool lets you add bits and pieces of text to your images.

8. Also, change your foreground color to something dark—black or navy blue works great (I picked black).

9. Click your *left* mouse button anywhere within your image and the Add Text dialog box appears (figure 2.14).

Fig. 2.14
From here, you can control the font, size, and style of text you add to your image.

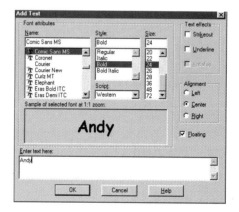

10. At the bottom of the Add Text dialog box is a spot where PSP asks you to Enter your text. Type in a short word or phrase—perhaps your name—and select a large font size and style, using other options in this dialog box. Click on the OK button, and Paint Shop Pro adds the text to your image, but puts a dotted selection line around it to indicate that you can use your mouse to drag it anywhere on your image.

11. Once you've found the right spot for your image, click on the right mouse button, and your text is placed on the image. Figure 2.15 shows my image with text placed on it.

Fig. 2.15
I am creating a simple button for my personal use.

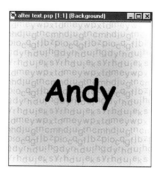

12. Almost done! Click on the Freehand icon (it looks like a miniature lasso). Now draw a rough outline around your image so that it circles your entire piece of text. You are selecting part of the image with which to create a button.

13. Now choose **E**dit, **C**opy from the menu bar to make a copy of the selected image on your clipboard.

14. Then choose **E**dit, **P**aste, As **N**ew Image from the menu bar. A second image appears on the screen containing only the section you selected. Figure 2.16 shows PSP with both the original and the pasted images.

Fig. 2.16
Notice that the pasted image has rough borders; these correspond to my selection with the freehand tool.

Original Image

Pasted Image

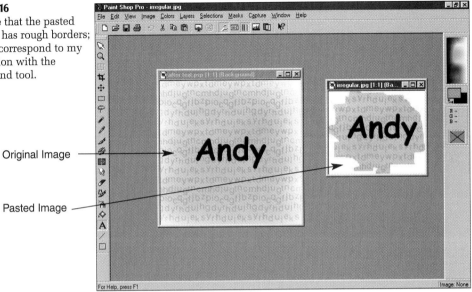

15. Now you can save your new image by selecting File, Save from the menu bar. Figure 2.17 shows the Save As dialog box. Make sure you use the GIF or JPG format so the image looks good on a Web page.

Fig. 2.17
Give your image a meaningful name so you can find it later.

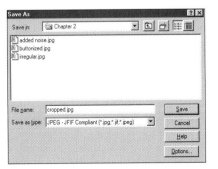

That wasn't difficult, was it? Now let's take a look figure 2.18, which shows how the image looks inside of a Web browser. This is a simple HTML page that loads up the image.

Fig. 2.18
Create a unique image
for your Web site in
just a few minutes.

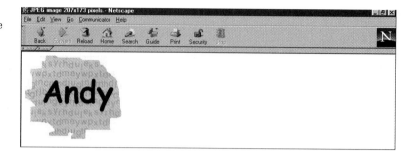

Just to give you a flavor of what to expect in this book, let's look at other
cool built-in features and deformations you can run on your graphics.
Again, these topics are covered in great detail later in the book.

NOTE

All the following deformations require you to edit an image with 16.7 million
colors or a 256 grey scale image. If you aren't using an image that's saved as a
JPG, choose Colors, Increase Color Depth, **16** Million Colors from the menu
bar. I'll talk much more about color depth later in this book.

In Table 2.1 is a set of three versions of the image I created above. All
three started with the same cut-out image shown in figure 2.18, then I
added extra Paint Shop Pro effects to each.

CAUTION

Be careful not to just hit File, **S**ave on the menu bar after you have modified
your image, or you'll lose the original version. Always use File, Save **A**s or
File, Save Copy As instead and give your new image a different name.

TIP

If you are unhappy with a change you make, choose **E**dit, **U**ndo from the
menu bar and Paint Shop Pro will quickly revert your image back to the
original size, or pre-crop state. You can undo many commands. In fact, you
are limited to the number of steps you can undo only by your computer's
memory.

Method	Image
Table 2.1 Paint Shop Pro Special Effects	
Image, Effects, **B**uttonize	
Image, **N**oise, **A**dd	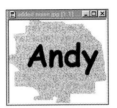
Image, **D**eformations, Circle	

Of course, you can save all these different images for your future use. Don't be afraid to explore other types of Deformations, Special Effects, and Filters available through PSP. Chapter 5, "Images and Special Effects" goes over these topics in much more detail.

Using Paint Shop Pro's Help System

As you read this book, you'll find many of Paint Shop Pro's advanced features discussed in detail. In addition to the Paint Shop Pro manual, use this book to guide you through deformations, special effects, saving and loading new images, and much more.

In addition, Paint Shop Pro 5 comes with a comprehensive and extremely useful interactive help system. Nearly any topic you can think of that relates to making or configuring images is presented. Paint Shop Pro functionality and many tips are also discussed in the Help System.

To access the on-line interactive help, choose **Help**, **H**elp Topics from the menu bar. Figure 2.19 shows the Help Index in action.

Fig. 2.19
Paint Shop Pro's Help system is a wonderful resource for creating graphics.

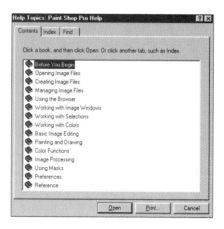

3
Creating Simple Graphics

Creating graphics is like doing any complicated task; you've got to learn how to walk before you can run. This chapter introduces you to many basic, but important techniques found within Paint Shop Pro 5. You'll soon see how you can build virtually any graphic you like once you become comfortable with this foundation.

You'll learn important details about the different options available when creating, saving, and drawing new images from scratch. I'll step you through several examples and teach you the best way to save and optimize your graphics for Web sites.

▶ **Create New Images**
There are several options available when making a new image. Understand how to choose the image size and the number of necessary colors for your Web graphics.

▶ **Save Your Images**
Creating your images is worthwhile only when you can save and recall them at a later date. I'll walk you through the entire process of saving a new graphic in the right format for the Web and familiarize you with all the different save options.

▶ **Understand Pixel Height and Width**
Knowing how to control the size and appearance of your images is critical to your understanding of graphics production. Learn what pixels are, how your computer measures them, and what to remember when making new images.

▶ **Draw Multiple Shapes**
Ovals, lines, and rectangles are all readily available with built-in drawing tools. Understand how to draw these shapes when building an image.

Making a New Image

At this point, you've already installed or upgraded to Paint Shop Pro 5 and toured PSP using several icons and palettes that house the drawing and painting tools. You've even seen some of PSP's advanced functionality for deforming and drawing great images.

Now it is time to thoroughly describe each step required to build and edit a graphic from scratch. In this section, I'll take you through the process of creating and then saving an image, explaining all the file options available through PSP.

Your first step in learning how to create and save a new file is to start up Paint Shop Pro 5. You can do this by double-clicking on the Paint Shop Pro icon that appears on your computer after installation. Alternatively, you can choose **Start, Programs, Paint Shop Pro 5, Paint Shop Pro 5** from the Windows 95 menu bar at the bottom of your screen. Paint Shop Pro will begin with an empty desktop, ready to get to work.

Once Paint Shop Pro is loaded, choose **File, New** from the menu bar to bring up the New Image dialog box (see figure 3.1). This dialog box is divided into two main sections—Image Dimensions and Image Characteristics, with several settings within each section. It is important that you understand exactly what these options indicate. Below, I describe and summarize the issues surrounding each option.

Fig. 3.1
All new images start from this dialog box.

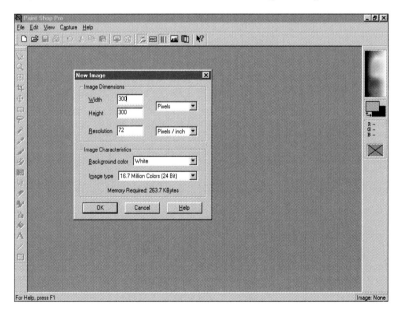

Understanding Image Dimensions

The first thing you need to decide when building a new image is how large you want it to be. Determining height and width is extremely important because image size affects how Web browsers display your image, and directly correlates to your image's file size. Thus, your image's height and width affect the time required for visitors to download and view your image on a Web page, an important metric in WWW usability. In general, you want graphics to be as small as possible so Web browsers can see them quickly.

Your computer screen's height and width is measured in pixels—which stands for *picture element*. For example, a standard VGA monitor can display 640 pixels across and 480 pixels vertically (640 x 480). Super VGA (SVGA) resolution offers 800 x 600 pixel resolution, and Enhanced SVGA offers 1024 x 768 resolution and better! Pixels are little dots going across your screen that make up the pictures and images that you can see. Usually, you can't see individual pixels, but you do see the words and images that are made up of thousands of coordinated pixels.

The higher the resolution (number of pixels), the more information a user can fit on one screen. Thus, creating a new image that has 320 x 240 pixel coordinates takes up approximately half a VGA screen, and about one-third of an Enhanced SVGA screen. Figure 3.2 shows how these three resolutions compare with one another.

NOTE

In this section, I talk primarily about screen resolution characteristics for PC compatible computers. Remember that the WWW is universal in computer access and that all sorts of computers will have access to the graphics and images on your Web page. Some Macintoshes and high-powered Sun or Hewlett-Packard workstations might have significantly higher screen resolutions available at their disposal. In general, though, the PC pixel sizings are a common denominator and should be used as a guide when creating your Web images.

Fig. 3.2
Compare the three
popular screen
resolutions.

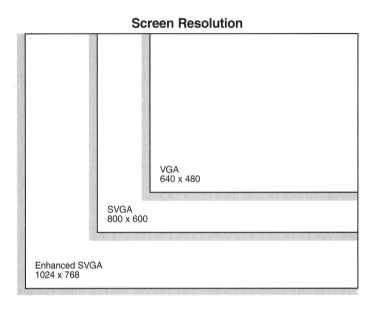

As a general rule, always design your Web page (and, consequently, your Web images) for the lowest screen resolution. This ensures that your images can be seen by anyone who surfs the WWW conveniently and easily. This means you should always size your image within the 640 x 480 height and width category. In fact, to properly ensure that your images can always be seen on a Web page, no image should ever be more than 600 pixels wide and 440 pixels tall. I removed 40 pixels from each axis to ensure that the graphic can fit within the Web browser's borders.

Figures 3.3 and 3.4 below show a sample headline image that is 300 pixels tall but 700 pixels wide. Although the two images look similar, they are taken in two different screen resolutions. Figure 3.4 shows this image on a monitor whose resolution is 800 x 600. The image looks fine here. However, in figure 3.3, the image doesn't fit on my Web page with a 640 x 480 screen resolution. As a result, the image looks good only to those using higher screen resolutions. One solution is to re-size my image to fit on the smaller screen resolution, thus making it work for all visitors who stop by. Like most images, this headline would easily fit within a 600 x 440 limit by changing the text size or spacing. I simply had to be aware of and stay within my upper limits to ensure that anyone who visits my site would be able to see the graphic as intended.

Fig. 3.3
My headline image at VGA resolution requires viewers to scroll to the right to see the entire image.

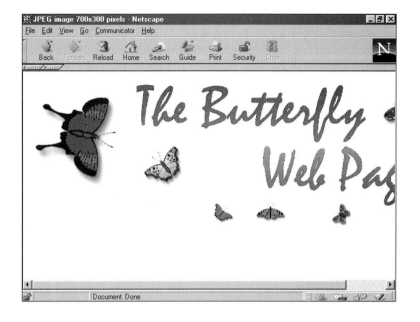

Fig. 3.4
The same image in Netscape, but at SVGA resolution

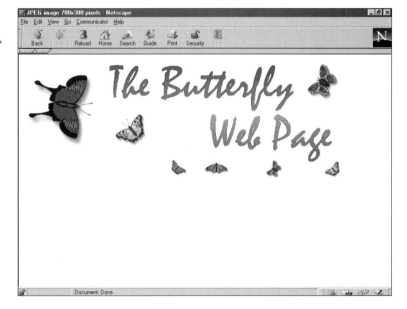

TIP

When using images that fit smaller screen resolutions, many Web developers follow the strategy of centering their images on the screen. By adding <CENTER> and </CENTER> around the HTML that displays the image, the Web graphic looks fine on higher screen resolution monitors because the white space flanking the image doesn't look like blank, wasted area on the Web site.

Other Web developers use HTML tables to center and lay out images on their pages to make sure that all visitors get a similar experience when they stop by.

Now that you are familiar with pixels and screen resolution, it's time to return to the New Image dialog box within Paint Shop Pro and figure out how big *your* image should be. Different types of images require different height and width coordinates. Table 3.1 gives general guidelines for the pixel dimensions you should choose when creating specific types of Web graphics.

Table 3.1
Dimension Guidelines
for Web Images

Image Type	Height and Width Coordinates (in pixels)
Small Icon	25 x 25
Medium-sized Icon	40 x 40
Large Icon	60 x 60
Horizontal Bar	10 x 500
Headline Graphic	150 x 600
Common WWW Ad Size	300 x 72
Logo or Photograph	300 x 400

In the New Image dialog box that appears in Paint Shop Pro (refer to figure 3.1), type in the appropriate **W**idth and He**i**ght in each labeled box. The default sizing in Paint Shop Pro is pixels, so typing in 300 for height and 300 for width will create a 300 x 300–pixel blank image. However, you can also size your image in inches and centimeters. To the right of the Height and Width boxes is a drop-down list that lets you select the units to which your Height and Width values correspond. Changing the units for a new image is useful only if you intend to create graphics to print, such as for a flyer or brochure. Since this book focuses on Web graphics, we'll always create graphics according to pixel size, not inches or centimeters.

NOTE

Below the Height and Width settings, in the Image Dimension section of the New Image dialog box, are two more available options. These two settings also relate to creating images for printing, instead of for the Web.

By default, the standard resolution for an image is 72 pixels per inch (PPI), which is standard for computer monitors. You can change both the quantity and units of resolution for creating printed images. When you want to create images to print, often you'll change this value to something like 600 or 1200 PPI. The higher the resolution, the more detailed your printout appears. That's why printed material often appears much crisper than on standard computer monitors—it has a much higher resolution—and why the graphics on printed Web pages often look fuzzy.

For your image to print properly, you must also have a printer capable of printing 600 x 600 or 1200 x 1200 resolution if you increase your image resolution.

Note that the size of your image in pixel coordinates is roughly proportional to file size. Although not always true, images that are larger and contain more pixels will be larger in file size than those containing fewer pixels (count your pixels by multiplying Height and Width). However, file size is even more dependent on the number of colors used in the picture, the file type you choose (GIF or JPEG), and how "busy" (full of different shapes and designs) your image actually is. Chapter 12, "Making Your Graphics Lean," focuses on this specific issue and offers tips to help you keep your final image file size down.

Understanding Background Color

Now that you've decided how big your image should appear on screen, the next choices in the New Image dialog box relate to color. You have to set the background color of the new image and decide how many different colors will be available when you work with Paint Shop Pro.

The **B**ackground color option simply refers to the default color in which your newly created image will appear. You can choose from several options, including white, black, red, green, and blue. In addition, you can set the background color to whatever is currently set as your foreground or background color from the Color Palette on the right-hand side of the screen or set it to be transparent. This lets you choose from over 16.7 million shades and hues of color. Before creating a new image, use your mouse to select the appropriate color from the PSP Color Picker. Set the color for either the foreground (using the left mouse button) or the background (using the right mouse button) by clicking anywhere within the Color Picker. Then, when you create a new image, the Background Color drop-down box allows you to select either your *Foreground Color* or *Background Color* instead of the handful of standard ones listed. A transparent background means that there is no color in the background of this new image.

In general, most Web images start with a background color of white and add more colors as necessary.

Choosing the Correct Number of Colors

The last choice available in the New Image dialog box is the Image type, meaning the number of colors available for this graphic. From this drop-down box, you have five options. Table 3.2 below lists each option and explains when you want to use each of them for your own graphics.

The number of available colors has a direct impact on how your image appears and its file size. You should choose an Image type that has a lot of colors available only when you really need many colors because file size can increase as the number of colors increases. Table 3.2 shows you a comparison of your five different Image Type options.

Table 3.2
Image Type
Explanation

Image Type	When you want to use this Option
2 Colors (1 bit)	In general, this image type is only useful for very simple and plain-looking graphics. It allows only two colors—black and white; not even shades of gray are permitted. Images in this format, however, are extremely small and efficient. Ted Turner's movie colorizing company would hate this file type, but you should use it if it meets your needs.
16 Colors (4 bit)	Sixteen colors are useful when you create simple drawings or line art (scanned hand-drawn images). Windows originally supported only 16 colors that roughly covered most of the rainbow and became the defaults for many applications and graphics. Many impressive images can be created with this many colors. Only the GIF format supports the limited palette of 16 colors. The JPEG, PNG, and PSP image formats automatically allow 16.7 million colors regardless of the number selected.
Greyscale (8 bit)	Offering the maximum number of shades that GIFs can support, this option allows more flexibility than just black and white by offering 256 different shades of grey. Because there is no performance incentive to using 256 shades of gray instead of 256 varied colors, you'll find yourself using this format sparingly. Chapter 8, "The Black and White Alternative," delves into several situations where greyscale images come in handy.

256 Colors (8 bit)	You'll probably choose this selection, the standard 256 colors that most GIFs use, often when creating your own images from scratch. It represents a compromise between the millions of colors you could never even name, and a reasonable number of colors with which to paint. Unfortunately, many of the cool PSP features don't support the 256-color option, so you'll only use this format when you know you have fewer than 256 colors in your image. The default 256 colors used are the same ones you'll find at the default VGA setting for most monitors.
16.7 Million Colors (24 bit)	With 16.7 million colors available, you never have to use a single color twice. This option is used when you plan to save your image in JPG form or need to use some of PSP's advanced features. Many of these features require that you have 16.7 million colors available because PSP mixes and matches thousands of colors for you automatically. For example, the images you created in "A Quick PSP Tutorial" in Chapter 2, "Using and Installing Paint Shop Pro 5," required 16.7 million colors. GIF images cannot be saved in 16.7 million color (24 bit) format. Paint Shop Pro will reduce the number of colors used in an image to only 256 if you try to save a 24-bit image into the GIF file format.

NOTE

Here's how computer programs such as Netscape, Internet Explorer (IE), and Paint Shop Pro know how many colors are available in an image. Computer files are saved in a format called binary, a bunch of ones and zeros concatenated onto one another. Large strings of binary numbers saved together are interpreted by a computer and then displayed as your image.

In table 3.2 above, each format is followed by a value within parentheses that lists how many bits are needed for that format. You can figure out how many colors are available for a format by multiplying 2 to the nth power, where n is the number of bits listed. So for 2 colors (1 bit), multiply 2 to the 1st power, for a total value of 2. For 256 colors (8 bits), multiply 2 to the 8th power, which is 256. And for 16.7 million colors (24 bits), multiply 2 to the 24th power—which results in 16,777,216 different colors available. Wow!

A 16.7-million color file requires 24 bits of disk space to recognize each color you refer to. However, when you use only 256 colors, it takes just 8 bits of disk space to recognize a specified color. Therefore, three different colors can be defined in the 256-color file in the same amount of space it takes to define just one color in the 16.7 million-color file. As you can imagine, the lower the number of colors you choose, the smaller your file size could be, because Paint Shop Pro doesn't have to waste 24 bits defining a single color when it saves your image. If your image is simply black and white, only one bit is needed to save each color, representing a savings of 95% in file size.

In general, always choose *16.7 million colors*. You can always reduce the number of colors used when saving your image to see if you can shrink its file size.

Now, select an Image type and click the **OK** button. Paint Shop Pro makes your new image appear on the screen. Figure 3.5 shows a freshly created blank image.

Fig. 3.5
So far, this 300 x 300 pixel image is pretty boring.

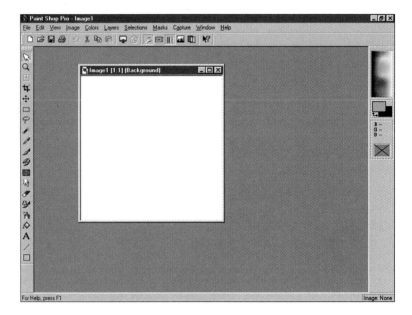

Dithering, the Web, and You

Just because you select 16.7 million colors for your image doesn't mean that everyone in the world will get to enjoy the images you created to their fullest extent. That's because many people have computers that only support 256 colors instead of all 16.7 million. In fact some people still use computers that support only 16 colors.

So what happens when someone with a 256-color monitor sees a full color image? That's when a process called *dithering* takes over. Dithering is the process of your computer interpolating how each color should appear by mixing together pixels from the limited palette it has available. For example, if the 16.7-million color palette contains a color that is bright green, the 256-color monitor might alternate the pixels on the screen between yellow and blue. When your eye looks at the image, it mixes the yellow and blue pixels together and fools you into seeing green.

While dithering is useful, the resulting image is rarely as exact or detailed as the original, and you have no control over what your visitors actually see when they stop by your page. Depending on how their computer or browser is set up, all your hard work on a full 16.7 million-color image might be wasted if that image dithers poorly.

Fortunately, many computer systems nowadays support 16.7 million colors or dither images rather well. But this is an important issue to consider when creating and publishing graphics to the Web. Paint Shop Pro has many advanced techniques that self-dither images down to 256 colors. Then you can save that image in 256-color mode to use on your Web page so that all visitors will see the same image when they stop by.

If you want to know how many colors your monitor supports, go to the Windows 95 desktop and click the *right* mouse button. Choose **Properties** from the pop-up window to bring up the Display Properties dialog box. Click on the tab labeled **Settings** and you'll see your current system color and screen resolution settings. Figure 3.6 shows mine—notice how I am at 24-bit color and 800 x 600 resolution.

Fig. 3.6
See how you can change your color and resolution system settings.

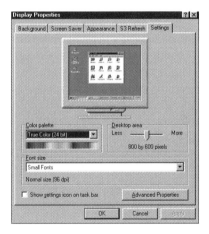

Saving Your Graphic

This section will show you how to save your newly made image so you can use it on your Web page or edit it again at a later date. You'll want to save often when creating Web graphics so your enhancements are permanently stored as a file.

Saving your images in Paint Shop Pro is rather easy. Choose File, Save **As** from the menu bar to bring up the Save As dialog box (figure 3.7).

Fig. 3.7
Name your file and tell Paint Shop Pro which image type to use.

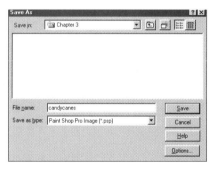

Two steps are required to save your file, both of which are explained in detail below. First you choose a file name; then you select an Image Type.

Naming your Web graphic file is easy. Simply type in a short but descriptive name in the box labeled File **n**ame. Although Windows 95 allows a name to be any length and to contain spaces and punctuation, try to keep your name short and sweet. You may have to enter in your file name as you create your HTML Web page, and a short name will be easier to type.

CAUTION

Some WWW servers and browsers have problems with file names that use spaces, commas, slashes, and the tilde (~) character. Unless you are sure your Web Server can handle the extended characters in file names, avoid using them in your file name to prevent problems when adding Web graphics to your site.

After naming your file, the next step is to select an Image type from the Save as **t**ype drop-down box. Although Paint Shop Pro allows you to pick from over two dozen different image types, your first choice is to use the new PSP image format. The PSP image format is the ideal place to store all your images as you work on them because it supports all the advanced Paint Shop Pro features, uses 16.7 million colors, and compresses in a non-lossy fashion.

Don't forget to save your image in the proper subdirectory on your computer. Once you are ready, click on the **S**ave button and voila, your image is saved!

The only problem with using the PSP image format is that it isn't supported within Web browsers. So, what you should do is always edit and save your images in the PSP format. Then when you are ready to publish a graphic to your Web site, choose either the GIF, JPG, or PNG image formats instead. This process lets you use all the great features in PSP to your advantage and keep a master set of images set apart from the images up on your Web site. You'll find this makes it much easier to manage and work with your images, especially as you start using advanced PSP features such as layering, masks, and filters.

TIP
To save a copy of your image with a different file name, you can also choose File, Save Cop**y** As from the menu bar.

Publishing Images to the Web

Once you are finished editing or creating your images in Paint Shop Pro, you'll need to convert them from the PSP file format into a GIF, JPG, or PNG.

Chapter 1 introduced you to these three formats and clarified when you'll want to use each of them. This section describes the various options available when you choose each image type from the Save As dialog box.

GIF Format

To save your graphic in GIF format, choose **CompuServe Graphics Interchange** from the drop-down box. Paint Shop Pro automatically adds the proper file extension to the file you name you typed.

Once you select GIF, click on the **O**ptions button to bring up the Save Options dialog box for GIFs (figure 3.8).

Fig. 3.8
There are several different ways to save a GIF.

In general, you'll want to accept the default settings from here—Version 89a and Noninterlaced. The Version number designates the year ("89" is 1989) in which the standard was adopted. Version 87a and 89a are very similar and all Web browsers (and PSP) support both types. Version 89a also enables you to take advantage of GIF animation (see Chapter 11, "Moving Graphics Creating GIF Animation") and GIF transparency.

The Interlacing option is more interesting. When an image is saved with interlacing turned on, Web browsers display the image in several passes, with each pass bringing the image into more detail. Displaying an interlaced image is similar to visiting an optometry office and having a few adjustments made to your glasses so that fuzzy letters become clear. Using interlaced images slightly increases your file size, but is an excellent option for Web developers who are creating large images. Such images give your visitors a feeling for how the image will look as it downloads from the Internet.

Interlacing is good for large GIFs, but is not needed for small icons, graphics, and buttons. Chapter 12, "Making Your Graphics Lean" covers interlacing in more detail with several examples.

JPG Format

Another available image type is JPG. Save your graphic in JPG format by choosing JPEG—JFIF Compliant from the Save as **t**ype drop-down list box (refer to figure 3.7). Remember that the JPG image type uses 16.7 million colors but is often more efficient when you are compressing large images that use many colors—such as photographs. PSP adds the **.jpg** extension to your file name automatically.

Similar to GIF, the JPG file type also has a few options from which to select. Click on the **O**ptions button to see the Save Options dialog box for JPG images (figure 3.9).

Fig. 3.9
JPG has fewer options from which to choose.

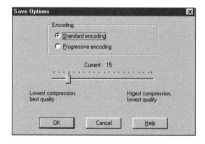

You can choose between Standard or Progressive JPGs and select the amount of compression you want to use for this file. Standard and Progressive JPGs correlate exactly with Noninterlaced and Interlaced GIFs, respectively. Progressive JPGs appear in several passes, while a standard JPG downloads one line at a time from top to bottom. Progressive JPGs also offer a 5% savings in file size from the standard JPG file type.

JPG Compression lets you trade off file size with image quality, another topic covered in Chapter 12, "Making Your Graphics Lean." JPG compression can be manipulated if you need to shrink your image size and don't mind losing some detail.

PNG Format

The final Web graphic type you might use is the PNG format. Choose **Portable Network Graphics** from the Save as **t**ype box, and Paint Shop Pro will add the **.png** file extension for you.

Be careful when using this image type; only the most recent Web browsers support PNG images and the thousands of people stopping by your site might not have the latest and greatest software.

Drawing Shapes

Making and saving images is only the first part of creating Web graphics. Once you have these two fundamentals down, it's time to start adding some shapes, text, and color to your actual graphics. Thus far, you've been working with boring graphics that are only a rectangular block of a single color.

Although Paint Shop Pro offers tremendous flexibility in saving and converting graphics of all types and formats, PSP originally got its start as a robust drawing and paint package. Whether you are a graphics artist or a new user, anyone can create great looking Web graphics with PSP's built-in tools.

This section shows you how to draw several different types of shapes and objects when you build your graphics from scratch. Most Web graphics are simple combinations of these basic shapes and objects.

Using the Grid and Ruler

Two important new tools will help you in your quest to create great-looking Web Graphics—the Grid and the Ruler.

The Grid is a set of lines that PSP displays on top of your image (they don't get saved with your graphic) to help you line up your cursor when drawing. To toggle the PSP grid on and off, select **V**iew, **G**rid from the menu bar.

Another feature you'll find handy is the Ruler. The ruler gives you an idea of image size (in pixels, inches, or centimeters); this can be useful when you are centering and drawing on your image. Toggle the Ruler on and off by choosing View, **R**ulers from the PSP menu bar.

Figure 3.10 shows an image with the grid and ruler activated.

Fig. 3.10
The grid and ruler are useful tools for building all graphics.

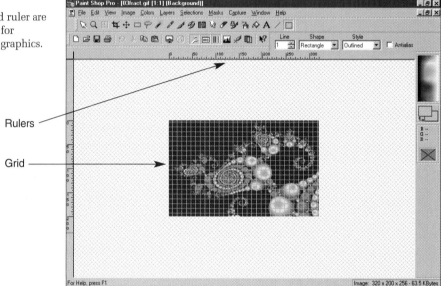

Rulers

Grid

You can set and change the units and width of the grid and ruler by choosing **F**ile, Pre**f**erences, **G**eneral Program Preferences from the menu bar to bring up the Paint Shop Pro Preferences dialog box. Select the tab labeled Rulers and Units (figure 3.11).

Fig. 3.11
Change the grid spacing or ruler units from here.

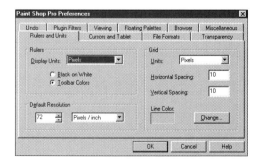

Choosing Colors

Before you can draw an object, you must choose the active colors for your drawing tools. Use the Color Palette on the right-hand side of the screen to select the different colors for your image.

Notice the two overlapping squares in the color palette. These represent your current foreground and background colors.

The foreground color corresponds to drawing something with your *left* (or primary) mouse button and the background color corresponds with the *right* (or secondary) mouse button. Whenever you draw or add an object to your Web graphic, it appears in the color selected, depending on which mouse button (right or left) you choose to draw with. Foreground and background colors have several different additional uses. For example, they are used when you choose to add a gradient color to your image or decide to buttonize a graphic.

You can change the current foreground or background colors in two ways. The easiest way is to click your left or right mouse button in the rainbow of colors known as the Color Picker, directly above the overlapping color squares. Your color is set according to whichever color you click in the rainbow. Clicking your left mouse button sets the foreground color and clicking the right mouse button sets the background color.

Often, it is hard to click on the exact color you want to use within the Color Picker. The other way to set your colors is by clicking on the foreground or background color squares. Paint Shop Pro brings up the Color dialog box as shown in figure 3.12. This color dialog box only appears if your image uses 16.7 million colors.

Fig. 3.12
Millions of colors are available.

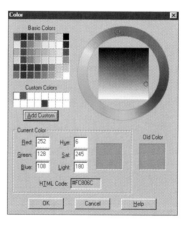

You can choose from one of the 48 basic colors or from the larger Color Picker on the right-hand side. Click the OK button to set your colors.

TIP

You can quickly switch your foreground and background colors with each other by clicking on the double-headed arrow between the two active colors you are using, in the Main PSP Window.

Drawing Lines

A line is the most basic object you can create on an image. Paint Shop Pro allows you to create a line by simply clicking the Line icon from the Tool Palette at the top of the screen and then drawing a simple line on your image. Use the left mouse button to draw your line in the foreground color, and the right mouse button to use the color defined as the background.

Once you click the Line icon, the Control Palette let's you modify the Width and Line Type options, which allow you to specify the thickness (in pixels) of the lines you want to draw and the type of line you wish to create. You can specify any whole number between 1 and 100 to select how thick your line will be. Two line types are available: Normal and Bezier. A Normal line allows you to simply create a line between two points while a Bezier line lets you create curved lines on your image. Bezier lines require that you to first draw the line, then add curve to it with your mouse.

When drawing, make sure you use a thickness that isn't too thin and difficult to see. Figure 3.13 shows a simple drawing I created from three straight lines and one Bezier line, each with a thickness of 10 pixels.

Fig. 3.13
Although only a few lines, all baseball fans should recognize this image.

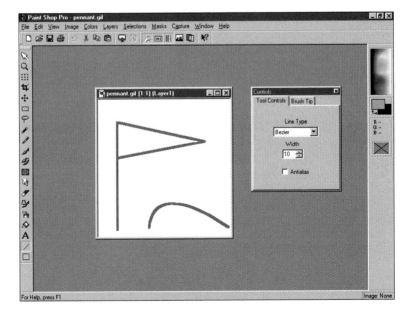

TIP
Practice using the powerful Bezier-lines tool. First you draw the line, then once the endpoints are fixed, you can add curvature to the line by clicking anywhere between the fixed ends and pulling away from the line. Paint Shop Pro automatically builds a full and natural-looking curve for you.

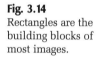

Drawing Shapes

Paint Shop Pro also enables you to create rectangular and elliptical shapes in any size and color. Simply click the Shapes icon in the Tool Palette. All you need to do is tell Paint Shop Pro which shape you want to draw in the Control Palette, and then click and draw the shape on your image with the mouse.

In the Tool Controls tab of the Control palette, you have several options. First, you can pick which of four shapes you want to draw (rectangle, square, ellipse, or circle), then you can select whether you want the shape to appear filled in or just as an outline, and finally you can select the thickness of the shape's border.

Rectangles and Squares

Any math major will tell you that a square is simply a special kind of rectangle in which all four sides are the same length. Fortunately, PSP lets you differentiate between the two, making it easy for you to create proportional squares or rectangles individually.

Choose rectangle or square from the Control Palette, then select a drawing color, and you are ready to start drawing. Figure 3.14 shows a handmade drawing created with only filled in squares. For each part of the pyramid, I chose a different color from the PSP Color Picker.

Fig. 3.14
Rectangles are the building blocks of most images.

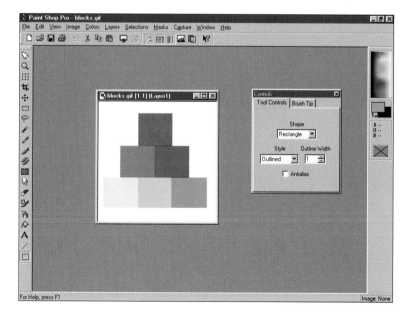

Ellipses and Circles

Using the same general procedure as you do when creating rectangles and squares, you can easily build ellipses and circles. Ellipses and circles have the same available control options discussed above, and you can draw any kind of oval, ellipse, circle, or round shape with the Shapes.

First click the Shapes icon, then decide the line thickness of your ellipse or circle, and choose whether you want it filled in or drawn as an outline shape using the Control Palette. Once you have selected your options, use your mouse to draw as many shapes as you need. Of course, you can also change colors for each new circle you draw. Figure 3.15 shows an inchworm made completely of ellipses. Sixteen ellipses filled with different colors combine to make this sample Web graphic.

Fig. 3.15
Using circular and elliptical shapes, any graphic imaginable is at your fingertips.

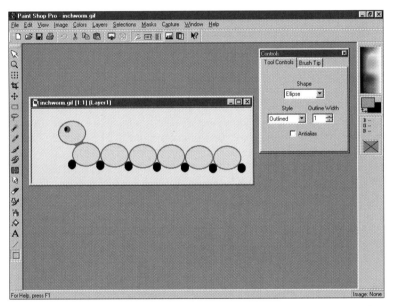

TIP

If you accidentally draw a shape or line of the wrong size, shape, or color, you can always choose **Edit**, **Undo** from the menu bar (or hit Ctrl-Z from the keyboard), and Paint Shop Pro will retract the last shape drawn or change made to your Web graphic. In fact, PSP lets you undo the last few commands, not just the most previous one issued.

Using the Paint Brush

Now that you are familiar with drawing shapes and lines for new Web graphics, it's time to look at some other important tools available with Paint Shop Pro. Leading that list of tools is the Paint Brush, a virtual marker that lets you draw freehand any shape, color, or pattern on your Web graphic.

You can draw literally any shape or design imaginable with the PSP Paint Brush. It's just like drawing on a piece of paper with a marker but you use your mouse and screen instead. You can draw a line, erase a smudge, change colors, accentuate a shape, save your changes, and choose different tools (chalk, marker, pen, and so on) with which to paint.

Out of all the available PSP tools, you'll probably use the Paint Brush most often. It can be used to add small touch-up details to a Web graphic, to create colorful and interesting patterns and backgrounds, and to paint shapes of all sorts on your screen. In fact, unless you are creating a specific line, oval, or rectangle, the Paint Brush is likely to be your tool of choice when you create Web graphics.

Click the Paint Brush icon from the Paint Shop Pro Tool Palette. Immediately, several options are available in the Brush Tip tab of the Control Palette. These controls give you flexibility over how your paint brush performs when you draw on the screen. They are tremendously useful and effective when you design graphics from scratch.

Using the Brush Tip Tab of the Control Palette

The Control Palette is the center where you can control most of the options and flexibility that the Paint Brush has to offer. Figure 3.16 shows the Brush Tip tab from the Control Palette.

Fig. 3.16
You can configure your Paint Brush in several different ways.

PSP always shows a preview of how your brush will appear when you start painting with it. The top part of the Control Palette lets you select the Size and Shape of your Brush while the bottom section gives you flexibility in setting four important characteristics of your Paint Brush.

Brush Size

Size, the easiest option to choose, is measured in pixels. You can type a number in directly, or drag the size bar left or right. Brush size ranges from 1–200 pixels

Brush Shape

When you paint your graphics, sometimes you may want to use a paint brush that has a slightly different or unique shape to it. With the Paint Brush tool, Paint Shop Pro provides six different shapes you can choose to paint with.

You can use all different shapes, depending on which you select from the **S**hape drop-down box in the Control Palette. Figure 3.17 shows you a sample of all six shapes and how they all appear using a standard paint brush.

Fig. 3.17
All six Paint Brushes are useful when building and editing images.

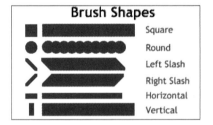

Brush Options

The easiest cool effect you can create will probably result from the Brush Options you select. Normally, you might select a standard paint brush that paints as you would expect.

Additionally, Paint Shop Pro lets you select from among seven different brush options, each of which emulate a different type of drawing utensil. Instead of a standard paint brush, you can choose from charcoal, crayon, pen, pencil, marker, or chalk.

Each brush option has its own unique flavor and style, which will allow you to add different appearances and textures to drawings by simply working with multiple brush options. For example, if you are creating a graphic for a Web page about or for children, you might choose the Crayon brush type to draw your image because it would create an appearance commonly associated with kids. Figure 3.18 lists all seven brush options along with an example of how each appears when used.

Fig. 3.18
Customizing your
brush type lets you add
unique personality to
your images.

NOTE

In case you're interested, creating the graphic in figure 3.18 required me to select each different brush size and manually draw a straight line across the screen with a steady hand.

I created images like this for my own personal reference and for this book. You can download them or see them yourself at the book's Web site.

Setting Brush Characteristics

At the bottom of the palette you'll find four settings that control different characteristics of your paint brush. These options affect how dark your paint brush appears, how well it integrates with the rest of the image, and other characteristics. Table 3.3 defines each of these characteristics.

Table 3.3

Characteristic	Explanation
Opacity	Controls how much of the background you can see through the paint brush stroke.
Density	Designates the number of pixels with which the Paint Brush paints, evenly spread across the whole brushstroke.
Hardness	Controls how hard the brushstroke will be. The lower the hardness settings, the softer around the edges your paint brushstroke appears, making it flow more smoothly into your background.
Step	Defines the distance between overlapping brushstrokes.

Figure 3.19 shows several example settings for each characteristic to give you a good idea of the flexibility you have when using the paint brush.

Fig. 3.19
Don't be afraid to mix and match settings across multiple characteristics.

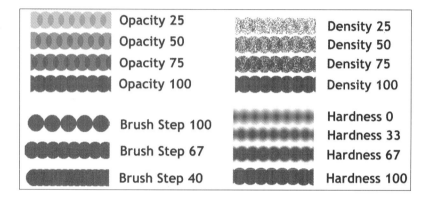

Changing Paper Textures

The final and most impressive option the Paint Brush tool gives you is the ability to select a particular Paper Texture. This option works much like the Brush Option described above, but offers significantly more flexibility and usefulness when you are painting. Normally your paint brush paints with a single color in the size and shape you specify.

Paint Shop Pro gives you nearly 30 different options other than painting with a solid color. Each paper texture has its own unique style that creates a different effect when used. You can choose any Paper Texture on which to paint your Web Graphics. Paper Textures are selected from Tool Controls tab of the Control Palette. Figure 3.20 lists each Paper Texture and shows a small sample of how it appears when painted.

CAUTION

To paint using Paper Textures, you must be in an image that has 16.7 million colors available. You can save images into 256-color mode after using the paper textures.

Fig. 3.20
With many different textures available, you'll never run out of stylistic options when painting and making new images.

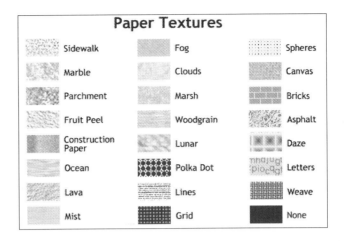

Paper Textures

Sidewalk		Fog		Spheres
Marble		Clouds		Canvas
Parchment		Marsh		Bricks
Fruit Peel		Woodgrain		Asphalt
Construction Paper		Lunar		Daze
Ocean		Polka Dot		Letters
Lava		Lines		Weave
Mist		Grid		None

Other Drawing Options

Paint Shop Pro is a truly robust graphics package. Artists and amateurs alike can create their own customized images from scratch using the tools provided. In this chapter you learned how to use Paint Shop Pro's general image drawing tools such as drawing Shapes and working with the Paint Brush. These two tools are critical functions that you will consistently use when creating your graphics with PSP.

In addition, several other tools may prove useful when you create new graphics from scratch. Some of the more popular Paint Shop Pro options are listed below with a detailed explanation of when to use each.

▶ **Airbrush.** This tool draws like you are using spray paint. Instead of drawing a crisp, solid line across the screen, the airbrush enables you to draw more indefinite patterns that aren't solid. You can use the airbrush tool when you paint the background of your Web graphics or when you want to add some texture and personality to an otherwise boring image. Some people refer to the airbrush as the "graffiti" tool because the resulting graphics often look like they were spray-painted on an image.

▶ **Flood Fill.** Another useful tool, flood fill allows you to paint an entire section of your image one color or pattern. The flood-fill tool is often used to paint an entire canvas one color. Figure 3.16 shows how I added a gradient flood fill to my large headline letters for a butterfly page.

Fig. 3.21
Each letter was filled with a gradient red.

▶ **Eraser.** Everyone makes mistakes. Even if you are a master artisan, eventually you'll color a square the wrong color or make some graphical equivalent to a typo. That's why you'll quickly want to get familiar with the built-in eraser. When used, Paint Shop Pro erases the section you mark and replaces it with the current background color, according to the Color Palette.

▶ **Retouch.** One of my favorite tools, retouch lets you add neat special effects to your image, such as smudging, embossing, or softening the lines of your image. These tools are great for blending images together or making modifications to existing ones.

Check out Appendix B, "Paint Shop Pro Tool Reference," for a more complete listing of Paint Shop Pro tools along with some of their available options.

4

Editing Images and Photos

Even when you want to create a unique Web page with original graphics, it may not be necessary to start completely from scratch. Thousands of excellent images are available for free on the Internet, with Paint Shop Pro, and on affordable CD collections of images and clip art. You will often find it easier and faster to modify, add to, or borrow from an existing image than to start with a completely blank slate.

This chapter will show you how to find and work with images that someone else has already created, or that you've digitized yourself. You'll learn how to adjust the details or images for your own applications, and will discover a number of handy techniques for customizing Web graphics.

▶ **Finding Graphics on the Internet or CD-ROM**
A world of graphics is waiting for you to explore, and to use when you get permission from the original artists or choose stock images and photographs.

▶ **Modifying Graphics for Your Pages**
Touching up color, resizing images, and rotating graphics are just a few techniques you'll learn in this chapter.

▶ **Capturing Screen Shots**
Sometimes the graphics you need are right in front of you. Paint Shop Pro makes grabbing and using them super-efficient.

Finding Existing Graphics to Use

Perhaps the best way to save time creating the graphics files is to avoid creating them altogether. Literally millions and millions of photos, images, animations, and graphics are available for use on your Web page; finding the right one(s) is the key.

This section describes several different popular and common methods for obtaining great images to start with.

Searching the WWW

With millions of images, photos, and icons available, you are virtually guaranteed to find useful images through a little exploration on the Web. Hundreds of sites have different sets and collections of images that work well for Web pages. You can download these images and edit them within Paint Shop Pro, or use them without making any changes.

Any graphic you see on any site is instantly reusable, as soon as the copyright holder grants (or sells) you the right to copy it, or if the owner indicates his or her images can be used free, without any restrictions. Many sites offer collections of free-to-use graphics.

One of the best sites on the Internet to find good images to use is Xoom (pronounced "Zoom"). Found at **http://xoom.xoom.com**, Xoom is the grandfather of affordable and amazing graphics on the Internet. Figure 4.1 shows the Xoom Homepage. At the time of this printing, Xoom had over 75,000 images, icons, photos, and graphics for you to use, free of charge, for noncommercial Web pages.

Fig. 4.1
Xoom is one of the best spots to find great graphics for the right price.

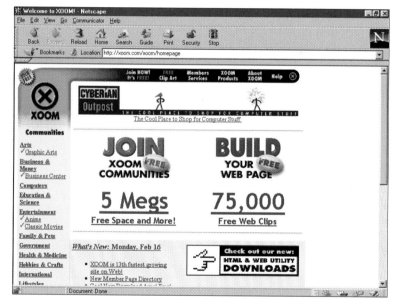

Here are a few more popular sites for innovative and free Web graphics:

▶ **Free Icon Collection**
http://members.aol.com/minimouze/private/ICONS.html

▶ **Iconz**
http://www.geocities.com/Heartland/1448/

Or, visit Yahoo! **(http://www.yahoo.com)** and search for **Free Graphics**. You'll find many Internet sites that have free images. This simple search yields over 1,200 different sites on the Web, each with hundreds or thousands of photos, backgrounds, icons, and more.

Finally, if none of these sites impress you, or you are overwhelmed by the returns from a search, visit this book's homepage **(http://www.muskalipman.com/graphics)**. On it, I list a handful of good, free sites at which you'll find images and photos you can use in Paint Shop Pro and on your Web site.

Grabbing the Graphics You Find

As you probably know, grabbing a graphic from a Web page is as simple as clicking it with the right-mouse button, then picking Save **I**mage as in Netscape Navigator or **S**ave Picture As in Microsoft Explorer. Figure 4.2 shows an image being saved with Netscape.

Fig. 4.2
Browsers let you save images from any Web site.

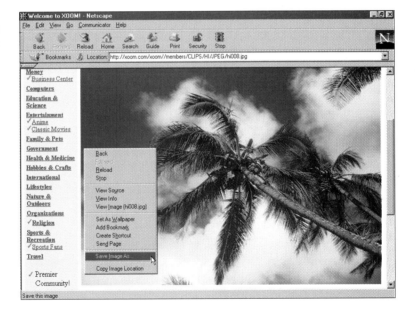

Similarly, you can also save background images from Web pages with your browser. Just move your mouse over an empty part of the Web page, click the right mouse button, and choose Save Background As. Figure 4.3 shows a background graphic being saved in Internet Explorer.

Fig. 4.3
Save a background
image to your computer.

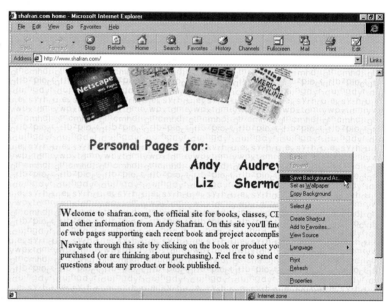

NOTE

The processes for saving images here used version 4.02 of Netscape Navigator and version 4.01 of Microsoft Internet Explorer. If you have a different browser version, the process for saving images might be slightly different.

Graphics from a CD-ROM

Because so many images are available on the Web, sorting through them to find the exact photo, icon, or image you want to use can be a slow and grueling process.

If you're like me, you probably don't want to spend hours finding images online. There are many other ways to find great images besides searching on the Web. Probably the best method is purchasing a CD-ROM or collection of images that you can browse at your leisure. Then you don't have to stay online while browsing, or wait for large HTML pages to download.

Go to your favorite computer store and find dozens of different clip-art and Web-art collections. Most have tens of thousands of images and are priced between $15 and $50, depending on the quality, quantity, and subject of the images contained.

Part I Web Graphics Basics

NOTE

A lot of people ask me which set of clip art and icons I use, where I download them, or how I create the examples in my books or on my pages. Personally, I use the Xoom Web Clip Empire CD. It costs under $50 and has nearly 100,000 different images on it, many of which can be seen and browsed online. Xoom Web Clip images are royalty free, of high quality, and the CD is easy to browse and explore. Many examples in this book originally come from the Xoom CD. You can purchase this CD at Xoom's home page **(http://xoom.xoom.com).**

In addition, my favorite set of photos is the *National Geographic Photo Gallery.* Purchased for $25 at my local computer store, this CD has hundreds of the vivid and colorful images we've come to expect from *National Geographic.* When learning some of the ins and outs of Paint Shop Pro, these images let me explore the true depth of image quality, color variation, and resizing techniques.

Digitizing Your Own

As the Web continues to grow in popularity, many people find generic images and clip art useful only to a point. Often, you need personal photos and logos scanned or digitized because they are the topic of your Web pages.

Paint Shop Pro makes it easy for you to manipulate and modify images once they are on your computer, but getting them there can be another story. Among the many popular ways for getting images from real life into your computer are scanning, using a digital camera, and using a personal video camera.

This section introduces you to several ways to bring images into your computer and Paint Shop Pro. For more detailed information on this topic, read Chapter 9, "Using Scanners and Digital Cameras."

Using a Scanner

Scanners are affordable tools that let you transfer an image from any book, paper, or photograph then store it electronically on your computer. Color scanners start from $79 and are priced based on their resolution and color quality.

Scanners are especially good for digitizing business logos and photographs. Once the images are scanned, you can customize them to fit your needs and then post them on your Web page. Figure 4.4 shows the logo of the company that published this book, after it was scanned into Paint Shop Pro. This scan was accomplished using a Microtek 600 x 1200 color scanner.

Fig. 4.4
This high-quality
scan can be used for
stationery, Web
pages, or electronic
documents.

TIP

Just because you want to scan a photo or logo doesn't mean you have to purchase your own personal scanner. Nowadays, many public libraries and universities have public workstations with scanners attached, free of charge. Or, local copy shops such as Kinko's let you use a scanner for a nominal charge.

If you decide to buy a scanner yourself, make sure you understand the quality of images you can expect to see. Don't forget to test your scanner immediately after getting it home or to your office to make sure it is adequate for your anticipated usage.

Using a Digital Camera

Recently, another technology has become popular for getting images directly into your computer—Digital Cameras. Digital Cameras work like standard cameras except they don't use film that needs to be processed. Instead, you take pictures with your camera, attach the camera to your computer, and save the images directly to your hard drive. This technique is perfect if you need to take a lot of pictures for Web pages or to store on your computer (realtors and insurance agents commonly use digital cameras).

Usually, picture quality is excellent. Paint Shop Pro lets you easily optimize pictures to take the red-eye out or to reduce a shadowing effect. Figure 4.5 shows a picture taken with a Kodak DC50Zoom Digital Camera.

Fig. 4.5
A Digital Camera
enables even an
amateur like me to
take great quality
pictures.

Unfortunately, digital cameras can be expensive, and price-prohibitive for most of us who are casual photo-takers. That's why Kodak invented the Kodak Picture Network (**http://www.kodakpicturenetwork.com**), shown in figure 4.6. This service lets you submit photographs to be developed. You get your prints back and also a private Web page that has digital versions and negatives of all the developed images.

Fig. 4.6
The Kodak Picture
Network is an
affordable way to get
your pictures in
electronic format.

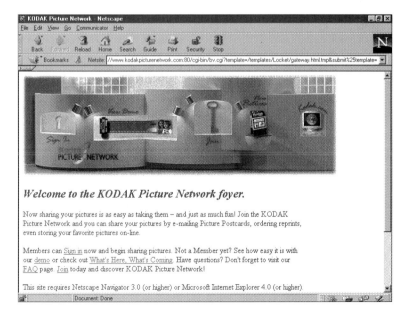

You can save your images, order reprints, see the negatives, and do more for a monthly fee. This solution lets you leverage your existing camera for Paint Shop Pro and Web pages.

CAUTION

One reason few people have purchased and used digital cameras yet is because printing out high-quality photographs is often difficult. Unless you have an expensive color printer or a special photo-only printer, even the best ink-jet printers will produce fuzzy and grainy printed images.

Other Technologies

Besides Scanners and Digital Cameras, you can get customized pictures into Paint Shop Pro in other ways, including:

▶ **QuickCam**

For $100, you can purchase a medium-quality camera that hooks up to your computer and can take video clips or still photos. Called the Quickcam, you can use it for photos or video-conferencing. You can't carry the QuickCam with you and the quality is limited, but the price is right for many people.

You can find out more about the QuickCam at **http://www.quickcam.com.**

▶ **Snappy**

The Snappy Video Capture unit lets you digitize still shots from any videocassette tape. You simply hook up the Snappy and a VCR to your computer. Don't worry, this process isn't too complicated and the instructions are provided. The Snappy costs $99 but has quality issues similar to those surrounding the QuickCam. Many people have or borrow a Camcorder, then digitize photos from the tapes they create, making this an affordable way to get images into your computer.

You can order and find out more about the Snappy at **http://www.play.com.**

Modifying Graphics for Your Pages

Now that you know how to obtain and create different images for your site, this section shows you how to edit. You'll learn how to resize, reshape, and select different parts of images with different PSP tools.

This section focuses on using scanned or digitized images once you've gotten them into Paint Shop Pro. Chapter 9, "Using Scanners and Digital Cameras," introduces you to how scanners work and shows you the best way for getting graphics into Paint Shop Pro for editing.

Print Graphics vs. Web Graphics

So you toss all those graphics together with a little HTML and you should be all set, right?

Wrong. Unfortunately, the requirements for Web graphics are radically different from requirements for printed graphics. In fact, almost all the rules are reversed:

▶ For paper, you want giant, high-resolution graphics files. For the Web, you want small graphics that load fast and look good on a relatively low-resolution computer screen.

▶ Printing color isn't cheap, and preparing color graphics for printing is a complex and often agonizing endeavor. On the Web, color is easy to work with, and almost free.

▶ Once a document is on paper, it doesn't change until the next print run. Web documents often need to be instantly and constantly updated.

▶ On paper, dark colors will bleed into the light colors, and it's a struggle to make bright colors shine. On a computer screen, it's the lighter colors that leap out and overwhelm nearby dark areas.

The bottom line is that graphics created for print publications seldom work unmodified for Internet publication. Since most clip-art and stock photography was originally designed for print publications, you will need to be aware of these differences even if you've never printed a paper page in your life.

Touching Up a Photo—Removing Red-Eye

Scanning images is great, but usually you'll want to touch up photographs to get them looking perfect for a Web page. For example, many times photos capture "red-eye," which occurs when someone stares directly into a camera as the flash goes off. With a print photograph, your options for fixing this phenomenon are limited, but once that photo is digitized, Paint Shop Pro gives you a lot more flexibility.

Figure 4.7 shows a sample picture that includes a bad case of red-eye. This photo was taken with a standard 35mm camera and scanned into Paint Shop Pro.

Fig. 4.7
Audrey was caught staring straight into the camera.

To correct the red-eye in this picture, zoom in on the eyes and select the Magic Wand tool. This tool lets you select multiple shades of color on an image, which is extremely useful when you are editing photographs and images. Often many different shades are used together to make up a larger image, and selecting this collection of shades manually can be difficult.

Figure 4.8 shows an up-close zoom on the cat picture with the Magic Wand tool selected.

Fig. 4.8
The Magic Wand makes image editing a breeze!

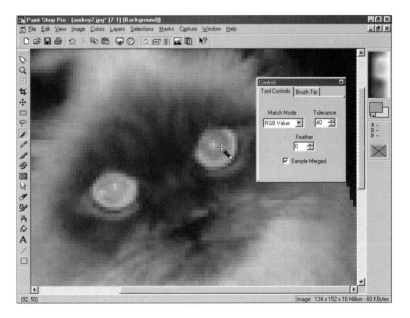

Now I am going to use the magic wand to select all of the red/orange color material in the eye. In the Control Palette, you have several settings for the Magic Wand, including Tolerance and feathering.

▶ **Tolerance**

The Tolerance setting tells Paint Shop Pro to select similar colors besides the one you click on. If you look carefully at figure 4.8, you'll notice that the eye is made up of several shades of orange, not just one. By changing the tolerance setting in the Control Palette, you are telling Paint Shop Pro to select all of the Orange colors that make up the eye, not just the one color clicked on. For this example, I'm using a Tolerance of 40, which means that PSP will select forty similar shades of Orange/Red when I use the Magic Wand. I can do this because all the colors around the eye are not even close to orange in color, so they won't be selected.

▶ **Feather**

The Feather setting tells PSP how many pixels outside of your color to select. Think of this setting as a buffer around the area you want to select. It's not useful here, because I only want to change the red-eye, not the whites of the eye or any other parts of the image. So, for this example my Feather value is set to 0.

Once my Magic Wand settings are selected, I am going to click anywhere within the eye. Paint Shop Pro now selects the entire section of the eye for which we are going to change color using the Magic Wand settings. Figure 4.9 shows one of the eyes selected.

Fig. 4.9
We are recolorizing the selected area of the eye.

The Selected Area ———

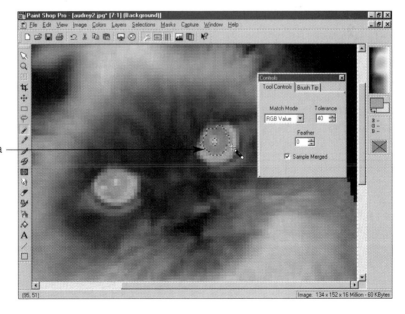

Once the proper area is selected, to change the color of the eye, I am going to use the PSP Color Adjuster. Choose **C**olor, **A**djust, **R**ed/Green/Blue from the menu bar. Figure 4.10 shows the Red/Green/Blue dialog box that appears.

Fig. 4.10
Only the selected part of the image will be affected.

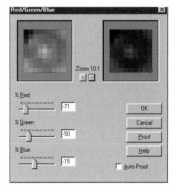

This dialog box lets you re-mix the amounts of Red, Green, and Blue for the selected part of the photo. Since the original eye had too much red, I am using the color bars to remove most of that color. The left side of this dialog box shows the original selected area, and the right side shows a preview of how your settings will affect that area.

For this example, I want to darken the entire eye to make it look more realistic. I selected –71% Red, -50% Green, and –15% Blue. Once I find the right mix and match of color percentages, I make my changes by clicking on the **OK** button. Paint Shop Pro changes only the area selected with Magic Wand. After repeating the same steps again for the other eye, figure 4.11 shows the final image, much improved and more realistic.

Fig. 4.11
Now this photo is ready to be used!

TIP
This is just one example of touching up a faulty photograph. Chapter 16, "Cool PSP Techniques," steps you through a more in-depth example of editing and fixing up a photograph.

Rotating Your Images

The Magic Wand and Color Changer are two very important tools that you'll use often. Another popular PSP tool is the Image Rotater, which lets you turn your images to any angle to fit your specific needs.

Figure 4.12 shows a text headline created for Audrey's Home Page. Normally, this headline would be fine; but for this page, I have a different design that I want to run up and down the left-hand side of the screen.

Fig. 4.12
A simple text-only GIF.

To turn this image, choose **I**mage, **R**otate, from the PSP menu bar. The Rotate dialog box shown in figure 4.13 appears. PSP gives you a few standard rotation values, or lets you select very precise turning coordinates. In addition, you can rotate the entire image, or just a single layer.

Fig. 4.13
You can turn this image in any direction imaginable.

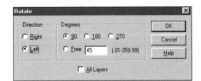

To figure out the right angle to turn your image, remember learning back in geometry class that circles are a total of 360 degrees round. So, to turn your image upside-down, you'd rotate it 180 degrees.

For this example, I want to rotate the image 90 degrees to the left. (Rotating *right* means turning the image clockwise, while rotating *left* means turning the image counter-clockwise. Thus 90 degrees left is the same as 270 degrees right.) Figure 4.14 shows the rotated image.

Fig. 4.14
This rotation is complete.

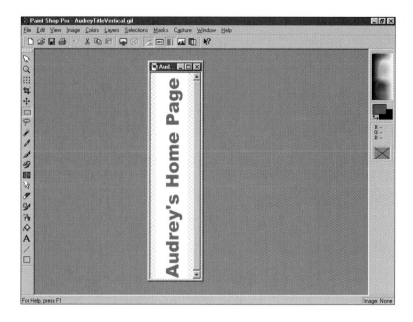

TIP
Besides the rotation tool, PSP also has image flip and mirror tools. The flip tool makes a vertical mirror copy of your image, while the mirror tool makes a horizontal copy of your image. This is different from rotating because the image is actually flipped around instead of turned.

Resizing Graphics

The final common technique you'll use when editing images is resizing. Often images and photos are too big to use on your Web pages because they take too long to download. You'll want to use PSP to reduce the size of your graphics to a manageable size. For example, figure 4.15 shows a sample photograph that I want to use for a Web page. Notice that the files are very large—the lower-right corner of the Paint Shop Pro window indicates that the image of the cat is 677 by 219 pixels. You'll also notice that the full-sized rendition doesn't add much detail or value to the image.

Fig. 4.15
This image is too large
for the Web.

Image size
in pixels

To resize this image, pick **I**mage, **R**esize from the menu bar. The Resize
dialog box appears and lets you decide how to change the height and
width of this image (figure 4.16).

Fig. 4.16
Images can be resized
to any height or width
imaginable.

Paint Shop Pro lets you resize by exact pixel coordinates, percentage of
the original image, or optimized to be printed out on paper. Table 4.1
compares these options:

	Options	Explanation
Table 4.1 Image Resize Options	**Percentage of Original**	Lets you specify a percentage of how the new Height and Width of an image will appear.
	Pixel Size	Lets you assign a specific Pixel Height and Width to a resized image. This setting is often used to make an image conform with a specific size for your page. For example, if you create a set of buttons for your page, you will want them all to be the same Width. So you'd resize them by Pixel Size and type in the exact coordinates for the image.
	Actual/ Pixel Size	Lets you have very specific control over the final image dimensions for printing purposes.
	Maintain Aspect Ratio	Calculates the correct Height in relation to the width once the original Height or Width has been modified. Enabling this setting will avoid the image from becoming distorted once resized.

For this example, we'll select **Percentage of Original** and type in 50%. Once the image is resized, save it and you'll notice a significant file-size savings. For this example, the photo went from 45K down to 5K—a 90% savings in file size!

Figure 4.17 shows the final image as part of a completed Web page.

Fig. 4.17
A final Web page with many edited and optimized graphics.

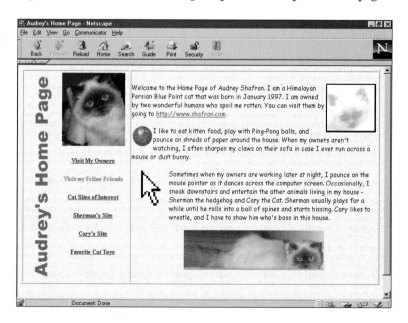

NOTE

It is important to note that resizing an image 50% means that both the Height and Width of the graphic are cut in half, and the original image is rescaled to fit that new size. This has the cumulative affect of creating an image 1/4 of the original size.

TIP

Here's another trick you should know to squeeze the absolute best out of images when you reduce their size. Always try to resize to exactly one-half, one-quarter, or one-eighth the original size if possible. The mathematical reasons this works better are beyond what I could explain in this little tip; but trust me—it works. Basically, Paint Shop Pro uses a complex algorithm to figure out which pixels to keep, and which ones to throw out. Using a standard resize value lets PSP work at its optimal levels.

Image resizing issues are discussed in more depth in Chapter 12, "Making Your Graphics Lean."

Capturing Screen Shots

It's quite likely that you use your computer for other things besides building Web pages. You may even use it to build old-fashioned paper pages with a word processor or page layout program. Or perhaps you've created or bought some other programs that display interesting graphics or type. In any of these situations—and in many others—it would often come in handy to transfer part of an image you see on your computer screen to a Web page.

For example, many times you'd want to take a snapshot of a program's dialog box or other features in action. The only way to do this is by taking a screenshot, or computer-screen snapshot.

You can do this in either of two easy ways:

▶ Use Window's built-in screen capture capabilities by pressing PRINT SCREEN to capture the entire screen or ALT+PRINT SCREEN to capture the active window. Then select Edit, Paste, As New Image in Paint Shop Pro to paste the image from the clipboard.

▶ Use Paint Shop Pro's Capture menu to grab the image directly. This is usually faster, and gives you a number of options that Windows' built-in screen capture doesn't provide.

To capture a computer screenshot, choose **C**apture, **S**etup from the menu bar. Figure 4.18 shows the Capture Setup dialog box.

Fig. 4.18
Paint Shop Pro offers a number of time-saving options for screen captures that the PRINT SCREEN key doesn't provide.

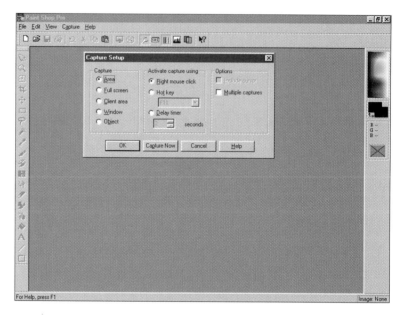

You can save the entire screen or just parts of the computer window. In addition, Paint Shop Pro has a built in Delay timer, which lets you prepare for a screenshot to be taken (that's how many images from this book were prepared).

Once your settings are established, click on the Capture Now button. If you selected to capture an Area, Paint Shop Pro waits until you click your *right* mouse button to start the capturing process. Then you use your *left* mouse button to select the area you want to capture. Figure 4.19 shows a screen capture in action.

Fig. 4.19
Here's a screen
capture of a screen
capture in action.

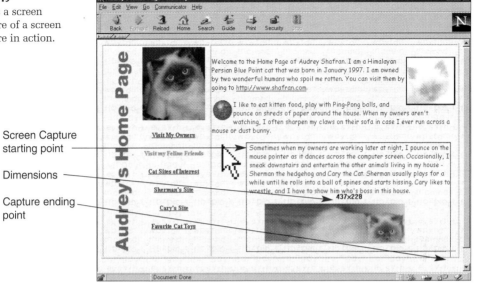

Screen Capture
starting point

Dimensions

Capture ending
point

If I had selected Full Screen, Client Area, Window, or Object instead of
Area in the Capture Setup dialog box, only the single right-mouse click
would have been needed to capture the image. Once you've defined the
area to be captured, Paint Shop Pro copies the selected area as an image
and let's you edit or manipulate it.

TIP

If you have other graphics software, such as CorelDraw!, Adobe Illustrator, or
a 3D-rendering program, it is probably capable of exporting some file format
that Paint Shop Pro can open.

However, the graphics files that your applications save may be at a resolution
better for paper printing or video production than for Web pages. This often
results in significant difference between the colors you see on the screen and
the colors you'll see when you open the resulting graphics file.

You may often find it faster and more reliable to simply capture images
straight from the screen while a graphics application is running. That way
you know the image will appear on your Web page exactly as you see it when
you do the capture.

Don't forget that you can use screen captures to grab still shots from moving
video clips, as well as animations as they play.

Finishing Touches

You've seen several of the four key steps involved in adapting almost any image for use on a Web page:

1.   Find or capture a promising image.

2.   Adjust the colors to match the other elements of the page.

3.   Resize the image and reduce the color depth.

4.   Touch up any colors or details that don't quite work.

Alas, the final item on the list is often the most time-consuming by far. The others will become pretty much automatic once you've created a few pages. But the more you explore Paint Shop Pro's powerful capabilities, the more tempted you'll be to spend half an hour touching up eye color, making changes to the background of an image, and playing around with **I**mage, **E**ffects, **D**rop Shadow for the precise 3D-look you're after.

But take my advice: Discipline yourself to spend only a few minutes "perfecting" the graphics on each page. I did indulge in a couple of worthwhile improvements to the completed page pictured in figures 4.17, but perfecting each image to look just right took a lot of time. Make sure you concentrate on the areas that will be of most benefit, such as image resizing or getting rid of nasty effects like red-eye.

Don't be afraid to play around with the Magic Wand and Color changing effects; they are the tip of Paint Shop Pro's power.

Part II
Making Great Images

5

Images and Special Effects

Computer users who have Paint Shop Pro at their disposal have a significant advantage over photographers and the tools they use to create special effects in images. Where's the advantage? Photographers can't change a print after it is developed, whereas computer graphic artists can make thousands of changes to images that already exist. The computerized image can be manipulated time and again while preserving the original image. Copies of the image can be saved at every stage of change.

This chapter will define and introduce you to these special features within PSP—deformations, filters, special effects, and image arithmetic. You'll see many examples of how images can be twisted, shaped, and manipulated with the built-in features of PSP.

Specifically, this chapter covers:

▶ **Deformations**
Deformation effects literally move image data (pixels) from one area of the image to another. PSP is capable of producing nine different deformations.

▶ **Filters**
Filters work differently than deformations. A filter affects an image or a selected part of an image by altering the color of the pixel based upon the current color and the colors that surround it. Filters can make a variety of changes that range from barely noticeable to dramatic.

▶ **Combining Images Using Image Arithmetic**
The Arithmetic function of PSP allows you to combine two images to create a third image. It uses the data (pixels) from two existing images and mathematical formulas to produce the third image. Thankfully, PSP is a mathematics genius and performs the computations for you!

Part II Making Great Images

Modifying Your Images

Before starting, be sure you understand several important concepts that will affect how these special techniques work:

Recognizing How Layers Work

By default, all the techniques in this chapter work only on the PSP layers you have selected. This means that if you have an image of a car driving on a road in which the car is one layer and the road is another, you can make changes to each layer separately. So, you could add a Blur effect on the car layer, making it appear to be going fast, while the road layer could stay perfectly clear. This example illustrates how powerful and useful layers in PSP 5 are when you're creating cool graphics. Remember that layers only work when you save your images in the **.PSP** file format or another format that suppports layers. You can always convert your graphics to GIF, JPG, or PNG when you're finished editing them.

Because layers are an important concept to understand in PSP, an entire chapter is dedicated to understanding them. See Chapter 7, "Using PSP Layers," for more information on this technique.

Having Enough Colors

With the exception of image arithmetic, all the filters and deformations require an image to be 16.7 million colors or 256 grey scale. This is because PSP does advanced image and color resizing, reshaping, and dithering, and needs a vast number of colors to make your new images look high quality.

To increase the number of colors in the images with which you are working, choose **C**olors, **I**ncrease Color Depth, **16.**7 million colors (24-bit) from the PSP menu bar.

Changing Colors

Many of these effects use the current foreground and background colors when PSP performs them. Don't be afraid to try different color combinations to see how PSP uses different shades and colors to create the resulting image.

Deformations

First we'll learn about deformations, techniques that take an entire image and change the perspective from which it appears. You can deform the image to make it appear circular, view it from a different angle, and more.

The magic of editing your own or existing images with great effects is not difficult to demystify. Remember that each image is made up of many tiny dots, called pixels. Paint Shop Pro's deformations analyze and rearrange the pixels in an image into a different, but related, image.

For example, figure 5.1a shows a sample picture of a colorful flower, while figure 5.1b shows the same flower with the vertical cylinder deformation applied.

Fig. 5.1a
The original yellow flower

Fig. 5.1b
The deformed yellow flower

a   b

Applying Deformations

This section walks you through a PSP session, demonstrating how you can use the deformation browser to modify your image.

1. Begin by either opening an existing image or creating a new image yourself. For this example, we will use this flower for its simplicity and highly contrasting colors. I selected the image from a collection of royalty-free images on a CD collection I purchased.
   Figure 5.2 shows Paint Shop Pro with the image ready to be deformed.

Fig. 5.2
This flower doesn't know what it's in for!

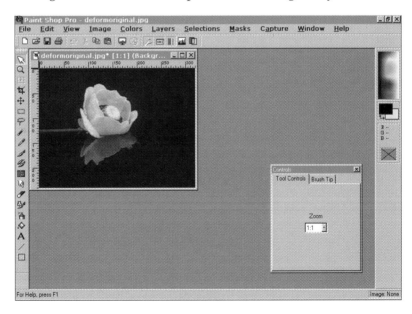

2. Paint Shop Pro lets you select from the nine different deformations individually, or use a graphical browser to see how the resulting image might appear. Usually, you'll want to use the graphical

Part II Making Great Images

Deformation Browser, which makes it easy for you to quickly see how different deformations might affect your image. Choose **I**mage, **D**eformations, **D**eformation Browser from the PSP menu bar, and the Deformation Browser appears (figure 5.3).

Fig. 5.3
From here, you can select the deformation to apply to your image.

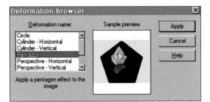

3. As you can see, the deformation browser allows you to scroll through and preview all available deformations. Beneath the list of Deformation names is a text description of the highlighted deformation. The preview window gives you an idea of the effect the highlighted deformation will have on the active (selected) image. Scroll through the different Deformations to see how each affects your image (or layer).

4. Choose **A**pply to tell PSP to go ahead and apply the highlighted deformation to the image. Some of the deformations will take several seconds to run, depending on the amount of memory in your computer. Of course, you can always choose **C**ancel to close the deformation browser without making any changes to the image.

Figure 5.4 shows the flower image with the Circle Deformation applied.

Fig. 5.4
Notice the round
effects on the flower.
I purposely set the
background color to
yellow for effect.

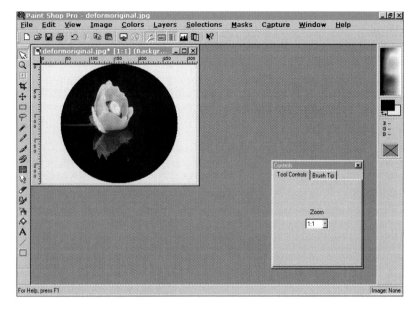

Some deformations have adjustable attributes that you can set before the
effect is applied to your image. These adjustable attributes let you control
how deformed your image appears. For example, when you choose to use
the horizontal cylinder deformation, PSP brings up the Horizontal
Cylinder dialog box (figure 5.5) so you can adjust how "strong" the
deformation effect is applied by sliding the % Effect bar.

Fig. 5.5
Use the sliding bars or
type in a specific value
to change the amount of
an effect you want to
apply.

Changes appear immediately in the preview window.

Part II Making Great Images

The % Effect setting controls how much perspective you want to add to your image. A setting of 5% will have far less effect than a setting of 50% will have on an image. Figures 5.6a and 5.6b show two different results of the Horizontal Perspective % Difference setting.

Fig. 5.6a
Using a 25% Horizontal
Perspective setting

Fig. 5.6b
Using a 75% Horizontal
Perspective setting

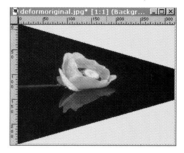

In addition to the % Difference setting and preview window, you have several other buttons available in this dialog box. The **Apply** button tells PSP to run the deformation, while **Cancel** quits your action without affecting the image. Clicking the **Proof** button will allow you to preview the effect on the full-size image without making a permanent change to it. As always, **Help** opens PSP's context-sensitive help file to the specific information for the currently selected deformation.

Image Deformation Comparison

Now that you are familiar with how Deformations work, you can choose from any of the nine included on the Deformation Browser or the PSP menu bar.

Table 5.1 presents a comparison of the nine different deformations applied to the same image. Remember that since some Deformations let you control their settings, your images might look slightly different.

Table 5.1
Comparing Image
Deformations

Deformation and Resulting Image

Circle

Horizontal Cylinder

Vertical Cylinder

Pentagon

Horizontal Perspective

Vertical Perspective

Pinch

Punch

Skew

Part II Making Great Images

Effects

Paint Shop Pro is capable of producing a number of special effects for you to use on images you create or edit. Objects or text in an image are brought to life with the addition of one or more of these effects. As we walk through these special effects, visualize how they might look on objects other than text. I chose to use text for example images because it shows the effects so well and is a great way to quickly jazz up buttons and graphics on your Web page.

CAUTION

Sometimes items in the PSP menu bar might appear greyed out. Don't worry! There's nothing wrong with your version of Paint Shop Pro. Remember that your image must contain 16.7 million colors or 256 shades of grey for these effects to be enabled. Also, the cutout, drop-shadow, and chisel effects require a selection within the image—they don't run on the entire image unless part of it is selected. You select a portion of the image with the Selection, Lasso, or Magic Wand tools.

Alternatively, you can select the entire image by choosing **S**elections, Select **A**ll from the PSP menu bar.

Four different Special Effects are available inside PSP: Buttonize, Chisel, Cutout, and Drop Shadow. I'll talk about each of these in this section.

Buttonize

The buttonize effect of PSP allows for quick creation of 3-D edges around square or rectangular selections. This feature lets you quickly create graphics that look like buttons you can click on—perfect for Web pages. This effect can be applied to the entire image or to a selected portion of it.

Buttonizing only part of the image requires that you select the area using the Selection tool. To demonstrate the effect, I am using a previously created image of text with a drop shadow applied to it.

1. Load the image you want to effect into PSP, then choose **I**mage, Effects, **B**uttonize from the menu bar. The buttonize dialog box appears, as shown in figure 5.7.

Fig. 5.7
The Buttonize dialog box offers a lot of flexibility.

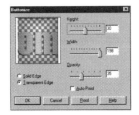

2. The Buttonize dialog box lets you set various options to determine how your selected area should appear after being buttonized. You can set the Transparency values, Opacity settings, and Height/Width dimensions. Use the preview window to see how your settings will affect your selected image.

3. The Height and Width sizing boxes are expressed in pixels and represent how far the buttonized borders should go in on your image. For a symmetrical border, use the same number in both the Width and Height settings. When you like the look in the preview window, click the **OK** button, and PSP changes your image instantly.

Figures 5.8a and 5.8b show two results of buttonizing.

Fig. 5.8a
This button has a symmetrical 10-pixel border with a solid background determined by the palette background color.

Fig. 5.8b
Created from a duplicate of the previous image, this border makes this button look very different.

a   b

Producing these effects "by hand" would take hours of tedious work. But creating these beautiful buttons using PSP's buttonize effect would allow you to make hundreds of buttons in the same amount of time!

Chisel

If you desire a border that looks like stone around text or another object in an image, the chisel function is what you are looking for. You may select from a transparent chisel that allows the colors in the image to "show through" or from a solid color.

Part II Making Great Images

To create a good-looking Web graphic with the chisel effect, follow these steps:

1. Begin by creating a new image 300 x 200 with a white background at 16.7 million colors.

2. Set the foreground color to Red and the background color to White.

3. Select the Text Tool and click inside the new image, which will bring up the Add Text dialog box.

    Choose some text attributes to add to your new image. Figure 5.9 shows the attributes and text I selected for this example (Impact font, 72 points with the text "Home").

Fig. 5.9
The text dialog box lets you choose from any of your installed fonts.

4. Click on the **OK** button to add text to your image. Center it in your graphic, and be sure to **leave the text selected** (figure 5.10).

Fig. 5.10
The scrolling marquee around the selection indicates the text or the area of an image or layer that has been selected.

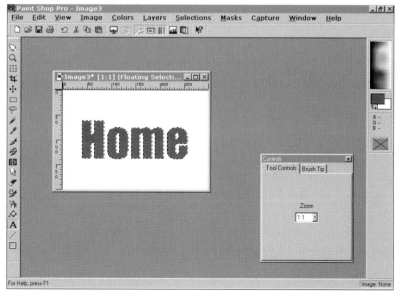

5. Choose Image, Effects, Chisel from the PSP menu bar to bring up the Chisel dialog box (figure 5.11). From here, you can choose the size of the Chiseled background and the transparency effect you want to use. The preview window allows you to see the effect before it is applied, and the view is interactive as you make changes in size or color.

Fig. 5.11
The Chisel dialog box allows you to easily adjust settings for the chisel effect.

6. Click on the **OK** button to accept your chisel settings. Figure 5.12 shows the final image.

Fig. 5.12
This chisel was made using a Width of 10.

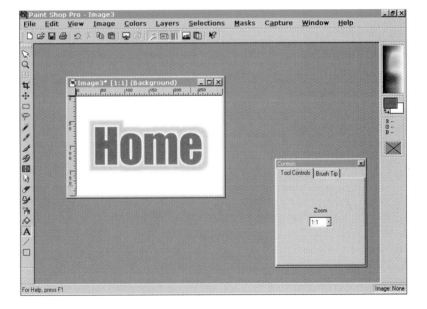

Cutout

Using the Cutout Effect can create the illusion that you can see through the image to a layer below it. To create a good-looking Web graphic with the Cutout Effect, follow these steps:

1. Follow the same procedure you previously used to create the chisel effect to produce a new image with the word "Home" on it. Remember to **keep the text selected.**

2. From the PSP menu bar, choose Image, Effects, Cutout to bring up the Cutout dialog box.

Fig. 5.13
This dialog box allows you to change settings that vary the look of the cutout.

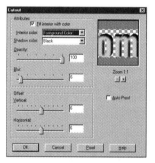

3. If you want to use colors other than those offered in the dialog box (black, white, red, green, and blue), you will need to change the foreground and background colors to the ones you want to use.

4. The opacity setting allows you to select how transparent the cutout effect will be. Changing the blur setting will affect how sharp (dark) the shadow will be. You can alter the appearance of the cutout to your taste by changing the interior and shadow colors.

    The offset setting affects where the shadow will lie in relation to the text. Change it by using the slide bars or by entering a number into the corresponding box. The preview box is interactive, so you will see the changes to the image as you make these various selections.

TIP

If you need to move your image up and down, or side-to-side, move the cursor to the preview window and drag the image with your mouse. Notice that the cursor has changed to a hand rather than a pointer. By left-clicking and dragging, you can get to any area of the image that is outside the preview boundaries.

5.   You can zoom in on a particular point of the image by moving your cursor to the point you want to see enlarged or made smaller, then click the + to enlarge or - to decrease the size. When you've chosen settings that appeal to you, click on the **OK** button. Figure 5.14 shows the resulting image for this Cutout.

Fig. 5.14
This image clearly shows the illusion of text being cut out.

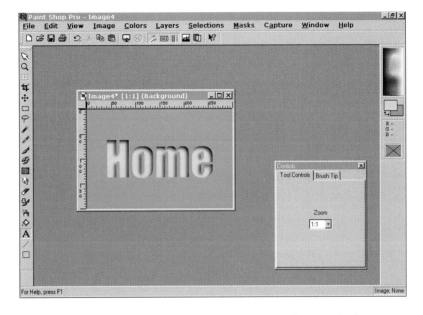

Some easy additions can significantly change the look of the basic image. Try using the Airbrush tool with a Paper Texture (figure 5.15a) to paint the text before applying the Cutout. Another fun way to fill text is with the Flood Fill tool, using another image as a pattern. In figure 5.15b, I used a complementing pattern before applying the Cutout effect.

Fig. 5.15a
Fig. 5.15b
Some very simple changes create entirely different effects.

a   b

Part II   Making Great Images

Drop Shadow

A drop shadow places a shadow behind the selected area so that the selection seems to "leap out" of the image, giving a 3-D effect. This effect is particularly desirable for use on the World Wide Web because we are all accustomed to seeing the effect on television.

To demonstrate the drop-shadow effect, we will again use the same image with the text "Home" prepared in the same manner as in the previous two sections. Remember to **keep the text selected.**

1. After setting the foreground and background colors to your liking, choose Image, Effects, **D**rop Shadow from the menu bar to bring up the Drop Shadow dialog box (figure 5.16).

Fig. 5.16
The Drop Shadow dialog box allows you to change the color, size, and placement of the shadow.

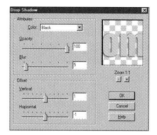

2. The various attribute settings will allow you to change the look of the drop shadow, including the shadow color, opacity, blur effect, and offset. You can use the slide bars or enter the numbers directly.

3. When you click **OK**, the dialog box closes and PSP creates the drop shadow. Table 5.2 depicts several types of Drop Shadows run on the same image.

Table 5.2
Drop Shadow Samples

Image	Image Settings
	Color Black, Opacity 100, Blur 10, Vertical 6, Horizontal -1
	Color White, Opacity 100, Blur 37, Vertical 0, Horizontal 0
	Color Black, Opacity 80, Blur 5.5 Vertical -9, Horizontal 9
	Color Black, Opacity 53, Blur 5.5 Vertical -10, Horizontal -10

These images show how varied a drop shadow can be. I particularly like the "glow" that resulted from using the white shadow with no offset.

Part II Making Great Images

Bullet Example

Now that you've seen how each of the four effects works with text, you will be able to envision how they can be used on objects other than text. Within an existing image, you can use the Magic Wand tool to select areas that you'd like to apply an effect to. Vary the tolerance if necessary to get the entire area selected.

Figure 5.17 shows two round buttons that can serve as bullets on Web pages. For the bullet on the left I created a gray oval and used the PSP Blur features. Then I added the highlights manually. For the bullet on the right, I used the selection tool to create the circle, filled it with a sunburst gradient, and then applied the Drop Shadow.

Figure 5.17
The image on the right shows that PSP can render a more realistic drop shadow.

Filters

Paint Shop Pro comes with a set of image filters that change the way a graphic appears. Running your image through the different filters lets you blur, sharpen, or emboss your image with a single command. Image filters are complex mathematical formulas applied to the pixels in your image that change the fundamental structure and appearance of the graphic.

In order to demonstrate PSP's filters in this chapter, I created many copies of the same graphic. This enables you to see how each filter affects the same image. The original image is a photograph scanned with a hand-held scanner with text added in PSP. Figure 5.18 shows my original image.

Fig. 5.18
I will bet the Chesapeake Bay waters have never been filtered like this before!

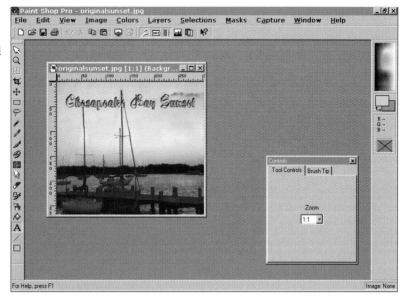

Like deformations, filters also have their own special browser built within PSP.

Applying Filters

This section walks you through a PSP session, demonstrating how you can use the filter browser to modify your image.

1. Begin by either opening an existing image or creating a new image yourself. For this example, we will use the image shown in figure 5.18.

2. PSP lets you select from over twenty different filters individually, or use the graphical filter browser to see how the resulting image might appear. Usually, you'll use the Filter Browser because it is easy to quickly see how different deformations might affect your image. Choose **I**mage, Filter Bro**w**ser from the PSP menu bar, and the Filter Browser appears (figure 5.19).

Fig. 5.19
Finding just the right filter for your image is easy with the preview window of the filter browser.

3. The filter browser allows you to scroll through and preview all the different filters. Beneath the list of filter names, you'll see a text description of the highlighted filter. The preview window to the right gives you an idea of the effect the highlighted filter will have on the active image. Scroll through the different filters to preview how each affects your image (or layer).

4. Choose **A**pply to tell PSP to go ahead and apply the highlighted filter to the image. Some of the filters will take several seconds to run, depending on the amount of memory in your computer. Of course, you can always choose **C**ancel to close the filter browser without making any changes to the image.

Some filters have adjustable attributes that you can set before the filter is applied. These settings let you control how the filter affects your image. For example, when you choose the Motion Blur filter, PSP brings up the Motion Blur dialog box (figure 5.20). From here you can adjust the intensity and direction of the blur filter.

Fig. 5.20
The direction and intensity of the motion blur are easily adjusted in the dialog box.

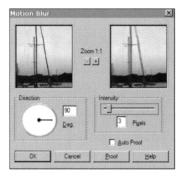

Image Filter Comparison

The next section shows the same image copied several times, with a different filter applied to each copy. Use this comparison chart to quickly see how each filter might affect your set of Web graphics. Remember that some filters let you specify the strength of their effects, so your images might look slightly different.

Keep your eye out for the Gaussian Blur filter, a new feature in PSP 5, which creates truly dynamic blurred images with a nice glow on them.

Table 5.3
Filter Comparison

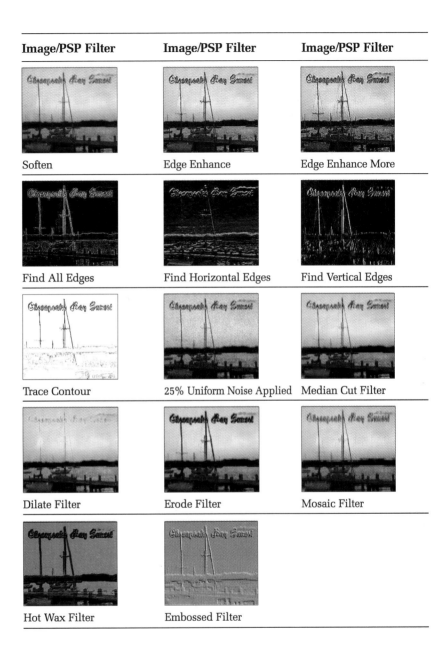

Image/PSP Filter	Image/PSP Filter	Image/PSP Filter
Soften	Edge Enhance	Edge Enhance More
Find All Edges	Find Horizontal Edges	Find Vertical Edges
Trace Contour	25% Uniform Noise Applied	Median Cut Filter
Dilate Filter	Erode Filter	Mosaic Filter
Hot Wax Filter	Embossed Filter	

Part II Making Great Images

User Defined Filters

Paint Shop Pro provides Web page designers with a way to create their own filters to use with images. Creating good-looking 3-D text without a program that specializes in 3-D effects can be a challenge. In this section I'll show you an easy way to create 3-D text by working with a User Defined Filter in PSP.

Choose Image, User Defined Filters from the PSP menu bar to bring up the User Defined Filters dialog box (figure 5.21). From here you will be able to create your own customized filters to apply to your images.

Fig. 5.21
This dialog box is needed for creating, editing, deleting, or applying custom filters.

Click on the New button to bring up the Define New Filter dialog box (figure 5.22). Although this dialog box looks complicated, don't worry. It simply consists of a 7 x 7 grid of boxes that allows you to specify different mathematical traits for your custom-created filter.

Fig. 5.22
Each of the 49 boxes accepts an integer only (no decimal numbers).

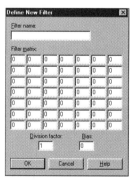

Enter the name you wish to give your new filter. I'm calling the one I'm demonstrating "3-D." Each of the 49 boxes will contain a zero when the dialog box opens. The values placed in the fields of the matrix must be an integer (a whole number—either positive, negative, or zero, but no fractions or decimals).

Place the following values in the fields of the matrix exactly as shown in figure 5.23. Note the change in the value from the default divisor of one to a divisor of two at the bottom of the dialog box.

Fig. 5.23
The changed Define
New Filter dialog box

Each value of the matrix is called a coefficient. In the formula used to calculate the desired filter effect, the coefficient and division factors you specify are entered in a complex mathematical formula. For our purposes, set the Division Factor to two (2) and the Bias to zero (0). Creating your own custom filters may require advanced knowledge of how all these factors affect one another. Although such details are outside the scope of this book, you can get a nice introduction to the variances for each matrix value in the PSP Help system. When you've finished changing the settings, click **OK.**

PSP automatically saves the filter with the name you gave it and returns you to the original User Defined Filters dialog box.

In order to use your newly created filter, first open the image to which you wish to apply it. Just as when using the other filters and deformations, the image must have 16.7 million colors. Figures 5.24a and 5.24b show the before and the after effects of a simple textual image with my 3–D custom filter applied.

Fig. 5.24a
Here's some text placed
on a black background.

Fig. 5.24b
You can apply this
great 3-D effect to any
of your text!

a   b

Part II Making Great Images

Plug-in Filters

PSP 5 also allows you to use most Adobe-compatible plug-in filters. These advanced filters let you create phenomenal effects on your graphics using a single command. You'll find many great, complex-looking images on Web sites that weren't painstakingly created; instead, designers used cool plug-in filters they purchased from graphics companies around the world.

The plug-in filters are available in three types: commercial, shareware, and freeware. The most widely used commercial filter set is Alien Skin's "Eye Candy for After Effects." Alien Skin filters, the industry leader for cool effects, are a fantastic enhancement for Paint Shop Pro 5. Figure 5.25 shows the Alien Skin Software homepage at **http://www.alienskin.com**.

Fig. 5.25
Alien Skin Software filters are a professional's first choice.

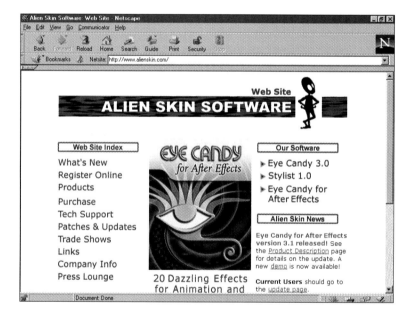

Besides the professional filters, multitudes of shareware and freeware filters can be found on the WWW. Since content on the web changes so frequently, I would suggest using one of the major search engines to find these sources. I keep an up to date list of the best filter sites at this book's home page (**http://www.muskalipman.com/graphics**).

Once you have obtained and installed the filters to your system, PSP needs to know where to find them. Instructing PSP where to look for the filter folders is easy. Choose File, Preferences, General Program Preferences from the menu bar. Then click on the Plug-in Filters tab from the PSP Preferences dialog box (figure 5.26).

Fig. 5.26
Version 5 of Paint Shop
Pro allows you to define
three sets of plug-in
filters.

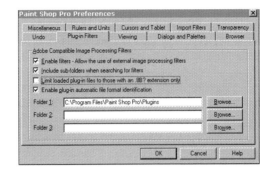

You can specify three different sets of plug-in filters for use with Paint
Shop Pro 5 at any one time. Once you've pointed PSP to a filter folder on
your computer, click the **OK** button. Paint Shop Pro will now remember
the location of all your filters in the folders and sub-folders you specify!
The next time you drop down the Image menu, you should find an entry
for the plug-in filters as well. Keep in mind that if you've added a large
number of plug-ins, loading them could take a few seconds.

Every set of plug-in filters has a different interface. Many allow for a lot
of adjustments, while others simply run on your graphics. You can find
literally thousands of different shareware and freeware filters when you
search the WWW. Figure 5.27 shows an image using a "Cut Glass" filter
downloaded from the Web.

Fig. 5.27
This cut glass effect is
just one example of the
filters you can
download.

Part II Making Great Images

Combining Images
Using Image Arithmetic

All graphic artists look for new and interesting ways to use existing or created images. The Arithmetic feature of PSP allows you to literally combine the pixels of two separate images to create a third image. Dramatic results can be achieved using this method to "layer" one image over another.

> **NOTE**
>
> Note that this use of the word "layer" (to combine images using image arithmetic) is different from the Layers feature that is addressed in Chapter 7.

I'm going to take you on a step-by-step journey through the creation of images using the Arithmetic function and then explain how this advanced and powerful feature works.

When you select the two source images, be aware that the final output image canvas size is determined by the size of the image you choose as "Source Image #1." Usually, you'll achieve better results when you use images of exactly the same height and width. Both images must be open in PSP before you can use the Image/Arithmetic function. Figures 5.28a and 5.28b show the two images I am going to combine for this example.

Fig. 5.28a
Fig. 5.28b
Using Image Arithmetic, we'll combine these two images to create a new image.

a   b

Once the two images you've chosen are open on the workspace, select Image, Arithmetic from the menu bar to bring up the Image Arithmetic dialog box (figure 5.29).

Fig. 5.29
All Image Arithmetic
starts here.

Select which file will be source image #1 and which will be source image
#2 at the top of this dialog box. The rest of the dialog box is broken into
three sections: Function, Channel, and Modifiers, each of which is
described below:

Function
Here you can select from any of the nine different arithmetic
functions that can be performed. The function you select represents
which logic PSP should use when combining the two source images.

Channel
You can choose to run the Arithmetic function on all colors in your
images, or across all three color channels (red, green, and blue).

Modifiers
The modifiers set the divisor and bias, which allow for altering the
effect of the function you select.

A checkbox allows you to change how PSP will handle the numeric
color values that are over 255 or below 0 after it has completed the
computations with the original formula and any modifications set.
If the Clip Colors checkbox is checked, any values less than 0 will
be changed to 0. Any numbers greater than 255 will be changed to
255. If the Clip Colors checkbox is not checked, any values less
than zero will be the difference between 256 and the value. Any
numbers greater than 255 will change to the difference between the
value and 256.

Figure 5.30 shows the results of combining the chicken and egg image with PSP Arithmetic.

Fig. 5.30
PSP did a great job combining these two images.

Image Arithmetic is an advanced concept worth your spending time learning. Experiment with the different functions and settings, and you'll see a variety of results from the two images you are trying to create.

6

Picture Tubes and Web Graphics

New to Paint Shop Pro 5 is the concept of a Picture Tube Brush. With this innovative tool, PSP enables you to paint graphics instead of colors and paint on your image. Picture Tubes are fun, easy to work with, and very effective for creating sets of graphics for your site.

Besides Picture Tubes, this chapter introduces you to building Web Graphics—icons, titles, bars, and more—that look perfect for Web sites. Most Web page designers establish the site's identity by creating a set of icons, buttons, accents, and graphical titles for its pages, in addition to any graphical content that may go along with the text itself. Generally, it's better to give your navigation icons a unique thematic look that reminds readers that the pages are all part of a single site.

In this chapter, I show you how to create the elements for a set of pages with Paint Shop Pro 5. You'll see how the techniques introduced in earlier chapters (and expanded on later in the book) are put to work in real-world sites.

▶ **Using Paint Shop Pro Picture Tubes**
Picture Tubes, the most entertaining and useful new feature in PSP 5, take painting to an entirely new level. Learn how to use Picture Tubes to your advantage.

▶ **Making Your Own Buttons**
You may be surprised how easy it is to create sophisticated-looking 3D buttons and navigational graphics from scratch.

▶ **Matching Titles and Bars**
Graphical headers and dividers set the mood of your site. Making them match your buttons and page content is key.

Using Picture Tubes

One of the most exciting features in Paint Shop Pro 5 is the Picture Tube Brush. This new type of paint brush changes the way you normally think of painting. Instead of painting a specific color, shape, or size, you instead paint from a set of creative and colorful images.

The best way to explain how the Picture Tube Brush works is to *show* you. First, create a new image that has a white background and uses 16.7 million colors. Picture Tubes require 16.7 million colors (or 256 color greyscale) in order to work properly.

TIP

When you download Paint Shop Pro 5 from the Web, the set of default Pictures Tubes must be downloaded and installed separately from the Jasc Software Web site **(http://www.jasc.com).** Of course, all the Picture Tubes come on CD-ROM when you purchase Paint Shop Pro through a store or directly from Jasc Software.

Hundreds more Picture Tubes have been created by Web developers like yourself. Stop by this book's home page to find a listing of some of the best sites from which you can download extra Picture Tubes to use.

To use the Picture Tube Brush, click on the Picture Tube icon from the PSP Tool Bar. Then open the Control Palette and click on the Tool Controls tab. From here you can select the Tube brush you want to use and the size of the graphics you are painting. For this example, I am going to select the **Airplanes** tube and keep the Scale at the default 100%.

Figure 6.1 shows the result of clicking my mouse on various parts of the graphic. Notice how each airplane looks related but has a different color, direction, and perspective. Every time I clicked on the mouse button to paint with my tube brush, a different airplane appeared. Tube brushes paint from a set of original images, like this collection of planes.

Fig. 6.1
Painting with the Tube
Brush is simple and
exciting!

Paint Shop Pro 5 comes with over twenty different Picture Tubes for you
to use and enjoy. Each Tube consists of a collection of different but
related images. When you paint with a Picture Tube, PSP automatically
picks one of the images associated with that Tube and paints it on your
image at the specified scale.

Viewing the Picture Tubes

You can easily open any Picture Tube file to see the full collection of
graphics that make up that specific Tube. Picture Tubes have the file
extension of **.TUB** and are intended to be used only by PSP.

Open a Picture Tube by selecting **F**ile, **O**pen from the menu bar and
selecting the Tubes subdirectory. The Tubes subdirectory is found within
the standard Paint Shop Pro directory on your computer (figure 6.2).

Fig. 6.2
Browse through your
system until you find
the Tubes subdirectory.

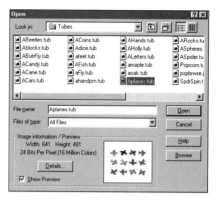

Select the Picture Tube you want to see and click on the Open button.
Paint Shop Pro loads the entire Tube on your screen, as shown in figure
6.3. This specific Tube is divided into twelve sections. Each Picture Tube
has a different amount of sections. Open each of them to see the images
that are available to paint with when you select that Tube.

When you paint with this airplane tube, PSP pulls out one of the twelve
sections every time you click your mouse. Of course, you can tell PSP
whether it should randomly select one of the tubes when painting, use
them in the order displayed (left to right, top to bottom), and more.

Fig. 6.3
Twelve different
airplanes comprise this
Picture Tube.

CAUTION

Do not make any changes to your default Picture Tubes images or they might affect the way your Tube Brush operates. Any colors or text you add to the Tube files will be reflected the next time you try to paint using that specific tube.

Comparing the Picture Tubes

You'll quickly learn to love using Picture Tubes when building individual and sets of Web graphics. Tubes are colorful, they save to efficient file sizes, and they are well sized for Web pages.

You probably noticed that I use various Picture Tubes as examples throughout this book. Later in this chapter, I'll show you how to build a set of icons and graphics from Picture Tubes for your Web site.

Table 6.1 below shows a sample image from the default Picture Tubes that come with Paint Shop Pro 5. Remember that Picture Tubes have a variety of different images, so many that I can't possibly show all variations here. For example, when you paint with the fish Picture Tube, a very diverse set of fish appears; the beetles tube also includes major variations.

TIP

It's important to point out that some Picture Tubes don't work properly unless you click and drag your mouse button when using them. Other Picture Tubes let you click once and paste one image from the tube.

Part II Making Great Images

Table 6.1
Sample Picture Tube Comparison

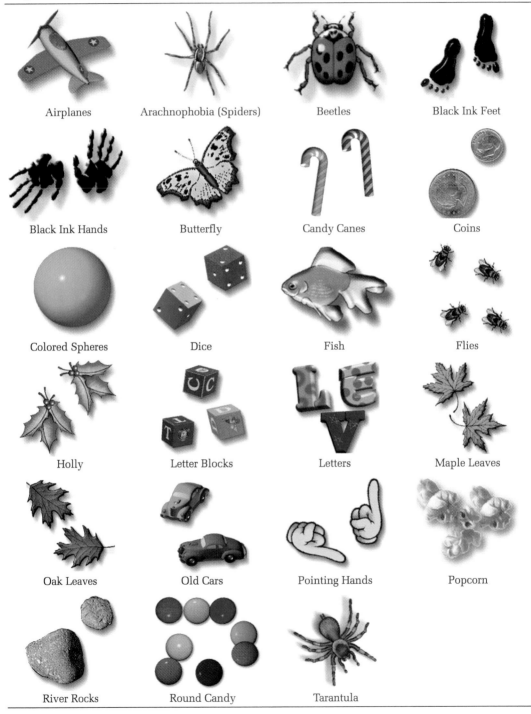

Airplanes	Arachnophobia (Spiders)	Beetles	Black Ink Feet
Black Ink Hands	Butterfly	Candy Canes	Coins
Colored Spheres	Dice	Fish	Flies
Holly	Letter Blocks	Letters	Maple Leaves
Oak Leaves	Old Cars	Pointing Hands	Popcorn
River Rocks	Round Candy	Tarantula	

Setting Your Tube Scaling

Now that you understand what Picture Tubes are and how to use them, it's time to learn how to apply some of the options PSP makes available to you.

The most flexible option with Picture Tubes is image scale. PSP automatically sizes Picture Tubes to fit your specifications. By default, PSP paints the Tube at 100% scale, or its normal size. But you can change the image scale to range anywhere from 10% to 250% of its original size.

Figure 6.4 shows an example of the same fish (from the fish Picture Tube) at three different sizes—50%, 100%, and 250%.

Fig. 6.4
Picture Tubes scale very nicely.

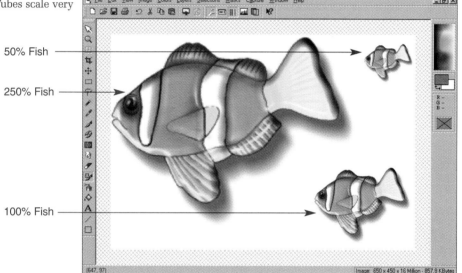

50% Fish

250% Fish

100% Fish

Part II Making Great Images

Other Tube Options

Besides Scaling, you can set several other options when working with Picture Tubes. Click on the Options button from the Control Palette to bring up the Picture Tube Options dialog box (figure 6.5).

Fig. 6.5
These options control how your Tube Brush operates.

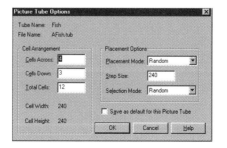

Usually these options are set when the Picture Tube is created because they affect how the Tube Paint Brush works. For example, you can change the Tube Step size, the distance between each painted tube as you drag your mouse. Figure 6.6 shows the fish Picture Tube at two different step sizes.

Fig. 6.6
This fish tube works better with a larger step size, otherwise painting with it becomes too confusing.

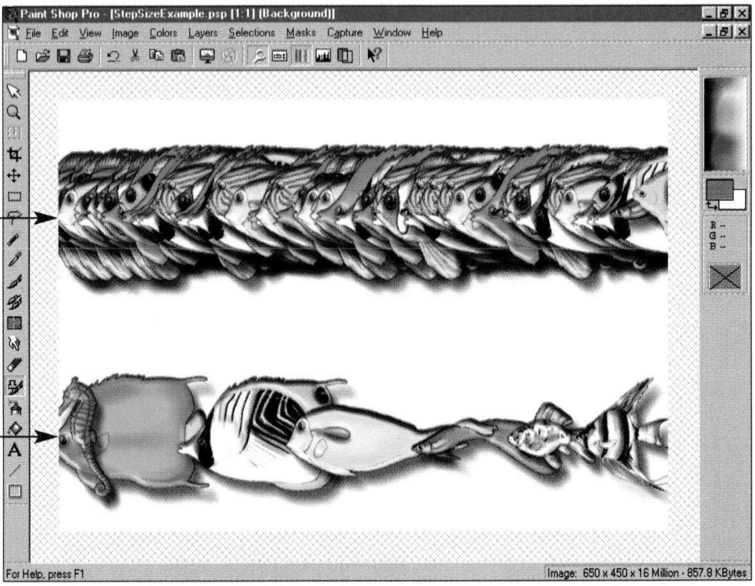

10 Pixel Step size

200 pixel step size

The other important option that you might want to change is Placement Mode. The Placement Mode variable has two options: Continuous and Random.

Continuous Mode
This mode tells PSP the order of images to place when painting with a specific tube. Remember the Airplane tube file in figure 6.3? With Continuous Mode, PSP would first place the airplane in the top left corner. The second image placed would be immediately to the right of the first image, and so on. After the fourth airplane got painted on your image, PSP would start pulling images from the next row.

Random Mode
Random Mode tells PSP to select any of the images in the tube at random every time you draw with the Tube brush and click your mouse button.

Both modes are useful when you work with Picture Tubes.

CAUTION

In general, most of the Tube options should be set only when creating a new Picture Tube from scratch, so be careful when you change them. The Cell Arrangement options are particularly dangerous to change, because they affect which part of the Tube image to paint from. For example, the Airplane Tube has 12 cells established (4 columns and 3 rows). Changing these values might affect which airplane or airplanes you see when painting with the Picture Tubes.

Web Graphics with Picture Tubes

Now that you've seen how Tubes work, think about some innovative ways to use them on your Web site.

One popular way to use Picture Tubes is to create a cool bar that goes across your screen. Figure 6.7 shows four separate button bars that could all be used on a themed page.

Fig. 6.7
Any of these four bars would be effective and professional looking on a Web site.

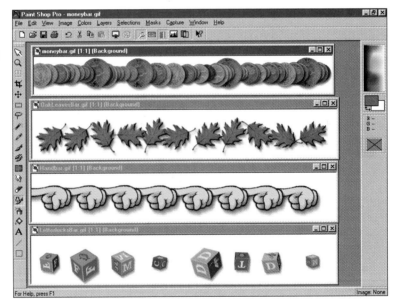

Similarly, you can also create a corresponding, or matching, title that uses Picture Tubes. Figure 6.8 shows two possible title images—one for a weather page and another for a child's page that were easy to create. For both of them, I used special fonts that carried the whole theme along with the images.

Fig. 6.8
These title images are just two of an infinite variety of graphics you can create with Picture Tubes.

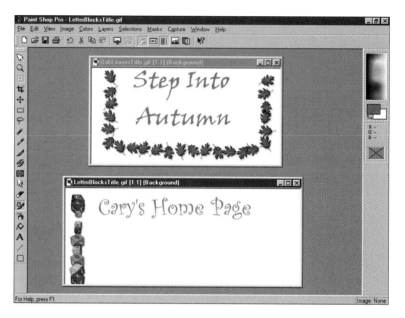

Creating Your Own Picture Tube

Using Picture Tubes to create cool graphics is an easy and effective technique. Besides using the default Picture Tubes, you can create your own from scratch to use yourself, or to share with other Paint Shop Pro users across the world.

This section outlines the steps required to create a PSP Picture Tube from scratch. Before you start, you need to have a set of graphics that will make up the Picture Tube. You can have as many or few images as you'd like when making a new Picture Tube.

1. Once you have the images you want to use to build your tube, choose **F**ile, **N**ew from the PSP menu bar to bring up the New Image dialog box (figure 6.9). This new image can be any size but must have the background color set to transparent and use 16.7 million colors. For this example, I'll create a small tube that is 400 x 400 pixels in size.

Fig. 6.9
The background of
Picture Tubes must be
transparent.

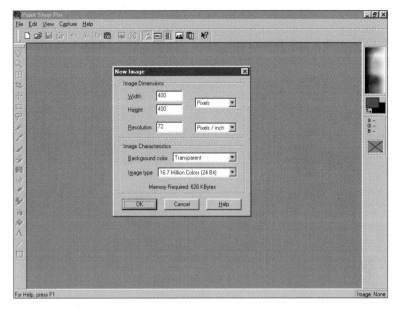

2. After creating your new graphic, open up all the images that will make up this Picture Tube. This sample Picture Tube is going to use the cover of this book rotated in four different directions. Figure 6.10 shows the four images that will make up the Tube and my empty larger graphic.

Fig. 6.10
This Tube will be
perfect for the book's
Web site when finished.

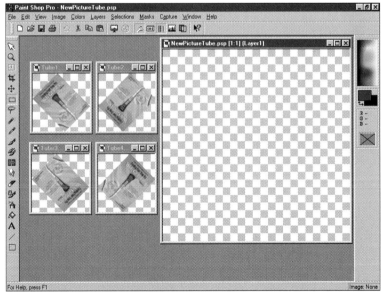

Part II Making Great Images

TIP

Picture Tubes divide the image up into rows and columns. You paint one cell at a time when using the Picture Tube brush. To line up your individual images when creating the Picture Tube, you may want to use the PSP grid system which adds navigational lines to work with. These lines aren't part of the image but used for placement purposes.

Grid lines can be toggled on and off by selecting **V**iew, **G**rid from the menu bar. PSP will display grid lines on top of your image.

You can change the interval of your grid lines by choosing **F**ile, **P**references, **G**eneral Program Preferences and clicking on the Rulers and Units tab (figure 6.11).

Fig. 6.11
Select a grid size that evenly divides your image into equal parts.

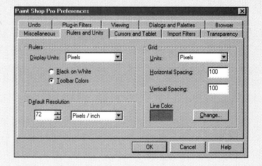

3. Now place each image making up your Picture Tube into the larger graphic. I'll use the copy and paste command to add all four of my individual images into the appropriate quadrant of the Picture Tube I am creating. Highlight the title bar of the image you want to copy and choose, **E**dit, **C**opy to copy each individual image to your clipboard. Select the Picture Tube image, and then choose **E**dit, **P**aste, As New **S**election.

    You must place each graphic in a different cell of the tube. This means you must have equally sized rows and columns with your tube image. When painting with the Picture Tube brush, Paint Shop Pro will select the contents of one cell each time you click on the mouse button. Figure 6.12 shows my nearly completed Picture Tube with all four images on it.

Fig. 6.12
This Tube is almost
finished.

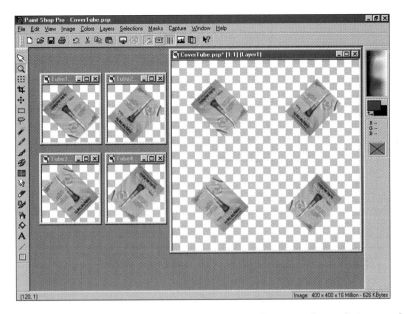

4. Choose **F**ile, **E**xport, **P**icture Tube from the menu bar to bring up the
Export Picture Tube dialog box (figure 6.13). You must tell Paint
Shop Pro how many cells are in this Picture Tube. For this simple
example, I have 2 cells across, 2 cells down, for a grand total of 4
cells. PSP tells you the height and width of each cell in pixels. In
addition, you can configure several default placement options which
control how users can paint with this Picture Tube. Don't forget to
name your Picture Tube. This name is the phrase that will show up
when painting with the Picture Tube brush.

Fig. 6.13
Set the default Picture
Tube options here.

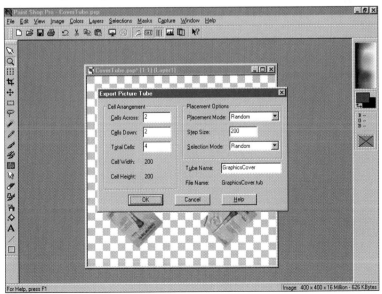

5. Once you've configured the Picture Tube options, click on the OK button and PSP creates the appropriate .TUB file. You can now paint with your Picture Tube! Figure 6.14 shows me painting with this newly created Picture Tube.

Fig. 6.14
Creating your own Picture Tube is a piece of cake!

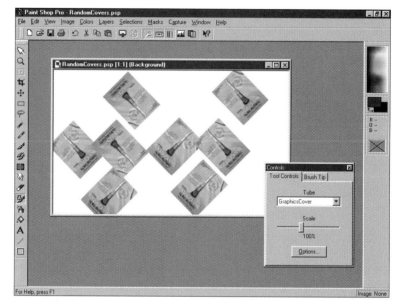

You can download this sample Picture Tube at the book's Web site. Feel free to experiment and make your own tubes from scratch.

Making Your Own Buttons

Picture Tubes are cool and effective techniques, but they aren't always perfect for creating individual and sets of Web graphics. This section looks at other ways and methods besides Pictures Tubes to create cool images for your site.

Themed Buttons

Usually, the old square-button-with-a-word-in-the-middle look is definitely *tres cliché*. In this section, I outline a general formula you can follow to create an unlimited variety of professional-quality buttons without hiring (or becoming) a professional graphics artist. To illustrate the principles in action, I explain exactly how you can create each of the buttons shown in figure 6.15, step by step.

For more detailed coverage of the special effects used in this chapter, refer to Chapter 5, "Images and Special Effects."

Fig. 6.15
Paint Shop Pro's special effects can help you produce a wide variety of button styles.

The first—and most important—step in designing a button takes place in your imagination. What colors, shapes, and textures best express the mood and message of your Web site? In the examples for this section, I use the same color scheme (electric blue and white) and text font (Parisian) throughout every example to highlight the other differences between the buttons. Naturally, you will want to select a font (or, at most, two) and a color scheme that reflect the style you're after.

1. **Select a shape.**
    First, you need to decide on a shape for your buttons. For now, though, let's stick to easily recognized button shapes such as rectangles and ellipses. But you should realize that good buttons can come in any shape or size, as long as they fit within the theme of the page.

2. **Fill in or shade it.**
    To make your shape stand out from the background, you need to fill it with some color. For a 3-D look with round buttons, use the Fill Bucket tool with Sunburst Gradient, as I did before adding the text to the icons in figure 6.15.

3. **Add a shadow.**
    The Image, Effects, Drop Shadow command can give almost any button more visual impact and "pushability." I used it to add a shadow to all three buttons in figure 6.15.

    Generally, you'll want to add a shadow before you label the button and then save the blank button as a full-color PSP file. That way you can use the same basic button many times simply by adding different labels. The exception to this rule is when you are going to distort or filter the entire button, including the text label. Then you'll need to wait and put the shadow on after you're done so its color and shape don't change in undesirable ways.

4. **Label it.**
    Use the Text tool to choose a font and put an appropriate label on your button. While the text is selected, you might consider using the Fill Bucket to shade the text with a Gradient fill that contrasts with the button.

Part II Making Great Images

5. **Add a cool special effect or filter.**

    Any of the filters, distortions, and effects discussed in Chapter 5 are available to make your button stand out and look smart. This is also where filters that you can purchase and download become effective. Figure 6.16 shows the same three buttons we've been working on, but with a special filter applied to each image. This filter is the Weave filter, which is part of the Eye Candy collection of filters from Alien Skin Software (**http://www.alienskin.com).**

Fig. 6.16
The same buttons now have a little bit of style to them.

6. **Reduce the color depth.**

    Fancy buttons don't do much good if nobody can see them until 25 seconds after your Web page starts loading. A key move for keeping button graphic files small is to reduce the number of colors used as much as possible. Almost any good button should reduce nicely to 16 colors; select Colors, Decrease Color Depth, **16** Colors, and choose Optimized Median Cut with the Nearest Color Reduction Method.

7. **Save as a transparent GIF.**

    Rectangular buttons with no shadow do not need to be transparent, but irregularly shaped buttons should be. That way, you can change the background on your Web pages any time you like without having to change the buttons.

    To save a transparent GIF, select the Dropper tool and click with the right mouse button on the region you want to be transparent. Then choose Colors, Set Palette Transparency and choose **Set the transparency value to the current background color** from the dialog box that appears. (You'll find more details on transparent GIFs in Chapter 10, "Creating Transparent GIFs.")

8. **Touch up anything that looks amiss.**

    Take a final look at your button. Don't be afraid to zoom in and paint a pixel or two if the button has some rough edges here and there.

By following these eight basic steps and adding your own choice of effects, you can create beautiful buttons that convey the unique flavor of your own Web pages.

Matching Titles and Bars

Web graphics are not simply buttons and icons. You'll almost certainly want some other matching graphics for your pages. Since the title is probably the first thing people look at on your page, you may want to make it a fancy graphic instead of a simple text heading. In fact, aside from graphical buttons, fancy titles are probably the most common use of graphics on the Web.

Almost as common are graphical bars, rules, or page dividers. If your page contains a lot of text, a thematic bar or rule is a great way to provide a visual break to readers. And, whether your pages are text-intensive or not, bars can add flair and help remind visitors where they are.

Figures 6.17, 6.18, and 6.19 are pages from a fictitious Web site I fabricated for this chapter. Notice how I created matching titles and bars across the screen to match my buttons. Each graphic in these examples was produced following the 8-step process outlined earlier.

Fig. 6.17
My title perfectly matches the Diner's buttons.

Figure 6.17 demonstrates how a little creativity can go a long way toward giving a page its own identity. By applying the same effects I used to make the buttons, I produced a title that conveys the same theme. By cutting and pasting one word over the other and using a slightly deeper shadow, I enhanced the three-dimensional effect.

Similarly, cutting and pasting a line of shaded and shadowed dots better fits the theme of the page than simply drawing a horizontal line.

Fig. 6.18
The Cutout Effect can make something drop into the page, while Drop Shadows make elements stand out above the page.

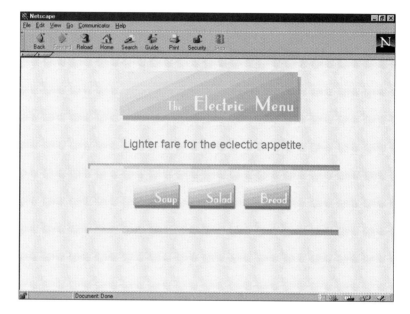

The title in figure 6.18 was a no-brainer once the buttons were designed. It uses precisely the same fill and shadow settings, which Paint Shop Pro remembers until you change them, even if you close down the program and start it up again. The only change in my procedure was saving the title as a 256-color image instead of a 16-color image. The color banding in the large region of gradient fill would have been too pronounced with only 16 colors. In fact, this title might look better if I were to use the JPG format and save it in 16.7 million colors. Then you wouldn't see the color banding across the icons and title.

The resulting Web page took only minutes to make, but looks sharp and loads fast.

Fig. 6.19
Embossing gives titles
and rules the stamped-
paper look.

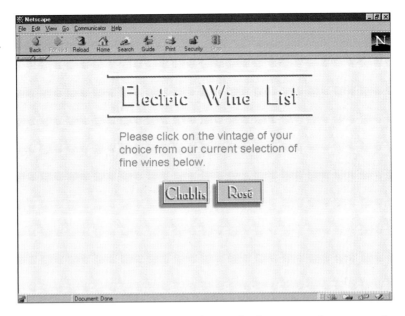

Of course, titles don't have to look exactly the same as buttons to give a
page visual consistency. In figure 6.19, I used the same Emboss and
Colorize filters on the title as I did on the buttons. Instead of adding a
Drop Shadow, I simply made the background color transparent. This is a
popular (and very easy) trick, which makes the title appear to have been
literally embossed onto the page.

The horizontal rules above and below the title are actually separate
graphics, which could be used anywhere on the page for dividers.

Web Graphics Tips and Techniques

Even if you are building a Web site with a much different look and feel from the examples shown in this chapter, the same principles that make these pages effective can work for you:

▶ Make all your buttons, titles, and bars convey the same mood and theme so that visitors recognize and remember your site.

▶ Use icons or repeating graphical elements as "landmarks" to help visitors keep track of where they are within the site.

▶ Employ every trick you can to keep file sizes to a minimum, especially for titles and navigation graphics.

Chapter 12, "Making Your Graphics Lean," includes many more tips on how to keep the size of you graphics files down.

Beyond these basic principles, the most important rule is that there *are* no cut-and-dried rules. The more unique you make your titles, accents, and navigation graphics, the more identifiable and memorable your site will be.

7

Using Paint
Shop Pro Layers

New to Paint Shop Pro 5, layers let you create and manage your Web graphics in a powerful manner. A *layer* is like a transparent sheet of acetate, with figures painted on the sheet. Several of these sheets can be stacked on top of one another, reordered, adjusted, edited separately, added, and subtracted. The image that results is a composite of all the individual sheets. This lets you work with different parts of each image individually. Although it's true that almost anything you can do with layers can also be done without them, layers make many image editing tasks a lot easier.

This chapter introduces you to Paint Shop Pro layers. You'll get a complete understanding of how they work, when to use them, and why they're the most exciting new feature in PSP 5!

Here's what you'll learn in this chapter:

▶ **Get to know PSP layers**
Although powerful, layers can be confusing until you know how to recognize and use them effectively.

▶ **How to add, delete, and restack layers**
You'll often want to add and remove layers to/from your layered images.

▶ **How to use several different tools to edit layers**
Paint Shop Pro includes many different tools that are useful for editing layers. You'll get the rundown of how to use each of them effectively.

▶ **How to adjust a layer's opacity and blend mode**
Since layers sit on top of one another, your final image depends on the opacity of each level.

Understanding How Layers Work

Every PSP image has at least one layer. A single-layered image can be as simple as a block of solid color or as complex as images like the one in figure 7.1, taken from the Paint Shop Pro 5 CD-ROM.

Fig. 7.1
A complex, single-layered image.

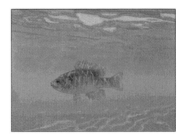

Editing the image in figure 7.1 can be difficult. You can't simply touch up the fish or make a change to the water color without affecting the entire image. As a result, editing non-layered images can be tedious and difficult.

With layers, editing this image would be much easier. You can make changes to each part of the image separately. When you're finished and save the image as a GIF, JPEG, or PNG, the layers will be "flattened" into one layer automatically.

NOTE
While you're working on a layered image, you'll want to save the image as a **.PSP** file. Created by Jasc Software, this advanced format is one of the few that support layering in images, and it's optimized to work with Paint Shop Pro.

When you're finished with your image, save it in a file format suitable for the Web. To do this, just choose **F**ile, Save **A**s to save the file as a GIF, JPEG, or PNG, just as you would for any Web graphic. There's no need to merge down the layers into a single layer beforehand, because Paint Shop Pro will do this automatically when you save a layered image to anything other than the PSP file format, or the few other formats that support layering.

PSP allows you to view all an image's layers at the same time or to hide one or more layers. Different layers can be edited independently of the others; this ability to manipulate certain parts of an image without affecting the other parts is what gives the layering its power.

Figures 7.2a, 7.2b, and 7.2c show an image with two layers—a background and a "higher" layer. Figure 7.2a shows the image with both layers visible. Figure 7.2b shows the same image with the background hidden. (The checkered grid that shows behind the ship is what shows up by default whenever PSP needs to represent an empty, or unpainted, area of an image.) Finally, figure 7.2c shows the same image with a Motion Blur applied to the sailboat layer but with the background (ocean) layer unchanged.

Fig. 7.2a
A two-layered image of a sailboat and sunset.

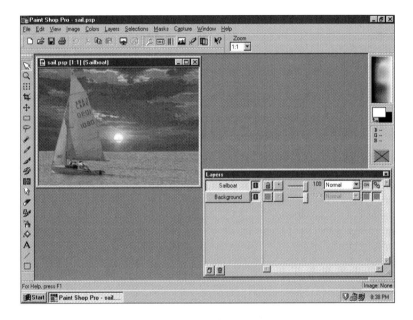

Fig. 7.2b
The same two-layered image with only the top layer visible.

Fig. 7.2c
The same two-layered image with a Motion Blur applied only to the top layer.

The Layers Palette

Layers are managed with the Layers Palette (figure 7.3). To toggle the Layers Palette on and off, click the Layers button on the PSP toolbar.

Fig. 7.3
The Layers Palette for an image with two layers.

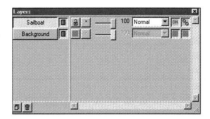

The Layers Palette has two panes. On the left are buttons for each layer, along with a Layer Visibility Toggle. By default, the Layer Buttons are named **Background**, **Layer 1**, **Layer 2**, and so on, but you can—and should—give your layers more meaningful names. The Layer Visibility Toggles allow you to temporarily "hide" layers so that you can see only some of your image's layers—maybe even just a single layer. Click a layer's Visibility toggle to hide that layer, and click the toggle again to make the layer visible.

TIP

You can view a thumbnail of a layer, whether or not that layer is currently visible, by positioning the mouse cursor over the appropriate Layer Button. Move the mouse away from the button, and the thumbnail disappears.

At the bottom left of the Layers Palette window are two more buttons, the New Layer button and the Delete Layer button. Use the New Layer button to add a new, empty layer or to make a copy of an existing layer. Use the Delete Layer button to remove an existing layer.

In the right pane of the Layers Palette are six more controls for each layer: a Protect Transparency toggle, a Layer Group toggle, a Layer Opacity slider, a Blend Mode selection list, a Layer Mask toggle, and a Link Mask toggle.

Don't let all these controls scare you away from layers. We'll look at most of them more closely later in this chapter. Once you start playing around with them, the layer controls are easy to use and remember.

Table 7.1 is a quick reminder of each control found in the Layers Palette.

Part II Making Great Images

Table 7.1
Quick-Reference for Layer Icons/Controls

Layer Icon	Icon Name	Description
Layer 1	**Layer Button**	Click on a layer button to make a layer active. Double-click on a layer button to open the Layer Properties dialog box, which is discussed in some detail later. Right-click on a layer button to open a menu that contains many of the commands available in the Layers menu bar.
	Layer Visibility Toggle	Click on this button to hide and then show a specific layer.
	Protect Transparency Toggle	Turn the Protect Transparency Toggle on when you want transparent areas of a layer to remain transparent, even if you paint into those areas. Turn the toggle off when you want to paint on transparent areas of the layer.
	Layer Group Toggle	Layer groups are sets of layers grouped together so they can be moved or reordered as a unit. When the toggle is off, it appears as an asterisk (*). Press this button to add the layer to the first layer group (the button will be labeled "1"). Press again to add the layer to the next group, and so on. Keep pressing until the button returns to off if you want to remove a layer from a group.
100	**Opacity Slider**	Move the Opacity Slider to the left to reduce the opacity of the layer, which will make figures on lower layers more transparent. Move the slider to the right to make the figures on lower layers more opaque.
Normal	**Blend Mode List**	The Blend Mode list allows you to specify how to "blend" a particular layer with the layers beneath it. The blend mode determines how the layer's pixels are combined with the pixels of lower layers. For example, in a two-layered image for which Darken is the Blend Mode of the upper layer, each pixel in the upper layer is compared with the pixel in the layer beneath it, and the darker of the two pixels is what is displayed.
ON	**Layer Mask Toggle**	Turn this toggle on to activate a layer mask; turn the toggle off to deactivate the mask. A layer mask allows you to adjust the opacity of different areas of a single layer without permanently affecting the layer. The mask can be edited or deleted, leaving the layer itself untouched. This advanced layer feature will not be detailed in this book.
	Mask Link Toggle	Turn this toggle on to link a layer mask to a layer, so that the mask and layer can be moved as a unit.
	Add New Layer Button	Press this button to add a new, empty layer. Drag the Layer Button of and existing layer to the Add New Layer button to make a copy of an existing layer.
	Delete Layer Button	Press this button to delete the current layer. Alternatively, drag a Layer Button to the Delete Layer button to delete that layer.

Naming a Layer

To change the name of a layer, use the Layer Properties dialog box. The Layer Properties dialog box appears whenever you add a new layer to your image by clicking the Add New Layer button or when you double-click on a Layer button.

Fig. 7.4
The Layer Properties
Dialog Box

This dialog box is split into three sections: Layer Properties, Mask Properties, and Blend Properties.

In the Layer portion of this dialog box, you'll see all the settings for the layer that you could also see in the Layers Palette itself. The Layer Properties box simplifies many of the changes that also can be made on the Layers Palette. For example, you can type in a Layer Group number instead of clicking on the Toggle button multiple times from the Layers Palette.

In addition, the Layer Properties dialog box also lets you rename a layer so you can more easily recognize and use it. Giving your layers meaningful names, especially when your image includes several layers, is a good idea. That way, you don't have to remember that "Layer 1" has the cactus and "Layer 5" has the blazing sun. Instead, name your layers "Cactus" and "Blazing Sun" and leave your brain free to focus on the great image you're creating with those layers.

To rename a Layer, simply type in a new name in the Name text box and click **OK** to return to the Layers palette.

Part II Making Great Images

When to Use Layering

Layers can be incredibly useful when you wish to do complex image manipulation, but you can go overboard with them. For simple operations, such as adding a solid-colored border around your image, you should probably forget about layers. But if you want to combine several image elements, and perhaps control their opacities independent of each other or apply special effects to some elements while leaving others untouched, then layers are the way to go.

You may also find layers helpful when you want to combine two or more elements but are unsure at first exactly how they should fit together. By giving each element its own layer, you can experiment with moving the elements around, positioning and repositioning each one until you've found an effect you like. You can also try out different opacities and blend modes on the separate layers.

How to Use Layers

Now that you understand how layers work and can find your way around the Layers Palette, it's time to use this cool feature within PSP. Let's begin with an uncomplicated example, the two-layered image displayed earlier in Figured 7.2a. For this example we'll add a reflection of the sun in the water. You can download this image from the book's Web site or find/scan one of your own to follow along.

Open the image and make sure the Layers Palette is open.

The first step in this example is creating a new layer by copying the Background layer of the original image. To copy the Background, drag its Layer button to the Add New Layer button. A new Layer button will then appear just above the Background's layer button. The new layer will automatically become the active layer, and its layer button will be labeled "Copy of Background." Don't forget to rename your layer (I called mine "Reflection" for easy use later). You won't be able to see any difference in the image at this point because the new copy is layered immediately on top of the original.

Hide all the layers except for the one labeled **Reflection**. This lets you ignore the other details on the image and focus on getting the reflection of the sun perfect.

Use the Selection tool to select around the sun in the copied layer. Make a rectangular selection about 75 pixels high and as wide as the image, as is shown in figure 7.5.

Fig. 7.5
Rectangular selection
around the sun in the
copied layer.

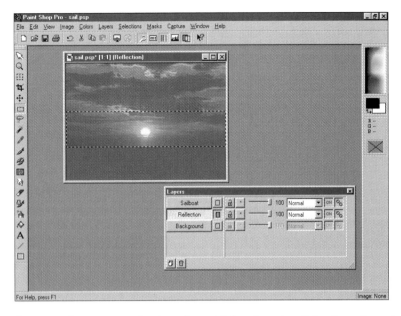

Once you have your selection, invert it by choosing **S**elections, **I**nvert
from the PSP menu bar. Then hit the delete key on your keyboard to erase
all but the selected area—everything but the rectangle around the sun.
PSP assumes that deleted parts of a layer will become transparent. This
situation is shown in figure 7.6, in which all other layers are still hidden.

Fig. 7.6
The copied layer with
everything but the
rectangular selection
deleted.

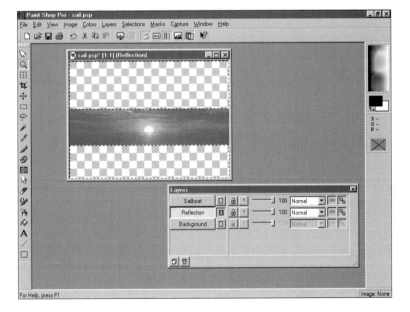

Part II Making Great Images

Turn off the selection by clicking in the image window outside the selection or by choosing **S**elections, Select **N**one from the PSP menu bar. Then, with the copied layer still active, you can manipulate the copied layer so that it's turned upside-down and positioned at the bottom of the image. Choose **I**mage, **F**lip from the menu bar to turn the copied sun layer upside-down.

Then choose the Mover tool and drag the layer to position it at the bottom of the image. You probably want to hide the Sailboat layer while you're doing this repositioning, but make it visible again once the Reflection layer is located where you want it.

If all the layers are visible at this point, that flipped-out sun will not be visible because the layer that contains the water is on top of the copied layer. What you need to do now is switch the stacking order of your layers.

The Layer buttons in the Layers Palette appear in the order in which layers are stacked on top of each other. The topmost Layer button corresponds to the uppermost layer, the Layer button below the top one corresponds to the next highest layer, and so on down. To restack the layers of this image so the Reflection layer is on top of the Sailboat layer, go to the Layers Palette and drag the Layer button of the Reflection layer above the button of the Sailboat layer, as shown in figure 7.7.

Fig. 7.7
Restacking the layers brings the sun reflection on top of the sailboat.

Dragging a Layer ——

Now you're just about done, but that fiery flipped-over sky looks more like a painted-on mess than a reflection, and it's covering up the bottom of the boat. To blend it into the water to make it look more like a reflection, adjust its opacity to around 50%, using the Opacity Slider on the Layers Palette. The result is the image shown in figure 7.8.

Fig. 7.8
The sailboat and water blend better with the sun reflection at 50% opacity.

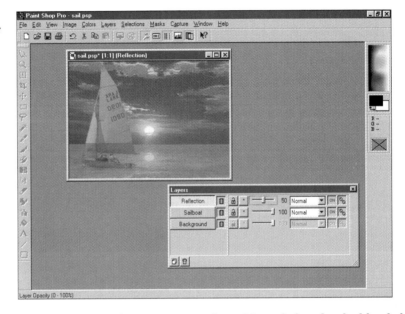

There's still room for improvement here. Not only has the sky blended in with the water, but it's also mixed with the sailboat! The effect on the body of the boat and the passengers is pretty good, but the bottom of the sails are a different color than the top of the sails. To correct this, you'll need to erase some of the Reflection layer so it doesn't interfere with the boat.

Make sure that Reflection is the active layer and that both Reflection and Sailboat are visible. Then Zoom in to 1:2 or 1:3 so you can get a better look at what you're erasing. Choose the Eraser tool and carefully erase the semi-transparent sunset from the sails. When you're done, reset Zoom to 1:1. The finished product is shown in figure 7.9.

Fig. 7.9
Every layer shows in
this image of the
sailboat with the sun
reflected in the water.

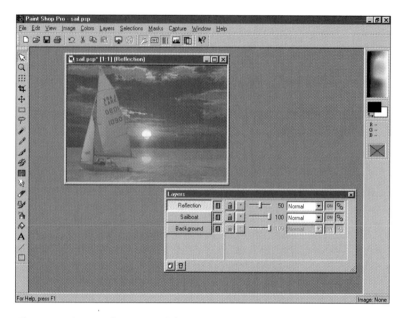

The manufactured sunset of the original image now looks much more
realistic.

Creating Your Own Layered Images

Now let's try creating a rather complex layered image from scratch,
instead of editing a photograph. This example shows you why you'll
want to use layered images when building most of the graphics on your
Web site, so that you can edit and change them easily in the future.

This new image will be a large masthead banner for a fictional Web site
called "The Lion's Roar." Begin by opening up a new image with the New
button, then set Width to 500, Height to 175, Resolution to 72
Pixels/inch, Background Color to White, and Image Type to 16.7 Million
Colors (24 bits).

Getting the Lion's Head

You can copy from an existing image to create a new layer. For example,
figure 7.10 shows an image taken from the Paint Shop Pro CD-ROM that
features a lion's head on a white background. Let's select the lion's head
and add it to our new image as a layer.

Fig. 7.10

This lion's head on a white background comes from PSP's CD-ROM.

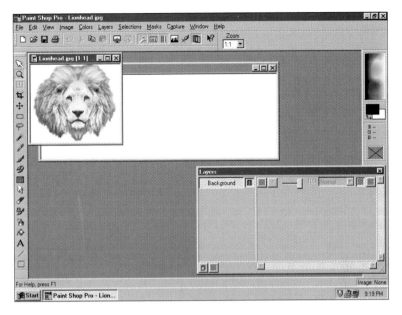

 First, select just the head by using the Magic Wand, a tool that lets you select based on pixel color. You'll want to select the lion's head, but the easiest way to begin is by selecting the white background. Since the white background blends a bit with the head, set the Magic Wand's tolerance to about 20 in the Control Palette. Then click on the white background to select all the White parts of the image. Since you really want to select the lion's head, choose **S**elections, **I**nvert from the PSP menu bar.

There's still a bit of background in the selection, so let's choose **S**elections, **M**odify, **C**ontract to tighten the selection a little by setting the number of pixels to 1 or 2 in the Control Palette. Now copy the selection to the clipboard using **E**dit, **C**opy; then close the lion's head image.

Click on the new banner image you created to make it active, if it isn't already. Then choose **E**dit, **P**aste, As New Layer. A new layer called "Layer 1" is created above the Background layer. This layer contains the lion's head surrounded by a transparent area, since only the pixels of the copied selection were added to the new layer. Rename the layer to something meaningful, such as "Lion."

Part II Making Great Images

You can then position the lion's head using the Mover tool. The result will look like figure 7.11, which shows both the Background layer and the Lion layer.

Fig. 7.11
The lion's head layer is now above the white Background layer.

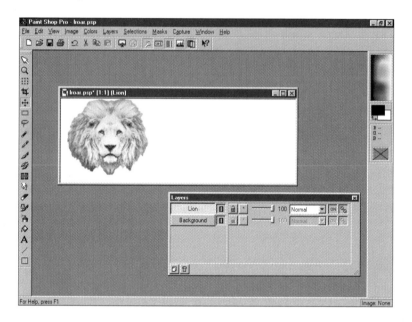

Integrating a Background

Once the lion's head is properly placed on your image, the next step is to add a new layer for a textured rectangle that will partly overlap the lion's head.

To make this new layer, you'll need to open up an image that contains the texture with which you want to fill the rectangle. I've used a handmade texture here, but you can use any texture you create or have on hand.

NOTE

Thousands of textures are available for download from the Web. Here are two URLs that have many textures you can use in your own Web graphics.

http://www.meat.com/textures/

http://infinitefish.com/texture.html

In addition, check out Chapter 14, "Background Graphics and Colors," for a step-by-step tutorial on creating your own textures.

Open the texture you want to use in Paint Shop Pro. Then switch to your banner image and press the Add New Layer button. The Layer Properties dialog box will appear, letting you name the new layer. Change the layer's name to "Texture" and click **OK** to close the dialog box.

> **TIP**
>
> You can bypass the Layer Properties dialog box when you add a new layer by holding down the Shift key while you press the Add New Layer button.

On this new layer, use the Selection tool to select a rectangular area that begins at the top edge of the image about 110 pixels from its left edge and ends at the bottom right-hand corner of the image. Then choose the Flood Fill tool, and on the Control Palette select Pattern as the Fill Style. Click on the Option button to bring up the Flood Fill Options dialog box. For the New Pattern Source, choose the name of the file containing your texture and click **OK** to close the dialog box. Then click in the selected area, and the rectangle will be filled (figure 7.12).

Fig. 7.12
A textured block layer is added above the lion's head layer.

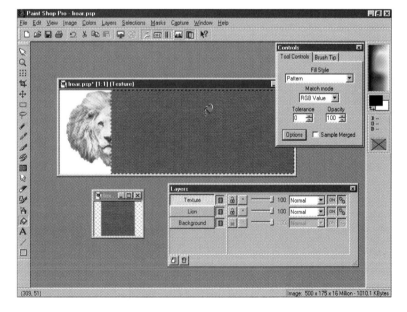

> **NOTE**
>
> If you try to fill a selection or paint on a layer but nothing seems to happen, chances are the layer you intended to edit isn't the active layer. Make sure that the layer you want to work on is active before you try to edit it. To make an inactive layer active, click on its Layer button in the Layer Palette.

158   Using Paint Shop Pro Layers – Chapter 7

Final Touches

You're almost done with this advanced layered image. This last section adds the finishing touches to your image so it will look like a professional-caliber graphic.

Suppose we want the part of the lion's head that is covered by the texture rectangle to show through somewhat. To get this effect, begin by making a copy of the Lion layer. Drag the Lion layer button to the Add New Layer button, and a new layer named "Copy of Lion" is created. Because this is descriptive enough, there's no need to change the name. You won't notice any change in the image's appearance yet, since the new layer completely overlaps the original lion's head layer.

Right now, the original lion's head layer and the copied layer are both underneath the textured rectangle. To make the copied layer overlap the rectangle, drag the Copy of Lion layer above the Layer button of the Texture (rectangle) layer, as shown in Figure 7.13.

Fig. 7.13
Dragging the Copy of Lion above the Texture layer button restacks the layers.

Restacking the Layer

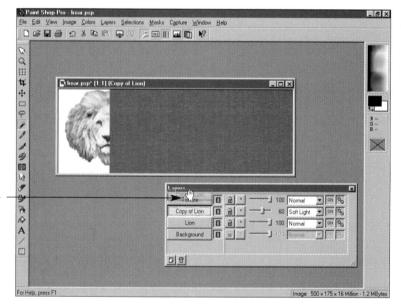

This makes the copied lion's head overlap the rectangle, letting none of the covered part of the rectangle show through. To make the overlapping part of the head seem to fade into the rectangle, set the Opacity slider for the copied layer to about 60, and for its Blend Mode, choose Soft Light. Figure 7.14 shows the faded image and Layer settings.

Fig. 7.14
Opacity and Blend
Mode adjustments made
to the copied lion's head
layer.

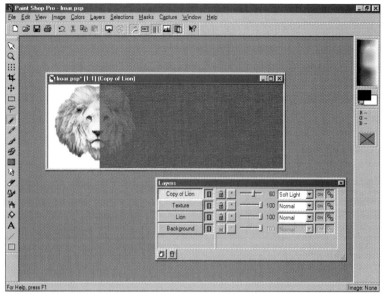

TIP

Several of the Blend Modes let you "meld" the colors and textures of two
images. Experiment with Multiply, Overlay, Soft Light, and Hard Light.
Each produces somewhat similar results, but all differ in their effect on
brightness and contrast.

To see why we want to have the Lion layer below the Texture layer and
the Copy of Lion layer above the Texture layer, try hiding each of these
layers one at a time while keeping the other visible. You'll see that the
Lion layer gives us the fully opaque left half of the lion's head, while the
Copy of Lion layer gives the blended right half of the lion's head. When
you're ready to continue, make both layers visible again.

Finally, add some text to the banner. Set the foreground color in the Color
palette by using the Eye Dropper to pick up some of the yellow in the
lion's coat so your text color coordinates with the rest of the image.

Click on the Texture layer button to make it active. Choose the Text tool
and click in the middle of the textured rectangle in your banner image.
When the Add Text dialog box appears, select the font and font size you
want, with both Antialias and Floating selected. Add the text "The Lion's
Roar," formatted as you wish, and click **OK.** The text might not be exactly
where you'd like it, but you can move it into place by clicking inside the
text selection and dragging it to where it belongs.

Normally, you'd then right-click when you have your text where you
want it, but don't do so here. We want to keep the selection active,

because we're going to turn this selection into a layer by using the Promote to Layer operation.

If you look at the Layers Palette at this point, you'll see above the Texture layer button something that looks like a layer button but is labeled "Floating Selection." To make this selection a layer, right-click on this layer button; then choose Promote to Layer from the menu box that appears. The text you added now becomes a layer.

The label on the button changes to "Promoted Selection," and any layer operation can now be applied to this new layer. Change the name of this layer to "Site Name" to remind yourself what the layer contains. The banner and the Layers palette now look like figure 7.15.

Fig. 7.15
The Lion's Roar banner now has a layer of text.

Now let's make the text more interesting than just solid yellow. Change the Blend Mode of the Site Name layer to Overlay. The texture of the rectangle will then show through the text a bit.

Our banner is almost complete. As a finishing touch, let's add a drop shadow to the lion's head. The shadow should show up on the white background, but not on the textured rectangle, so make the Lion layer the active layer. Then, choose **I**mage, **E**ffects, **D**rop Shadow. The result is shown in figure 7.16.

Fig. 7.16
The banner is completed by adding a Drop Shadow to the lion's head.

Suppose you're not quite happy with the placement of the lion's head and want to reposition it. You have two copies of the head, though, and you'll want them to move together so that they don't get misaligned. This is easily accomplished with the Layer Group toggles.

To group the layers together, first click on the Layer Group toggle for the Lion layer. A "1" appears on the toggle button. Now click on the Layer Group toggle for the Copy of Lion layer. A "1" then appears on that toggle button as well. Now if you move either of those two layers, the other will also move along.

The only thing left to make the banner ready for the Web site is to save it in a Web-recognizable format. This image will look good as either a GIF or JPG file, and can easily be added to any Web site. Figure 7.17 shows the final image on the Web site.

Fig. 7.17
This professional-caliber image couldn't easily be created without using PSP Layers.

CAUTION

Once you flatten an image, the separate layers cannot be retrieved. Your JPEG, GIF, or PNG will have only a single layer. If you want to keep a copy of your project with all layers intact, save a copy as a PSP file before the layers are merged.

As a general rule, always save your original image in the PSP file format then save it as a GIF, JPG, or PNG when you need to publish it to the Web.

Layer Tips and Tricks

Before you leave this chapter, let's review a few points you should keep in mind when working with layers:

▶ Any 256-color greyscale or 16-million-color image can have layers added to it in an editing session, but layers can only be saved in the PSP file format (or the PhotoShop .PSD file format).

▶ When you save your layered image to a file format that does not support layers, the file saved to disk will be flattened into a single layer. For the layered images that you create in order to make sophisticated Web graphics, save in PSP format if you want to keep a copy for future editing.

▶ Don't panic when you see how large your multi-layered PSP files are. These files contain all the layer information, which will not be saved in your Web-ready versions. The file size of your Web images will probably be *much* smaller once you save them as GIFs, JPEGs, or PNGs. For example, the Lion's Roar banner created here was over 100Kb in PSP format, but became less than 20Kb when saved as a JPEG.

▶ Spend time exploring Layer Blend modes and Opacity. These two enhancing features let you create powerful graphics with minimal effort.

8

The Black and
White Alternative

Back in 1994, when *Schindler's List* was released, all the pundits predicted it wouldn't be successful, no matter how well done it was, because it was a black and white (B&W) movie. For years, Technicolor had colorized the glamour and glitz of Hollywood and nobody dreamed of filming and releasing a big-screen picture that lacked color through almost the entire movie. Even the all-time movie classic *Gone with the Wind*, originally shot in black and white, had been colorized by Ted Turner and his creative production companies. Fortunately, Spielberg demonstrated that B&W movies weren't hopeless when well planned, produced, and filmed.

On the WWW, you'll notice a similar philosophy in action. Color images are the de facto standard, with B&W Web graphics few and far between. But, as you'll learn in this chapter, colorless graphics aren't necessarily yesterday's news. Web pages around the world use B&W pictures for a variety of reasons.

In this chapter, you'll learn all about using B&W graphics on your Web pages. You'll learn to decide when to consider using B&W pictures, how to create them, and what interesting tips Web browsers use when working with B&W images. Most importantly, you'll realize that B&W images have an important place on the WWW in terms of artistic impression and have significantly smaller file sizes than their color counterparts.

▶ **Knowing When to Use Black and White**
B&W images often evoke a unique feeling and setting when used on a Web page. Learn why many people use B&W pictures to offer artistic or thematic Web pages.

▶ **Create New B&W Images**
Paint Shop Pro lets you draw new graphics using 256 shades of grey instead of the full-color spectrum. See how to make new colorless images and use a grey color palette.

Part II   Making Great Images

▶ **Convert Color Images into Shades of Grey and vice-versa**
Saving full-color pictures in B&W means that each unique color is
matched up to a different shade of grey. Learn how PSP manages this
conversion process so you don't lose any details in your image.
Colorize your B&W images to make them bright and eye-catching.

▶ **Use Only 16 Colors without Distortion**
Unlike color images, B&W graphics can easily reduce the number of
colors used in an image from 256 to 16. Learn how to take advantage
of this tremendous file-savings bonus geared for B&W images.

▶ **Overlay Images on Top of One Another**
Overlaying two images allows users to quickly get a feeling for how
Web graphics look, without waiting for extremely large files to
download. Learn to use the LOWSRC keyword as a valuable graphics
tool on the Web.

Finding a Place for Black and White

In general, most images and graphics available on the Web use lots of
different colors. Green, red, purple, yellow, orange, and blue are all part of
everyday life for most people exploring the Web. That's because colorful
and vibrant graphics on Web pages tend to catch visitors' eyes, and make
them come back again and again. Imagine visiting the Walt Disney Web
site. You expect to see information about new movies and animated films,
and you'd be sorely disappointed if you had to look at their cartoon
characters in only shades of grey.

Much of this book is dedicated toward instructing you how to create these
colorful images. You've learned that working with the Paint Shop Pro Color
Palette to manage and match colors is critical when designing good Web
graphics.

Since most people can see full-color images without a problem, designing
color graphics tends to enhance a Web site. However, just like in real life,
Web pages also offer a smaller, yet important, place for B&W images. For
example, visit the online Black and White World magazine at
http://www.photogs.com/bwworld/index.html, which sponsors a B&W
photo-of-the-month contest (figure 8.1). This site focuses on the art and
effect of using B&W images in a high-quality manner.

Fig. 8.1
Black and white
photos are the way
things work at this
Web site.

B&W photography has its own distinct place in the art world. Famous photographers such as Ansel Adams and Robert Mapplethorpe are world renowned for their stunning ability to capture images on B&W film; both feared that color photographs would detract from the image. The overall effect of their photos speaks for itself as they let viewers imagine how the colors might actually appear.

Online art galleries aren't the only sites that use B&W images and graphics. Many sites include them because they are usually smaller files than full-color Web graphics. When properly created, B&W graphics can offer tremendous file savings over their color counterparts. To reduce download time for visitors, these sites only use B&W headlines, icons, and images.

When to Use Black and White

The most difficult part about working with B&W Web images is deciding when and where to use them on your Web site. These decisions are important because effective use of B&W graphics can add class and style to your site, and possibly offer powerful performance advantages for visitors.

On the flip side, by overusing B&W graphics, you run the danger of making a boring and unexciting set of pages. The best method is to plan out your Web site and decide why, where, and how many B&W images to use.

This section discusses several reasons you may want to consider creating B&W images for your site.

Artistic Emphasis and Value

When Steven Spielberg put together *Schindler's List*, he realized he was tackling a difficult and emotional topic—The Holocaust. Instead of filming a colorful and bright movie, he chose to produce a movie shot almost entirely in B&W film. The overall effect was tremendous. The B&W nature of the movie incorporated a dignified thoughtfulness that helped make the movie an Academy Award winner. You simply couldn't have achieved the same effect with color film.

Similarly, you may encounter situations in which your Web pages relate to a specific topic that allows, or even requires, you to consider using B&W images. For example, if you were to create a memorial Web page for victims of a plane crash, a set of B&W photographs might better fit the mood for such a solemn topic. On a lighter note, one site uses only B&W images because the creators are showing their life from their dog's point of view.

Other artistic and practical times to consider B&W pictures might include a botanist's Web site that depicts several different tree leaves, emphasizing the shape of a leaf instead of its color and hue. Or, a movie purist might create a Web page for her favorite old cinema stars—Clark Gable, Ingrid Bergman, and Humphrey Bogart. You can only find these actors in B&W movies, so using B&W images at this particular Web site would fit with the theme and artistry of the topic. Figure 8.2 shows a B&W Web site dedicated to The Jazz Singer (**http://www.cwrl.utexas.edu/~nick/e309k/texts/jazzsinger/jazzsinger.html**), the first movie that used sound.

Fig. 8.2
This site's creator
knew his topic only
comes in B&W.

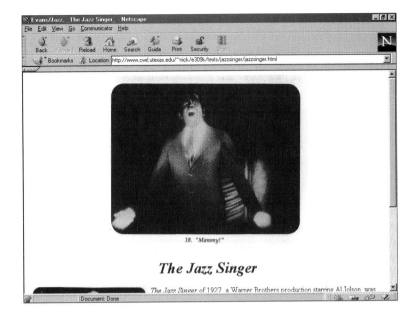

Theme Coordination

Another popular reason for keeping color out of your Web graphics is to
follow a particular theme or topic for your site. Many common ideas and
themes make you think solely of black and white. When creating a Web
page about one of these topics, it may be creative to play on these
colorless concepts.

For example, a zoo might have a page dedicated to zebras or albino
monkeys, or perhaps include a photo of a white tiger. There's simply no
purpose for a full-color photo of an animal that exists only in shades of
grey. Similarly, imagine creating a wedding Web page. Often a wedding's
colors are simply black and white. Nothing could be more appropriate for
a Web page than matching that particular theme.

Be careful not to overload your Web page with only B&W images. Even
an appropriate topic can get boring when everything is colorless.
Choosing black and white for theme-based Web pages can quickly lose its
novelty, leaving too many visitors longing for colorful images.

One example of a Web page that could use black and white to follow a theme can be found at the Dalmatian Club of America site found at **http://www.dalmatians.com/dca**. This site mixes color and B&W graphics but could easily use colorless images to follow the theme of everyone's favorite spotted dog (figure 8.3).

Fig. 8.3
You might expect this Web page to be only in black and white, with a hint of red for fire engines.

Performance Considerations

The third popular reason for using B&W graphics on a Web page instead of color pictures is to increase performance and reduce image file size. Often B&W pictures are smaller in file size than their color counterparts. As you will learn in Chapter 12, "Making Your Graphics Lean," file size is highly dependent on the number of colors used in an image, and converting a color image into B&W can significantly reduce the number of colors in an image.

Additionally, many Web sites take advantage of a new HTML tag that allows you to integrate high-resolution and low-resolution graphics on a Web page. These Web sites create lower resolution B&W images that load quickly on a Web page. Then your WWW browser goes back and reloads a color, higher resolution picture, replacing the original B&W image. You'll learn more about this performance-enhancing technique later in this chapter under "Overlaying Images."

Creating B&W Graphics

Now that you are familiar with several possible scenarios to create and use B&W Web graphics, it's time to see how you can build some good ones for yourself. In this section, you'll see how Paint Shop Pro allows you to build new images from scratch and convert color pictures into shades of grey, and vice-versa.

You'll see that making B&W graphics is very similar to creating Web graphics that use a full set of colors. Converting existing color images into those that are black and white is an important part of building Web graphics because many images you'll want to use will originally come in full color.

It is important to note that in Paint Shop Pro, B&W images aren't exactly just black and white. Usually, they are really 256 different colors/shades of grey. This means that you have many different colors to work with and get very high-quality and detailed images without using any other colors.

Making New Images

Creating a B&W image in Paint Shop Pro is easy. Simply choose File, New from the menu bar to bring up the New Image dialog box (figure 8.4).

Fig. 8.4
Creating color and B&W images starts here.

In the Image Type drop-down list box, choose **Greyscale (8 bit),** then click on the **OK** button. Paint Shop Pro sets the image size depending on your selection. This example is sized at 500 x 500 pixels. You now have 256 colors—all different shades of grey ranging from black to white, available to draw and design with.

Set your drawing color by clicking on either the foreground color box or the background color box, the overlapping boxes found in the Color Palette. The Edit Palette dialog box appears, letting you choose from a plethora of different intensities of grey (figure 8.5).

Fig. 8.5
Every shade of grey under the rainbow is available here.

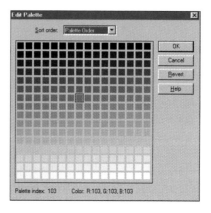

NOTE
When you click anywhere in the rainbow of colors available in the Color Palette, Paint Shop Pro translates the color you clicked on into a corresponding shade of grey.

Now you can create a B&W image just as you would any other Web graphic. All the techniques you learned through the other chapters in this book for drawing and using Paint Shop Pro work identically using B&W, as if you had a full-color palette available to you. In fact, all advanced PSP functions—such as filters, effects, and deformations—work with 256 shades of grey, just as they did with 16.7 million colors.

One important note is that when you create B&W images in this fashion, your file size may be very similar to the file size you would have if using color graphics. That's because file size is dependent on the number of colors available and the number used in the image.

But reducing the number of colors used is easier when working with B&W images. So reducing an image from 256 shades to use only 16 shades of grey often results in a high-quality image—better than you can often expect when working with full-color Web graphics using 16 colors.

To achieve this file savings, choose **Colors**, **Decrease Color Depth**, **16 Colors** from the menu bar. The available color palette now lets you use only 16 different shades of grey instead of the default number of 256. Don't reduce the number of colors on a blank image. Paint Shop Pro will provide you with a blank palette (all white). Instead, only reduce the number of shades on a Web graphic that has some text or a drawing in it.

For most practical purposes, when creating Web graphics from scratch, you'll find 16 shades of grey plenty of variety for making buttons, bars, headlines, and other types of Web graphics.

When you are finished with making your image, choose **F**ile, **S**ave to store your new graphic on your computer. Remember that only the GIF file format allows you to save in the 256-color mode. The JPEG file type uses 16.7 million colors and incorporates all of the shades of grey. B&W images tend to be saved in GIF format. That's because you don't get to take advantage of the reduced usage of colors. Of course, as you might expect, detailed photographs are still saved in the JPG format because of the massive amount of greyscale-switching in the image. For a detailed discussion on how colors affect file size, check out Chapter 12, "Making Your Graphics Lean."

Converting Color Graphics to Black and White

Although you'll occasionally create new B&W graphics from scratch, many useful B&W images come from pictures that were originally in full color. Using Paint Shop Pro, you can convert color images into greyscale format quickly, and vice versa.

You'll still be able to detect subtle shadows, brighter and darker shades, and different lighting effects. It's really just like watching a color television show on a black and white TV. You're watching the same program, but seeing slightly different scenes. Paint Shop Pro does a nice job of completing the conversion for you, so you still end up with a high-resolution image.

To convert a full-color image into a B&W one, load your color graphic into Paint Shop Pro. Then choose **C**olors, **G**rey Scale from the menu bar. Paint Shop Pro will perform a special algorithm to match up each color to an appropriate shade of grey. Once Paint Shop Pro is finished, you can save your newly converted graphic. Be sure to give it a different file name so you don't overwrite your original, full-color graphic.

CAUTION

Transforming color to B&W images can be a memory-intensive operation. Converting a large color graphic into a B&W image can take several moments for PSP to calculate.

When converting color images to the B&W format, you'll reduce file size by 5–25% from the original size. In general, you can expect your new file to be around 10% smaller than the original color image. That's because the conversion often reduces the number of colors used in the newer image.

Part II Making Great Images

Figure 8.6 shows an example of two images from the same photo. The image on the left uses 256 colors and the image on the right uses the greyscale palette. The B&W image is exactly 10% smaller than the original, with no other compression techniques or file-savings tips applied.

Fig. 8.6
The same image in color and B&W. Both use 256 different colors or shades.

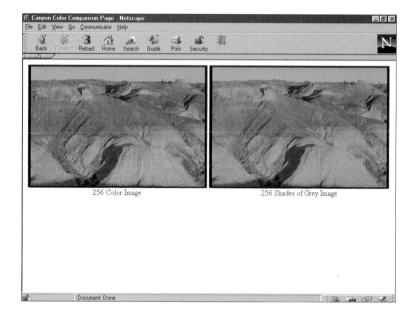

Using 16 Shades of Grey

In Chapter 12, "Making Your Graphics Lean," I talk about reducing the number of colors in your graphics from 256 to 16, to realize a significant savings in the overall file size. Unfortunately, a drawback to using only 16 colors in a graphic is that it produces a lower quality image. Often, you lose detail when you reduce the number of available colors, which makes your Web graphics less enjoyable to look at and less suitable for inclusion on your Web pages.

When working with B&W images, you can likewise reduce the number of grey shades from 256 to 16 and get quite a savings in the file size—often with little to no loss in image detail and quality (unlike color images). That's because the human eye has more difficulty separating different shades of grey when looking at a computer graphic. With color images, it's easy to discern different colors, even between individual pixels, because our eye notices the differences easily. B&W images work in a slightly different way because all shades of grey are so similar in nature. Therefore, greyscale differences between pixels are less pronounced and noticeable.

Additionally, Paint Shop Pro is slightly more optimized when working with greyscale because it doesn't have to do the work of mixing different values of red, green, and blue when interpolating a color. Instead, it only has to decide upon a single shade of black, a much easier task, which results in higher quality and better resolution images in the B&W format.

You'll find that the problems you encountered when reducing color images to 16 colors simply don't exist with B&W graphics (as you'll see momentarily in an example). To reduce the number of colors used in your Web graphic, choose **C**olors, **D**ecrease Color Depth, **16** Colors from the menu bar to bring up the Decrease Color Depth dialog box shown in figure 8.7.

Fig. 8.7
Converting 256 to 16 shades of grey is a piece of cake.

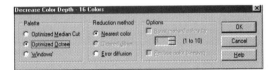

This dialog box allows you to make an important decision on how Paint Shop Pro should convert each of the original 256 colors into the remaining 16. You have several options in the Reduction method section of this dialog box. Each option is covered in depth in Chapter 12.

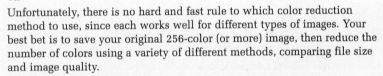

TIP

Unfortunately, there is no hard and fast rule to which color reduction method to use, since each works well for different types of images. Your best bet is to save your original 256-color (or more) image, then reduce the number of colors using a variety of different methods, comparing file size and image quality.

With B&W images, the results of the error diffusion, or dithering, are astounding. You'll lose virtually no detail in your image but will get tremendous file savings. I recommend always choosing this setting first when reducing the number of shades of grey in your image.

Once you've selected a Reduction Method, click on the **OK** button to continue, and PSP runs the color/shade reduction algorithm through your Web graphic.

Part II   Making Great Images

Figure 8.8 shows the same canyon pictures reduced to only 16 colors. Notice how the greyscale image came out much more detailed than the color image at 16 colors. Both 16 color images represent over a 65% file savings image from their respective color originals.

Fig. 8.8
The B&W image reduced colors much better than the color photo did.

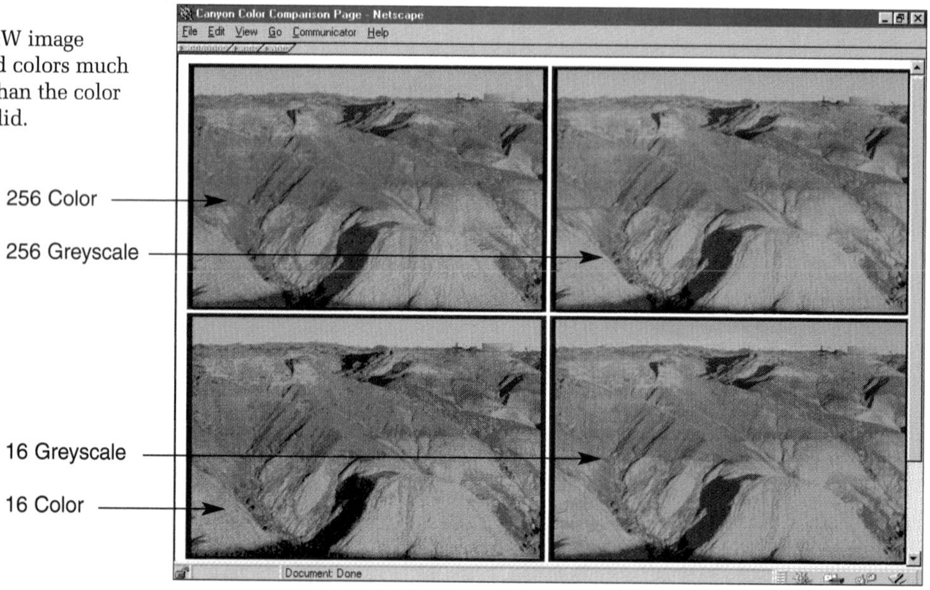

256 Color
256 Greyscale
16 Greyscale
16 Color

Colorizing an Image

The previous section of this chapter showed you how to effectively take a color image and reduce it to B&W format. This technique usually gives you a performance/file size boost and is appropriate for many different types of Web pages.

Often, you may want to reverse the process and convert a B&W image (or at least part of one) back into color. As you probably imagined, Paint Shop Pro supports an effective way to colorize B&W images and photos.

In this section, I'll step you through one method for editing and colorizing an image. Take a look at my original image in figure 8.9, a full-color picture of a dandelion. Although this image is decent, the green background is distracting. I want to make the background black and white, but keep a vivid yellow for the flower.

Fig. 8.9
An okay image for a
Web page on weeds.

You can use many different ways to make the background of this image in grey, but keep a bright yellow for the flower. The set of steps below describes one method:

1. Use the Magic Wand to select only the Yellow part of the image. Since the Yellow is such a stark contrast to the green background, I can use a high tolerance on the wand to make sure I select the entire dandelion. Magic Wand tolerance is set in the Control Palette (figure 8.10).

Fig. 8.10
The flower is selected.

2. Once the flower is selected, let's convert the entire image to be 256 greyscale. Choose **C**olors, **G**rey Scale from the PSP menu bar. I selected the dandelion before greying the image because it was easier to use the Magic Wand to select all the yellow because of the high image contrast. Selecting the flower after greying the image makes it much more difficult to select *only* the flower in the image. Figure 8.11 shows the greyed image.

Fig. 8.11
Notice how the flower is still selected.

3. With the greyed image and flower still selected, choose **C**olors, **I**ncrease Color Depth, **16** Million Colors. When colorizing an image, Paint Shop Pro needs to have all 16.7 million colors at its disposal. If this menu bar option is not available, your image is already set to use 16.7 million colors.

4. Now choose **C**olors, **A**djust, **R**ed/Green/Blue from the PSP menu bar to bring up the Red/Green/Blue dialog box shown in figure 8.12. This dialog box will enable you to add different hues of red, green, and blue back to an image, or a selected area of an image.

Fig. 8.12
Carefully select the
amount of red, green,
and blue to colorize
your image.

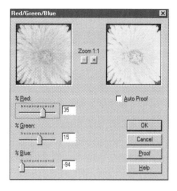

5. The Red/Green/Blue dialog box in figure 8.12 shows before-and-after
    images. The before image on the left is the original image/selected
    area of the photo. The right-hand image shows the results after I
    selected how much red, green, and blue to add to the image. Use the
    slide bars to decide how much color to add to your images.

    When you are finished deciding how much color to add, click on the
    OK button and PSP performs the colorization immediately. Figure
    8.13 shows the resulting image. Notice how only the selected flower
    got colorized.

Fig. 8.13
The colorized result
looks pretty good.

Besides greying out then recolorizing an image, you can accomplish a
similar effect in several other ways:

Copy and Paste

When you have the original yellow flower selected, copy and paste it to a new image. Then grey the entire dandelion picture, and copy and paste the yellow flower portion back. You have to line up the pasted color flower perfectly onto the greyed image, but the quality is very good.

Use PSP Layers

Layers are perfect for editing one part of an image while leaving another part alone. You could have moved the flower of the dandelion to a new layer then greyed out the rest of the image. Layers are a powerful way to edit complex images and photos such as this one. Check out Chapter 7, "Using PSP Layers," for more information on this technique.

Overlaying Images

As you can see, creating and working with B&W images often has significant performance enhancement opportunities for Web developers. It's easy to take a detailed color image and convert it into one that is black and white with slightly less quality. This saves up to 75% from the original file size without losing much detail from the original picture. That's even before you consider resizing, cropping, or thumbnailing your image to save even more in file size.

However, many Web developers still prefer using bright and colorful images on their Web pages, even when given the performance options of B&W pictures. Visitors tend to enjoy colorful images more and will come back to visit more often when they remember and like a particular Web site. Web developers are often in a quandary of whether to choose brilliant colors or great file performance.

To solve this dilemma, a new HTML keyword was added to the <IMG> tag which allows Web developers and visitors to experience the benefits of both worlds. Called the Low Resolution keyword (LOWSRC=), this bit of HTML lets you instruct your WWW browser to first load and display a smaller, low-resolution image file and then, when the whole page has finished loading, begin displaying a normal, high-resolution image.

In practice, Web developers often have a large color image that is simply too big to use on a Web page. Instead, they follow the steps outlined in this chapter and create a significantly smaller B&W image that can load and be displayed for visitors immediately. Once the whole page is loaded, the Web browser overlays the original B&W image with the higher resolution color image. This allows the visitor to read and explore the Web site while the colorful pictures are being downloaded.

For example, let's say I have two images, one called <u>LOWCAR.GIF,</u> which is a 16-color, less detailed, B&W picture of two automobiles. My colorful, high-resolution image that uses all 256 colors is named <u>HIGHCAR.GIF</u>. To use the new <u>LOWSRC</u> keyword, I add the following line of HTML:

```
<IMG SRC="HIGHCAR.GIF" LOWSRC="LOWCAR.GIF">
```

That's it! Figure 8.14 below shows this process in action. Netscape first loaded <u>LOWCAR.GIF</u> and then <u>HIGHCAR.GIF</u>, which figure 8.14 shows in the process of being displayed on top of the B&W image.

Fig. 8.14
Half of this image is in color and half is in low-resolution black and white.

Many professionally designed Web sites use this method to achieve a great effect.

CAUTION
If you use the low-resolution keyword method, make sure that your high-resolution image is not interlaced (GIF) or progressive (JPG). Although these two techniques usually are good for large images on the Web, they create distortions when images are overlaid on top of each other. Check out Chapter 12 for more information on Interlaced and Progressive images.

Part II Making Great Images

Spot Color and B&W

Another popular way of using B&W images on the WWW is by mixing them with limited use of spot color. By mixing a primarily B&W set of graphics with complementary graphics and color, you achieve the file savings and theme-based intent of B&W images.

One example of a site that uses mostly black and white, with just a hint of color, can be found at **http://www.zebra.com** (figure 8.15). This high-quality site represents a company that makes bar-coding machines. Many of the images on their home page are appropriate in B&W, but they use a hint of red along the left-hand side of the screen to attract subtle attention to important information and to break up simple monotony.

Fig. 8.15
This Web site designer knew when to add a splash of color to keep visitors interested.

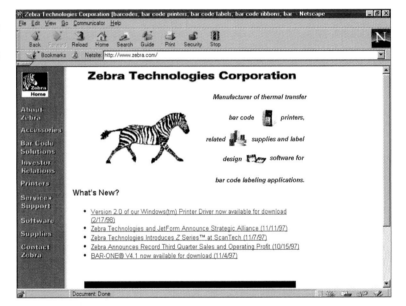

Using mostly B&W images with slight color is a useful technique. You can add simple color to your existing images, integrate multiple images on a single Web page, or simply change the color of your text to something creative. See Chapter 15, "HTML Tips for Web Images," for more information on coordinating color and using tables with your Web graphics.

Part III
Advanced Image Techniques

9

Using Scanners
and Digital Cameras

If you plan to incorporate photographic images into your Web pages, you'll need some type of digital camera or scanner to transform the colors of the photo into bits that the computer can handle. These devices make it easy to take or use photographs for your Web pages.

Digital cameras and scanners have been around for years, but only recently have they become relatively affordable and of sufficient quality to be effective for most home or small business users. High-quality scanners and digital cameras allow you to digitize excellent images and use them directly on a Web site.

In addition, Paint Shop Pro has built-in support for popular scanners and digital cameras. This integration enables you to load the digitized photo directly into PSP to edit or resize the image, touch up the colors, or combine multiple images.

This chapter is all about digitizing your images effectively. You'll learn the basics behind both scanners and digital cameras, and see how PSP makes them part of the Web Graphics experience. Specifically, this chapter will give you information on:

▶ **Understanding How Scanners and Digital Cameras Work**
This interesting technology lets you capture images directly into your computer. See how it works and integrates with PSP.

▶ **Choosing the Most Suitable Photos**
Learn to pick the photo that will look best online—not the one that looks best on photographic paper.

▶ **Digitizing from Paint Shop Pro**
PSP makes scanning with any TWAIN-compatible scanner or Kodak digital camera a simple operation.

Part III Advanced Image Techniques

▶ **Using Other Scanning Options**
Even if you don't own a scanner, you can easily get your own photos into electronic form.

▶ **Correcting and Retouching Images**
Take a crash course in PSP's professional-caliber image correction and enhancement features—and you don't have to be a pro to put them to work.

Understanding and Using Scanners

You can scan virtually any photo, piece of paper, page from a book, or other item that can be laid on top of the scanner. Connected to your computer, scanners come in a variety of shapes and sizes. Some are small—hand scanners—and look like computer mice, while others are large—flatbed scanners—and closely resemble printers or copiers.

Scanning images is the process of saving a copy of a physical piece of paper or photograph on your computer. Scanning works a lot like a photocopy machine, except that the copy you make will sit in your computer, not on another piece of paper.

Important Scanner Characteristics

Understanding how a scanner works is relatively easy. Finding the right type of scanner for you to use or purchase can be more challenging.

When you go into a store to look for a scanner to purchase, you're likely to be overwhelmed by the number and variety of options available to you. Below is a laundry list that describes several different characteristics of scanners. Use this list to help identify the type of scanner most appropriate for you:

Brand Name
As with all things in the world, brand name carries a lot of weight in the scanner market. Hewlett-Packard is typically recognized as the market leader, but you pay a premium for their scanners. Mustek, Umax, Microtek, IBM, and Logitech are all well-known brands in the scanner market and have won awards for their quality, technical support, and ease of use.

PC/Scanner Integration
Scanners can be hooked up to your computer using several different connections: SCSI, Parallel, or USB (Universal Serial bus). SCSI connections require you to have or install a special card inside of your computer. Make sure you understand the inner workings of your system, or hire someone to do the installation for you if you choose this route.

Parallel scanners share your printer port. You hook your printer up to the scanner's cable, then hook that cable into the back of your computer. This scanner type is easy to install and relatively portable.

USB scanners are new to the market and work only with Pentium II caliber machines. They hook into a special cable connection behind your computer, are very fast, but are not widely available.

Scanner Type

Scanners come in all shapes and sizes:

Hand-Scanners—Compact and portable, hand-scanners are the size of a computer mouse. They require a steady hand because you drag the scanner across the item you want to scan. Hand-scanner popularity has dropped as other scanner types have become affordable.

Flatbed Scanners—The most popular type of scanner is the flatbed, on which you lay a book, paper, or photograph so the scanner can digitize the image for you. Known for their high quality, flatbed scanners are the premier choice for good photograph and color-image scans.

Document Scanners—A new phenomenon, document scanners are very small, portable, and affordable. They allow you to feed one or more sheets of paper (or photographs) through an oblong-shaped device. They are well used for scanning documents and pieces of paper for electronic storage and offer adequate photo-scans.

All-in-One Machines—Ideal for home office usage, all-in-one machines serve as copiers, printers, fax machines, and scanners in one compact package. They hook up directly to your computer and phone line to give you robust functionality at an affordable price. These machines have two drawbacks: 1) If the printer breaks, so does your fax machine, copier, and scanner. 2) Scanning resolution is often good, but not great.

Drum Scanners—Costing upwards of tens of thousands of dollars, drum scanners are the true professional tool of the desktop publishing industry. You probably won't use one yourself, but be aware that's how professional publishers and advertising companies scan/digitize images. The cover of this book was drum-scanned from an original piece of artwork.

Part III Advanced Image Techniques

Color or Black and White

Nowadays, color scanners are affordable and of good quality. Don't even consider getting a B&W–only scanner. Color scanners can also digitize B&W/greyscale images with high precision and quality.

Resolution

The most important scanner characteristic—resolution—is measured in dots-per-inch, and two dimensions are usually given—300 x 300 or 600 x 1200, for example. Resolution directly corresponds to the quality of the scanned image. A 300 x 300 scanner looks at every square inch of scanned material and picks up 90,000 dots for that square. This offers pretty good quality and means that your scanned image closely represents what the actual photo looked like. But a 600 x 1200 dpi scanner takes in 780,000 dots for every inch scanned, almost nine times the quality of the 300 x 300 scanner! `

This means that the higher the scanner resolution, the better your scanned images will appear. For scanning photographs and images with a lot of detail, better resolution means a better and more professional set of images for your Web pages.

Software Interpolation

Scanning resolution is only part of the story when it comes to image quality. The other aspect is software interpolation. Most scanners come with special software that makes guesses about images that are scanned to increase their effective resolution to be much higher. For example, a 300 x 300 dpi scanner might include special software that brings scanned images up to 2400 x 2400 resolution.

Software interpolation is a good feature of scanners, but be careful when shopping around. Don't be fooled by large letters on a box that say "4800 x 4800 Resolution" for a phenomenal price. You are likely getting an average scanner with good interpolation software, and interpolation software is only as good as the resolution of the original scan. So, software interpolation on a 600 x 1200 scanner is likely to be much better than the same software on a 300 x 300 scanner because it started with better quality scans.

NOTE

Many people have asked me what type of scanner(s) I have and use, and why. In real life, I have three scanners in my office, each of which I use for different reasons.

First, I own a Logitech PageScan Color scanner. The first scanner I ever owned, the Logitech is small and has a great set of software for a home office user. At 200 x 200 resolution, the scanner sits right next to my keyboard and lets me feed single sheets of paper or photos through it. I used it to scan all the images on http://www.shafran.com. If I could afford just one scanner, this all-purpose tool would be the one, unless I absolutely needed amazing quality scans.

Second, I have a Microtek ScanMaker V600. A 600 x 1200 scanner (with software interpolation up to 9600 x 9600), this scanner delivers unbelievable quality. It sits on its own computer because of the heavy memory and processor requirements to achieve high quality. Many of the images used in this book were scanned using this equipment, and the results show amazing detail and resolution. I use it when the scans absolutely, positively have to be great.

Finally, I have a Brother MFC 1770 printer/copier/scanner/fax. Hooked up to my computer, I use it to scan large quantities of documents to store in my electronic filing cabinets. Of course it also answers my fax line and makes a decent photocopy when necessary.

Choosing the Most Suitable Photos

Now that you know about the different types and characteristics of scanners, the next step is finding a good image or photograph to scan.

In general, most photographs scan well, depending on the quality and resolution of your scanner. But rarely will you simply scan an entire image then use it directly on your Web page. Usually, you'll crop or resize the image for more appropriate use.

For example, figure 9.1 shows a scanned photograph in PSP of a famous spot in Paris, the Church of Sacred Heart (Eglise de Sacrée-Coeur). Although it is a decent photo, I don't need all the background distractions or people. The image on the left was scanned in at 200 x 200 resolution (my Logitech scanner) while the other image was scanned in at 600 x 1200 resolution (my Microtek scanner).

Part III Advanced Image Techniques

Fig. 9.1
This church in
Montmartre, an
arrondissement of Paris,
is world renown. Which
scan looks better?

200 x 200 resolution   600 x 1200 resolution

Since I only want to use the photo of the church on my Web site, I'm
simply going to use PSP to crop away the extraneous parts of the image.
Figure 9.2 shows my revised image. The cross-hatching surrounding the
photo isn't part of the image, just empty area within the PSP window.

Fig. 9.2
A much better picture,
without the people
and car.

Before you scan—or even before you take a picture—you should
remember that many details will be lost when a photograph is scanned.
Notice how the image quality of the scan is very good and will fit nicely
on a Web page, but it is still slightly blurred.

When looking for images to scan and use on your Web page, don't be constrained to accept or reject the entire photo. If I hadn't thought of using just the church from figure 9.1, I would not have had a good image to use because the entire image doesn't work well on the Web.

Scanning from PSP

Once you've identified an image to scan, the next step is to scan, or Acquire the image into Paint Shop Pro. PSP handles virtually any scanner imaginable, as long as the scanner is TWAIN-compliant. TWAIN is a scanning standard that allows software programs and scanners to communicate with each other in a standard fashion. PSP includes the standard TWAIN interface for scanners, so you can scan images without leaving the program.

CAUTION

This chapter assumes that you have successfully obtained and installed a scanner for your computer. There are literally thousands of different scanners, each with their own installation and configuration routines. Paint Shop Pro can work with just about any of them once they are properly installed.

If you have problems using or installing your scanner, your best bet is to call the manufacturer's technical support phone number.

To scan an image, select **F**ile, **I**mport, **T**WAIN, Ac**q**uire, from the PSP menu bar. PSP launches your scanning software for you automatically. Figure 9.3 shows the scanning software for the Logitech PageScan Color scanner.

Fig. 9.3
I'm ready to scan!

The dialog box that *you* see when you select the Acquire command is probably going to look different from mine because each scanner manufacturer provides its own dialog box. The exact interface will depend on which scanner you use and on the software drivers you installed when you connected the scanner to your computer.

Even though figure 9.3 shows the elements for my scanner, your options are likely to be similar. Basically, I can scan a color photo or a black and white image. Then I make sure the paper or photo is already loaded into the scanner and click on the Scan Now button. After a few moments of thinking and whirring, the image gets sent into PSP where I can then edit and manipulate it to my heart's delight. Figure 9.4 shows me in the process of scanning.

Fig. 9.4
The scan is in process.

NOTE

If you get an error message or if nothing happens when you select **File**, **Import**, **TWAIN**, **Acquire**, check to make sure your scanner was turned on before you started your computer. Many scanners need to be on before the computer starts so they can be recognized and accessible.

If you still have problems, try using the vanilla scanning software that comes with your scanner. Then save the images you scanned individually and load them into PSP, instead of scanning them directly into PSP.

You will want to add the Acquire Image button to your toolbar if you plan to scan images often. To do so, select File, Preferences, **C**ustomize Toolbar to bring up the Customize Toolbar dialog box (figure 9.5). Highlight the Acquire Image icon from the left and click on the **A**dd button. While you're at it, you also might want to add the Brightness/Contrast, Adjust RGB, and Gamma Correction buttons to your toolbar, because they are useful tools for editing scanned images, as I explain later in this chapter.

Fig. 9.5
If you scan and correct images frequently, you'll want to add the Acquire and color adjustment buttons to PSP's toolbar.

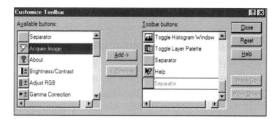

TIP

Several other methods of getting images into your computer are available if you don't own or have access to a scanner. Check out Chapter 4, "Editing Images and Photos," for other ways to digitize images in an affordable fashion.

Gaining More Scanner Information

Many books and magazines exist to teach you about using scanners and advanced color optimization and enhancement techniques. Below is a set of URLs that may be of interest to you for more information. This book's home page has a comprehensive listing of scanner URLs and references.

http://www.hp.com/peripherals/main.html
Home of HP printing and imaging products

http://www.microtekusa.com/
Home of Microtek scanners and accessories

http://www.hsdesign.com/scanning/
Sullivan's On-line Scanning Resources and Tips—great place to learn some advanced scanning techniques

Understanding and Using Digital Cameras

Besides scanners, digital cameras are another way to get an image into your computer. Gaining momentum, digital cameras are quickly becoming affordable and usable for the nonprofessional photographer.

Digital cameras work like normal cameras do when it comes to taking pictures. The difference is what you do with the pictures afterward. With a normal camera, you'd drop the film off to be developed and eventually get a physical set of prints and negatives to pick up and enjoy.

Part III Advanced Image Techniques

Digital cameras work differently. When you are finished taking pictures, you hook your digital camera up to the computer and transfer all the images to your hard drive. Digital cameras are different in other ways as well. You don't have 12-, 24-, or 36-exposure rolls of film. Instead, pictures are stored in memory inside the camera; so the more memory you purchase, the more pictures you can take before hooking the digital camera to your computer to transfer the images. In addition, most digital cameras let you take photos at varying quality, or resolutions.

Like scanners, all digital cameras come with special software to transfer images from the camera to your computer. Paint Shop Pro 5 then lets you use the transferred images to edit and touch up your photos like any other image. In addition, PSP 5 also has special support for Kodak digital cameras and comes with special commands that only work with the Kodak line of cameras.

As a result, you can directly import and manipulate images on your Kodak camera within PSP, instead of using the separate software program that came with the camera. PSP 5 only works with the Kodak DC40, DC50 (with Zoom lens), and DC120 in this advanced and integrated fashion.

Acquiring Images with Kodak Cameras

If you have a Kodak Digital camera, the first step is to connect it to your computer via its special cable. Once your cable is connected, and you have pictures on your camera that have been taken, the first step is configuring PSP to work with your camera.

Choose File, Import, Kodak Digital Camera, Configure from the menu bar to bring up the Kodak Digital Camera Configuration dialog box.

Fig. 9.6
You must tell PSP which Kodak Digital camera you are using.

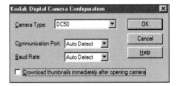

The most important option here is to designate which camera you are using, since PSP will give you an error message if you select the wrong type of camera. Specify your Kodak digital camera in the Camera Type drop-down box and click **OK** to continue.

Once your camera is configured within PSP, choose File, Import, Kodak Digital Camera, Access from the menu bar to bring up the Kodak Digital Camera dialog box (figure 9.7).

Fig. 9.7
Access your images
directly with a digital
camera.

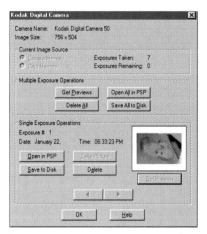

Figure 9.7 shows a lot of information. First off, in the top part of the
dialog box I see information about my camera and photographs, as well
as how many exposures I have taken with my camera that can be
downloaded and/or viewed. Since I am using a Kodak DC50Zoom with
no extra memory cards, and images at the highest resolution, I only have
seven exposures available to me (I'd have many more at a lower
resolution).

The rest of the Kodak Digital Camera dialog box is split into ways to
access my pictures, or exposures. The Multiple Exposure Operations
section lets me download, delete, open, or preview all the exposures in
PSP.

You can open all of your images directly into PSP or save them all
directly onto your computer. Your best bet is to click on the Open All
button in PSP. PSP will download all your images and open them up for
you to view. Then you can save the good images yourself. Figure 9.8
shows PSP downloading an image from my camera.

Fig. 9.8
It takes a few
moments to download
each image.

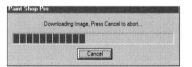

When you are sure you are finished with the current set of photos, click
on the Delete button to erase the set of images in the camera.

CAUTION
When you click the Delete button, your digital photographs are permanently
removed from your camera's memory. Make sure that you have the images
you want saved on your hard drive before you delete them from your
camera!

Part III Advanced Image Techniques

I can do similar tasks one exposure at a time in the bottom of the Digital Camera dialog box. If I had any free exposures left, I could even take a picture from this dialog box—a good technique if your camera is on a tripod.

NOTE

With *my* Kodak digital camera, I cannot delete one exposure from my seven. I can delete either all or none of them from the camera's memory. With extra memory, I would be able to delete selected pictures and keep others on my camera.

Once you've imported the photos into PSP, you can resize them, crop them, or edit them however you like. Usually digital picture resolution is quite good. For example, figures 9.9a and 9.9b are sample pictures taken at leisure. Both would crop and resize very well for Web pages.

Fig. 9.9a
Even cats get red-eye.

Fig. 9.9b
All the colors captured nicely with the Kodak camera.

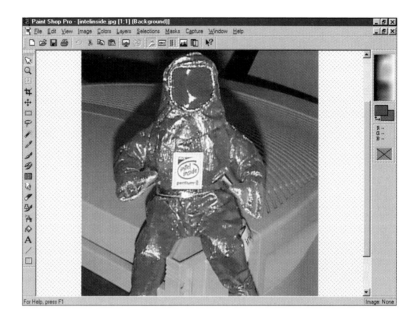

Correcting and Retouching Images

Many of the snapshots you scan are likely to need some repair work. However, you don't have to be a highly trained professional to learn the basics of correcting and enhancing images. The quick-and-dirty rundown that follows isn't going to qualify you for a degree in graphics arts, but it will show you how to use PSP to polish almost any image you plan to put on a Web page. Make sure you check out Chapter 4, "Editing Images and Photos," for more techniques on cropping, resizing, and common edits you can do on pictures, such as removing the red-eye.

Color Correction

Almost all photographs and many computer-generated pictures will benefit from color correction. An image designed to be printed on paper will almost always look bleak and washed-out when viewed on a monitor.

Also, plenty of poorly scanned snapshots on the Net need color correction to look good on display devices or printers. Let's use the worst-case scenario: Pretend you found a poorly scanned snapshot on the Net that you really want to use for your Web page. For example, figure 9.10 is a rather dull image of a flat-coated retriever that I downloaded from the **alt.binaries.pictures.animals** newsgroup. Pictures of flat-coated retrievers are hard to come by, so if someone wanted a masthead for the *Flat-Coated Retriever Breeder's Journal*, they might just have to make do with this inadequate shot.

Part III Advanced Image Techniques

Fig. 9.10
A bad picture of a
good dog.

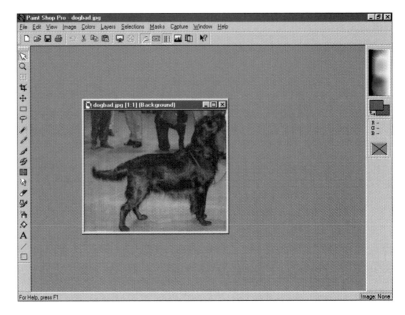

Since I don't know this dog's name, and "the flat-coated retriever" may
get stale after a while, I'll use the nickname of a similar dog I once
knew—"Fry-Brain." (The original Fry-Brain liked to keep his head under
the wood stove until he singed all the hair off the top of his head.) There
wasn't much the real Fry-Brain's owner could do to fix his dog's fur, but
we can bring this version of Fry-Brain into PSP for some graphical
grooming.

Brightness and Contrast Enhancement

Fry-Brain's primary problem is that he's too dark. In PSP, the **C**olors menu
and the **C**olors, **A**djust submenu gives several options for correcting this
problem. You might be tempted to rush right in and select
Brightness/Contrast, which certainly could do Fry-Brain some good, but
you should consider a few other choices as well. To analyze your choices
intelligently, carefully note the range of tones in the image rather than
simply glancing at it and pronouncing it "dark."

When you look closely, you'll notice that Fry-Brain appears too dark for
these specific reasons:

▶ His coat lacks highlights.

▶ He doesn't have a wide tonal range. That is, his darkest color is too
   similar to his lightest color.

These distinctions may seem like "hair-splitting," but they are actually essential in adapting an image for successful display, especially on a low-resolution device like a computer monitor. To see the range of tonal values in an image, you can view the Histogram Window by clicking on the Toggle Histogram Icon. The *Histogram* is a graph of the relative amount of each brightness level in the image, as shown in figure 9.11.

Fig. 9.11
Opening the Histogram Window gives you a graph of the relative brightness of an image.

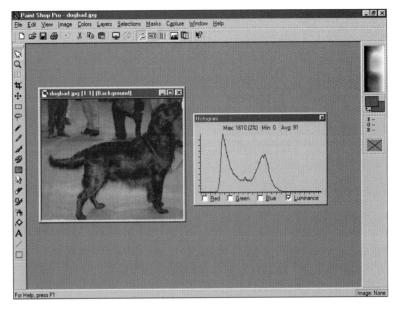

TIP

When you first display the Histogram Window, you will see four separate colored graphs, all displayed at once. These represent the amount of red, green, and blue light in the image and the sum of all these colors, called the *luminance*. It will be easier to correct the brightness and contrast of the image if you display only the luminance graph, and turn off the others by clicking in the Red, Green, and Blue checkboxes at the bottom of the Histogram Window. Figure 9.11 shows the Histogram Window with only the luminance displayed.

The histogram of a good image almost always covers the entire range of tones from the far left of the graph to the far right. The histogram is a graph of how much color and brightness appears on the image and should be read as if it has an X and a Y axis. You can see from figure 9.11 that Fry-Brain's histogram is bunched in two very small areas. In the next few figures, you'll see how each of the available color adjustment controls affects the image and its histogram.

Part III Advanced Image Techniques

Adjusting the brightness and contrast are intuitively the easiest corrections to apply and are quite effective for many images. As you might expect, increasing the brightness simply moves the entire histogram to the right, and increasing the contrast spreads the histogram out horizontally.

Figure 9.12 shows the Brightness/Contrast dialog box that appears when you choose Colors, Adjust, Brightness/Contrast from the menu bar and the image being edited. There are separate sliders for percentage brightness and percentage Contrast. This dialog box shows the before and after effect of changing the brightness/contrast. Figure 9.12 is actually more complicated than a single dialog box. You should also notice how I have the Auto Proof checkbox turned on so I can see the results on the image as I change the sliders, and how the histogram of Fry-Brain changes when the sliders change.

Fig. 9.12
You can see the dialog box, image, and histogram that result when the brightness and contrast change.

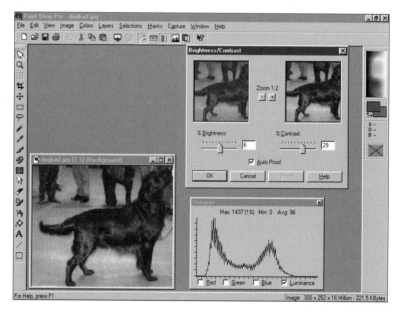

This resulting image makes Fry-Brain look much better and lifelike.

Gamma Correction

Another common tool for adjusting the balance of light and dark in an image is gamma correction. If you choose **G**amma Correction from PSP's Colors, **A**djust menu, you have several sliders which affect the overall image brightness. Gamma correcting lets you change brightness on the image by color (Red, Green, or Blue).

The Gamma Correction sliders range from .2 to 5.00. Load an image and drag the sliders left and right to see the resulting image. By default, all three colors are linked. But you can unlink them and change the brightness of the image from a single-color perspective. Figure 9.13 shows Fry-Brain being gamma-corrected a little too much.

Fig. 9.13
I've over-gamma-corrected the Blue and under-corrected the Green!

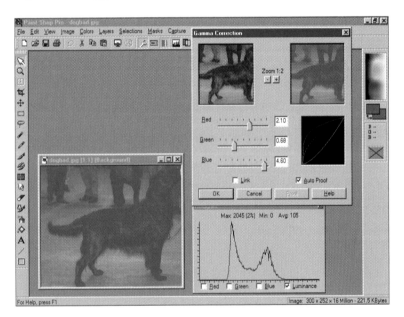

Generally, gamma correction alone will leave an image too "flat," or lifeless. Gamma correction is usually most helpful when used in conjunction with contrast enhancement. The pros will often use the combination of gamma correction and contrast enhancement instead of the more obvious combination of brightness and contrast.

Tonal Corrections

As you get used to looking at histograms and correcting the tonal range for images, you may start to think in terms of the specific regions of the histogram, and the role each region plays in the overall image. The brighter tones (or highlights) tend to add spark and character to the image, while the darker tones (or shadows) provide the visual anchor and underlying mood. In between are the mid-tones, which give an image a

Part III Advanced Image Techniques

pleasing range of tonal variety. With the **H**ighlight/Midtone/Shadow control on the **C**olors, **A**djust menu, you can manipulate each region independently or in conjunction with one another. Although this technique takes a bit of practice to get used to, it's the most powerful way to really improve most images, and therefore worth the time and effort to learn.

Essentially, these controls let you horizontally stretch the histogram any way you like. When the dialog box pops up, Highlight will be set at 100%, Midtone at 50%, and Shadow at 0%. If you leave them at those values, the image will not change at all. But if you set Highlight to, say, 80%, then the right-most part of the histogram will be "pulled" to the right, making the bright tones brighter and turning any tones in the far right 20% of the graph to pure white. Similarly, if you set Shadow to 20%, the bottom part of the histogram will stretch to the left and the dark tones will get darker. Changing the Midtone setting pulls the center of the histogram to the left or right, making the middle range of tones either darker (for settings below 50%) or brighter (for settings above 50%).

If I were going to prepare Fry-Brain's image for inclusion on a Web page, I would start with **H**ighlight/Midtone/Shadow adjustments, then apply slight contrast enhancement and gamma correction. Figure 9.14 shows the Highlight/Midtone/Shadow dialog box, histogram window, and resulting Fry-Brain image from some of my experiments. Notice the significant histogram changes from the original image.

Fig. 9.14
Adjusting the highlights, midtones, and shadows gives you more flexibility than simple brightness and contrast controls can provide.

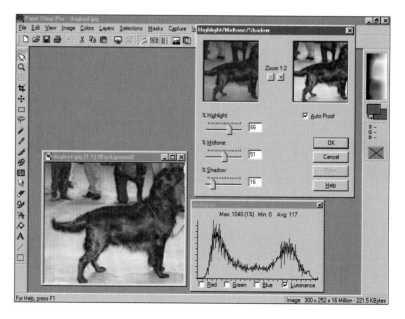

Color-Correction of Images Using HSL and RGB Controls

Two more color correction tools are available in PSP. These color correction tools are the Hue/Saturation/Lightness (HSL) Controls and the Red/Green/Blue (RGB) Controls.

Select Hue/Saturation/Lightness from the Colors, Adjust menu in PSP, and you get a dialog box like the one shown in figure 9.15. By adjusting the settings for % Hue, % Saturation, and % Lightness, you can move your whole image through "color space" to a more desirable location. Increasing the lightness is essentially the same thing as brightening the image. Saturation controls the richness of color, and you will often find that photographic images greatly benefit from increased saturation. By adjusting the hue, you can eliminate a "color cast" caused by the film or lighting conditions where a photo was taken. You can also adjust the hue to deliberately give the image an artificial or surreal coloring.

Since Fry-Brain is predominantly black, his image didn't need much color correction, other than bumping the lightness way up. I also pulled the hue over a little bit to make the ground brown instead of pale green, and I enriched the colors slightly by increasing the saturation.

Fig. 9.15
By adjusting hue, saturation, and lightness, you can eliminate color problems in an image.

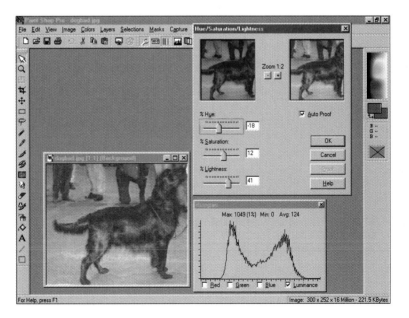

Part III Advanced Image Techniques

Hue, saturation, and lightness aren't the only ways to describe color. Any image can be represented on a computer screen or TV by combining the three primary colors: red, green, and blue (RGB).

In fact, since RGB is what your computer monitor uses, you may prefer (as I usually do) to adjust the RGB values of a photo rather than the HSL values. When doing RGB color adjustments, you may find it helpful to turn the red, green, and blue graphs back on in the Histogram window. I talked about RGB values more in Chapter 8, "The Black and White Alternative."

Equalization

Now that you have graduated from my crash course in color theory, you may feel that color correction is either an attractive career choice or a quagmire to be avoided. You might also wonder if some of this could be automated somehow. If the basic procedure for most images is merely to spread out the histogram to use the full range of tonal values, why can't the computer just figure it out and do it for you? Well, it can—quite often with spectacular results. But alas, at other times the results are disastrous and some hand-correction is almost always necessary.

To automatically redistribute the tones in your image over the entire histogram, select **C**olors, Histogram Functions, **E**qualize. Fry-Brain's response to this is typical: The range of tones is dramatically improved, but there aren't enough colors in the image to fill all the "gaps" that the histogram tries to equalize. Therefore, the transitions between colors becomes too abrupt.

Selecting **C**olors, Histogram Functions, **S**tretch also modifies the histogram and image, but much more gently. Occasionally, this is enough to correct an image completely, but it's usually more of a place you can start, before you further massage the image with the other tools we've discussed. Figure 9.16 shows the results of Fry-Brain being equalized and stretched.

Fig. 9.16
Stretching the
histogram is gentler
than equalizing it.

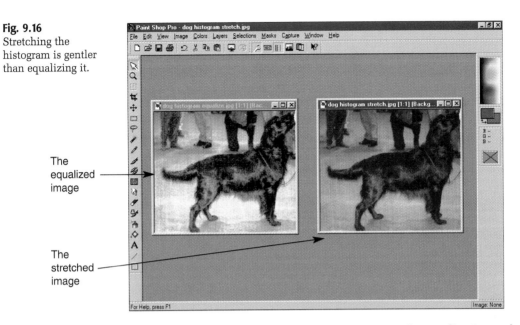

The
equalized
image

The
stretched
image

When used with the tone- and color-correction tools, equalization and
histogram stretching are essential tools that can save you a lot of fussing
and fiddling.

All of these important color correction tools will come in handy when
editing photos that you've scanned or digitized into your computer.

Part III Advanced Image Techniques

10

Creating Transparent GIFs

Throughout much of this book, you've focused on the primary image types of the Web—GIF, JPEG, and PNG. Because all three formats offer different advantages over one another in various situations, part of the process of creating high-quality Web graphics is choosing the correct image format for the circumstances.

In general, GIF, JPEG, and PNG images have many of the same features and much of the same flexibility. The main difference is the way each handles image compression and large numbers of colors. In this chapter, I change gears and show you how to take advantage of a powerful GIF-only feature for your Web images called transparency. Although PNG images also support transparency, they aren't covered in depth here—mainly because few browsers enable PNGs to display inside of them.

GIF images allow you to specify one color within the file that WWW browsers will ignore and treat as transparent. The end result is that your WWW browser displays the normal GIF image but ignores the color designated as transparent; instead of displaying the designated color, the browser shows the Web page's background color or pattern. Much like an overhead machine displays transparencies with its projector, Netscape and Internet Explorer display transparent GIFs on Web pages as more natural-looking images.

Transparent GIFs are a powerful tool in a Web developer's toolbox. Creating effective images for the World Wide Web requires that you understand and use transparent GIFs to enhance your entire Web page experience for viewers.

▶ **What Transparent GIFs Are**
Learn the technical specifications for how transparent GIFs work, are saved, and are displayed by WWW browsers.

▶ **When to Use Transparent GIFs**
Like all new features, transparent GIFs are ideal only for certain situations. Learn to determine when creating transparent GIFs is worth the time and effort.

Part III Advanced Image Techniques

▶ **How WWW Browsers Treat Transparent Characteristics**
Netscape and Internet Explorer both recognize transparent GIFs and
know how to correctly display these images on a Web page.
Understand the mechanics of how browsers treat these new images.

▶ **Specify a Color to Be Transparent**
Only one color in a GIF file can be designated as transparent. Learn
how to identify and indicate that a particular color be transparent by
using built-in Paint Shop Pro tools.

What Are Transparent GIFs?

It's easy to understand what transparent GIFs are and how they work by
thinking of how an overhead projector works. An overhead projector
takes pieces of clear plastic with writing on them and displays only the
writing on a screen. Since the plastic is transparent, it isn't projected onto
the screen. Transparent GIFs work in a similar fashion. The GIF file
format allows you to specify that one of the 256 available colors from a
GIF file appears transparent when shown within a WWW browser.
Typically, GIF transparency is only supported by browsers, and not other
programs found on your computer.

So, instead of appearing normal, the specified color allows whatever is
behind it on the Web page to be displayed. You can choose only one
color to appear transparent on a GIF. With Paint Shop Pro, identifying
and saving the color that you wish to appear transparent is easy.

Often, transparent GIFs are used in images that normally use the color
white in the background of the image. The white part of the image
represents area not being used in the image and is saved as a section of
blank white area. By setting white to be transparent, Netscape ignores this
color in the image and makes the image appears to "float," or fit in with
the actual Web page better. The white, which is part of the image,
becomes transparent, or see-through.

Figure 10.1 shows an example of this phenomenon. On this Web page I
have created a simple tic-tac-toe board using two repeated images—*X* and
O. For this example, the background color of the Web page is set to grey.

Fig. 10.1
The O's fit in much more nicely with the screen than the X's do because the background of the O's is transparent.

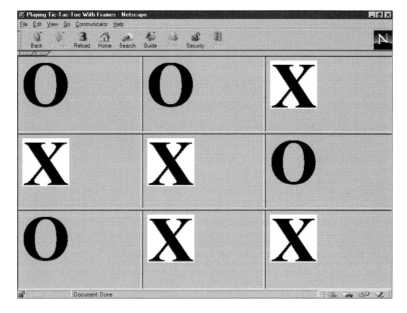

The images are nearly identical. Both are the same size in pixel height and width and use only two colors—black and white. I used Paint Shop Pro 5 to create both of them. The only difference is that I instructed Paint Shop Pro to make the white on the O's transparent—so we can see right through the center of the O's when they're added to the Web page. For the X's, I did not instruct PSP to make the white transparent. As a result, the browser ignores the white for the O's, but not for the X's. You can easily recognize which image looks and fits in better when used on a Web page.

Transparent GIFs improve the appearance of images on your Web page. Nontransparent images sometimes look awkward and out of place because they display the Web-page background graphic or color behind your image and interfere with the overall result of using images on Web pages. In general, you want to explore using transparent GIFs when you define any background color or use a background image on your Web page. This allows your Web browser to ignore parts of an image that are not necessary.

Part III Advanced Image Techniques

The creation and use of icons on Web pages represents another situation in which transparent GIFs are extremely practical. Many people like to create their own colorful bullets and lines instead of using standard ones available through HTML. Web-page bullets often appear as round or another nonrectangular shape, but GIF images can only be saved as rectangles. The result is that an odd-shaped bullet might not fit with the design of the rest of the page because it looks like a rectangle when displayed. To compensate for this problem, icon designers make the background of their round bullets transparent. Figure 10.2 shows an example of a Web page using transparent and nontransparent icons—both depicting a dollar sign. Which would you rather use?

Fig. 10.2
Transparency functionality is one reason most icons and bullets are saved as GIFs instead of JPEGs.

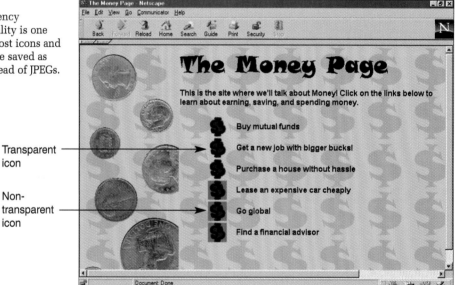

Transparent icon

Non-transparent icon

How Web Browsers Treat Transparent GIFs

When you select a color to be transparent, Paint Shop Pro saves that information into the actual GIF file. Since it is part of the file that is downloaded and displayed on your Web page, WWW browsers can easily recognize and ignore that particular color.

When you design GIFs, you can choose from literally millions of colors to colorize your image. A grand total of 16.7 million shades and hues of reds, greens, and blues are available. While you have millions of options, only 256 different colors can be present at any one time in a GIF file.

Fig. 10.3
Counting the number
of colors in your
image is easy.

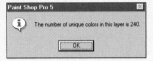

For more information on color specifics and limitations, see Chapter 3,
"Creating Simple Graphics."

Each color is assigned a number from 1 to 256. Paint Shop Pro doesn't
recognize "blue," for example; instead, it knows color number 175.

When displaying an image, your WWW browser displays the pieces of
the image according to the color used. It's just like painting by number, as
you probably did when you were a kid. The image is broken into many
different numbered sections in which each number corresponds to the
color of paint chosen for that section. Although WWW browsers have 256
colors from which to choose, the concept is still the same. Each part of
the Web image is painted according to the number of the color specified.

Here's where the transparency issue comes into play. With transparent
images, you can instruct your WWW browser *not* to paint one particular
color of an image—but to leave it blank instead. Since nothing gets
painted, that particular part of the image is left transparent so you can see
right through it. Web browsers allow you to place colors and images in
the background of your page, behind all the images and text. With a color
designated as transparent, you see the background designs, if any, instead
of the particular color assigned to that section of the Web image.

As you can see, Web browsers aren't very complicated pieces of software
when it comes to displaying images and graphics. Understanding how
Web browsers display transparent GIFs provides insight into how Web
graphics can be designed to take advantage of the Web browsers'
flexibility.

Part III Advanced Image Techniques

Making Transparent GIFs

Now that you know what transparent GIFs are and how WWW browsers such as Netscape and Internet Explorer display them, it's time to learn how to create your own transparent GIFs.

Making transparent GIFs doesn't have to be tricky, but some steps in the process can be confusing if you aren't positive how to proceed. In this section, I'll lead you through a step-by-step process for making a transparent GIF for your own Web page. You'll learn how to make transparent GIFs from scratch, how to convert existing images into transparent ones, and how to identify which color to make transparent.

Creating a Transparent GIF from Scratch

First, I'll show you an example of how to make a simple transparent image from scratch. We'll look at how to create a transparent X to mate with the O used earlier in this chapter. I'll walk you through creating the graphic from start to finish.

1. First, start up Paint Shop Pro and choose File, New from the menu bar to bring up the New Image dialog box (figure 10.4 below).

Fig. 10.4
Creating transparent images is just as easy as working with any other type of GIF file.

2. In the Image type drop-down list box, choose 256 Colors (8 bit) because the GIF file type limits us to a maximum of 256 colors. GIF transparency only works within PSP when you are working with 256 colors. Even though Paint Shop Pro can reduce the number of colors to 256 when you save the image as a GIF, you create extra work for yourself by trying to manage all those extra colors when producing transparent images.

3. Choose the appropriate Height and Width for your new image. Although transparency features work on GIFs of any size, I'll choose 100 x 100 for this example. Then click on the **OK** button to continue. A new blank image is created.

4. Click on the Text icon at the top of the screen so you can add an *X* to your image.

5. Click your mouse cursor in the image to bring up the Add Text dialog box (figure 10.5).

Fig. 10.5
Text can be added in any font, style, and size.

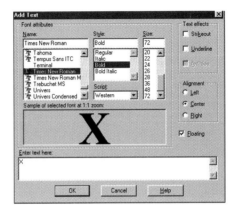

6. Choose the Font attributes you want your text to appear in by selecting the **N**ame, the St**y**le, and the **S**ize of the font. Now type your desired text in the **E**nter text here window. I am adding an *X* that is in Times New Roman, Bold, and at 72 points in size. Click **OK** after making your selections.

7. Your text appears on top of your Web graphic. Move your mouse over the graphic until the pointer becomes a cross with arrows on each end. Click your left mouse button and drag the text to the spot on the image where you want the text placed. Then click your right mouse button to permanently add the text to your image in that spot. Figure 10.6 shows my newly created *X* image.

Part III Advanced Image Techniques

Fig. 10.6
Making this simple
image has been a piece
of cake so far.

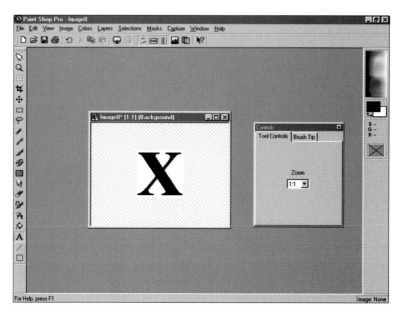

8. The next step is to set your transparent color. The easiest way to set a transparent color is to tell PSP to use whichever color is currently shown in the background in the Color Palette on the right-hand side of the screen. You need to ensure that the color deemed transparent is the current background color in the Color Palette. To do this, click on the eyedropper icon from the Tool Palette.

9. Now move your mouse to anywhere in the background of your image (the white part of the image in this example) and click the *right* mouse button. The eyedropper lets you select colors by pointing and clicking on them. The left mouse button controls the foreground; the right mouse button controls the background. Remember to switch the mouse buttons you click on if you have set your system up for left-handed usage.

    Notice how in the Color Palette on the right-hand side of the screen, the background color switches and becomes whichever color you click on. For this example, my background color is white; but it would work the same if I had clicked on blue, red, green—or any other color. If I wanted to make the background color black, I would have clicked on part of the X instead.

    Finally, you are ready to mark your transparency settings. Choose Color, Set Palette Transparency to bring up the Set Palette Transparency dialog box (figure 10.7).

Fig. 10.7
PSP gives you three
transparency options
from which to select.

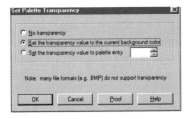

TIP

Although you are saving your image as a transparent GIF, be aware that the image will only display transparent characteristics in a Web browser that supports transparency, such as Netscape or Internet Explorer.

In Paint Shop Pro, to see how your transparency settings look, you must choose **C**olor, **V**iew Palette Transparency from the menu bar. Paint Shop Pro will make the color marked as transparent invisible – instead you will see the PSP checker boxes which indicate a deleted or transparent area.

You can choose from three options: No transparency for this image, set the current background color to be transparent, or set a different color to be transparent by typing in its color number for this image (from 1 to 256).

Select the option button labeled: **Set the transparency value to the current background color**. This tells Paint Shop Pro to make a special note that the current background color (as we defined in the Color Palette during step 9) is now the one that should appear transparent for this image. For more information on the other choices in this dialog box, see "Setting the GIF Options" in the next section. Click **OK** to save your settings.

NOTE

When you edit your graphic in the future, Paint Shop Pro automatically remembers the color, by number, that you've defined as transparent.

12. Give your image a file name and save it. Now this graphic is ready to be used on a Web page with the correct color marked as transparent. Figure 10.8 shows my newly created transparent X on the same tic-tac-toe board Web page.

Fig. 10.8
Making that X look good wasn't too hard, was it?

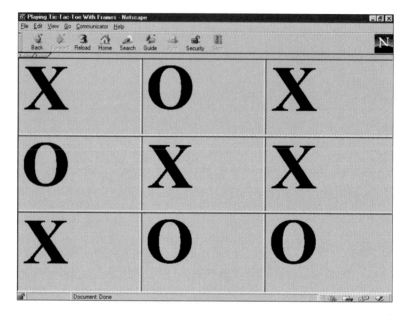

Working with Existing Images

Creating new transparent GIF images from scratch is relatively easy. All you do is make your new image, draw or add a design to the graphic, and indicate the transparent color. Then save your image as a transparent GIF and voila, you are done.

You will often want to modify an existing image that lacks indicated transparent values by converting it to fit better on your Web page. You may want to incorporate an existing image onto your Web page from CD-ROM graphics collections or from elsewhere on the Web.

In general, converting a GIF into transparent GIF format follows the same process outlined above. First, you load the existing image into Paint Shop Pro. Then, using the dropper icon, click your *right* mouse button on the color you want to make transparent. This sets the color you select as the current background color. Finally, choose **C**olor, Set Palette **T**ransparency from the menu bar, and make sure the background color is marked as transparent.

NOTE

If an existing image has many intricate details, the eyedropper tool can sometimes be difficult to use without a little extra help. If you have trouble selecting the correct background color, try zooming in on the picture to get additional detail. Choose View, **Z**oom **I**n from the menu bar, and select a magnification from the available list. When you are finished, you can again choose View, then **Z**oom **O**ut.

Setting the GIF Options

When you save your transparency options, Paint Shop Pro gives you three selections to indicate which color should appear transparent on your Web pages. I described one option earlier. Here's a brief summary of the other two options in the Set Palette Transparency dialog box:

▶ **No transparency**
As the name suggests, this option tells the GIF not to make a color transparent for Web browsers. This selection is often used for photographs and images with lots of colors that are saved in the GIF file format. You don't affect your image file size by ignoring transparency settings, just its appearance.

▶ **Set the transparency value to palette entry**
This selection allows you to designate any one of the 256 colors (including the default background color) as the transparent color by specifying its corresponding number rather than the name of the color. As I discussed earlier, using the paint-by-numbers analogy, each color in a GIF is assigned a corresponding number. You can see a color's corresponding number in the Color Palette by double-clicking either the foreground or background color and selecting the color you want to use. Paint Shop Pro shows that color's palette number in the bottom of the Edit Palette dialog box (figure 10.9).

Fig. 10.9
Each color in your image is numbered and can be marked as transparent.

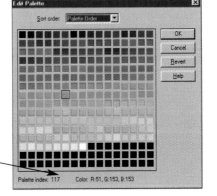

Color
Number

Part III Advanced Image Techniques

More Transparent Examples

Now that you understand how transparent images work, this section shows you a few more examples of creating and using transparent GIFs within Paint Shop Pro.

A Transparent Icon

In the previous example, where I made the X image transparent, you can easily see how the background of the X was transparent. Basically, I told Paint Shop Pro not to display any of the white when putting the image on a Web page.

My next example will show you that any color, not just white, can be marked as transparent. Here's another example with a small GIF—the bullet icon used in figure 10.2. This image is a 40 x 40 graphic. To build it, I used the Fill tool to paint the whole image light green. Then I added a darker green U.S. Dollar sign ($) to the small icon. Figure 10.10 shows me zoomed in 5:1 with Paint Shop Pro.

Fig. 10.10
This background of this icon will become transparent in a moment.

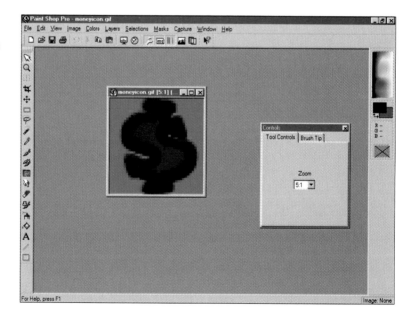

Now I am going to make the green outside of my dollar sign transparent by using the same process described earlier. Using the dropper, I will select the background of my icon then choose Color, Set Palette Transparency. I'll choose to make the background color transparent and then save my image. Figure 10.11 below shows how the icon appears in Paint Shop Pro and how it looks in a browser.

Fig. 10.11a
The Dollar Sign icon displayed in Paint Shop Pro.

Fig. 10.11b
The same icon displayed transparently on a Web page.

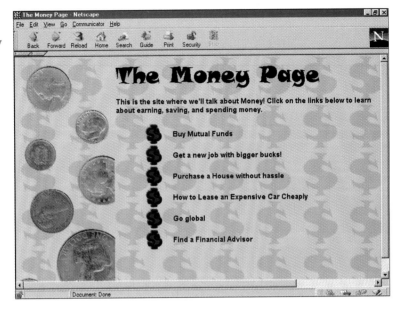

NOTE
It's important to point out that the graphic shown down the left-hand side of figure 10.11b is also a transparent GIF. Created using Paint Shop Pro Picture Tubes (the Coin Tube), this decorative graphic sets the feeling of the page. The coins were placed on an image with a white background, set to be transparent.

A Floating Photo

Transparent GIFs are commonly used when making your own buttons, icons, drawings, and bars for your Web page. When you set the background color to be transparent, your images display correctly on your Web pages. You don't actually change the way an image appears in a paint program like Paint Shop Pro; you merely redefine how a WWW browser interprets and displays the GIF.

Part III Advanced Image Techniques

Another popular way to use the transparency feature in GIFs is to create a "floating" photograph. Like JPEG files, GIF images can only be saved in rectangular shapes. Each file has a defined height and width, regardless of whether you use the whole space of an image. Therefore, with an image shaped as a circle, your GIF file is actually still saved in a rectangular shape but part of the image is left blank—as unused white space.

As you've seen with other icons and images, the GIF transparency feature is commonly used because it makes the icon appear to fit directly into the Web page. A "floating" photograph expands upon that approach. Often, you will not want to use the whole photograph for your Web page. One useful technique is to first crop the photograph to the smallest possible rectangular area needed and then erase the unnecessary part of the remaining picture. You can then set the background of the photograph to be transparent. Now, when added to a Web page, the resulting effect is a floating photograph that appears irregularly shaped and uniquely placed to fit the page.

Let's look at an example of this phenomenon at work. In the following example, I want to crop out only the head in a particular photograph to add to my home page.

Scanning the Picture

The first step is to select and scan a photograph. I'll use the scanning program that installed itself with my Logitech PageScan Color Scanner. Of course, you can use any scanner and software to digitize a picture onto your computer.

I talk about scanning pictures in more detail in Chapter 4, "Editing Images and Photos," and in Chapter 9 "Using Scanners and Digital Cameras." In those chapters you'll learn more about using Paint Shop Pro to *acquire* images directly from a scanner.

Cropping the Picture

Once your image is properly scanned, open it up in Paint Shop Pro. Figure 10.12 shows my scanned photograph, ready for manipulation. Remember that you can only set transparent values for images saved in the GIF file type. JPEG images tend to have smaller file sizes for photographs and use more colors, but they don't use the transparent options described in this chapter.

Fig. 10.12
I'm ready to "float" my photograph.

Once loaded in Paint Shop Pro, the first step is to crop your photograph into the smallest useful rectangular area. Since GIF images must be saved as rectangles, use the Paint Shop Pro crop tool. Click on the Crop tool icon and draw a box around the portion of your image you want to keep. Figure 10.13 shows the image with the area to be cropped marked.

Fig. 10.13
I only need a small part of this image for my Web page.

My Crop Box ——

Part III Advanced Image Techniques

Then click on the Crop Image button in the Controls Palette. Alternatively, you can double-click in your image to crop to the selected area. Only the selected area will remain. The resulting image will be a working file that is not saved until you choose **F**ile, Save As from the menu bar. Paint Shop Pro lets you undo multiple commands, but save often in case you make a mistake on your image.

Sculpting Your Image

The next step in creating a floating image is to cut away the unnecessary parts of your newly cropped photo. Just like a sculptor, you want to whittle away the extra parts of the image so you are left with the final, clean image for display on your Web page. You are sculpting your image so that the unnecessary part of your Web graphic is all the same color. For my image, I sculpt around the head by making the image's background color all white so I can set white as transparent.

Sculpting around an image can be tedious and time-consuming. Although you have cropped your image to a compact rectangle, you probably don't want interference from the background of your image. For this example, I want to display only my head on the Web page, not the person and the wall behind him. Therefore, I need to patiently cut away the excess part of the image until only the section of the photograph I want to use remains.

PSP has many tools that are useful when you are sculpting away parts of an image. You can use your Paint Brush, Magic Wand, or Lasso Tool to effectively sculpt. For this example, I'll use the lasso tool so you can see how it works.

Click on the selection "Lasso," which lets you select irregularly shaped areas. Using the lasso, mark the areas on the image that you want to "cut" away from your final product. Now choose **E**dit, **C**ut from the menu bar; and Paint Shop Pro removes the selected area and replaces it with blank area. By default, your blank area is set to the background color defined in the Color Palette on the right-hand side of the screen. Be careful not to select a background color that is part of the image itself. Otherwise your Web browser might ignore other parts of the image, not just the background. In general, white is an excellent color to use for transparent images.

Additionally, you may want to use the paint brush tool to paint over smaller sections. I used a combination of the lasso and paint brush to cut away all the extra parts of my image.

CAUTION

Even the most talented sculptors don't recklessly chip and manipulate their carving. Take care to slowly cut away the unnecessary parts of the image, one piece at a time. Don't rush and attempt to cut away the entire background part of the photo in one fell swoop. You're likely to accidentally cut an important part of the picture.

If sculpting and doing detailed work on photos seems to require a lot of patience, that's because it does. Often professional and amateur graphics creators will spend hours sculpting and painting over detailed sections of an image to achieve the perfect effect.

You can choose to zoom in on your image so that you can sculpt in detail. To zoom in on your photograph, choose View, Zoom In from the menu bar. Figure 10.14 shows me whittling away part of the background wall from my photograph while zooming in for more detail. You'll find that constantly zooming in and out will help you monitor your progress in the sculpting.

Fig. 10.14
I zoom in considerably when sculpting my photographs.

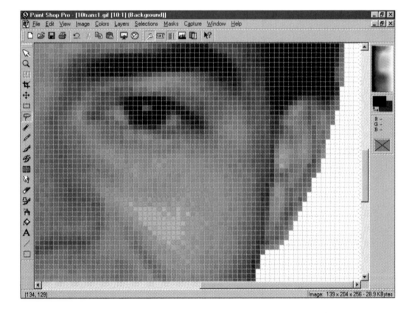

Sculpting is by far the most difficult step in creating a floating photograph for your Web page. Fortunately, Paint Shop Pro makes it easy for you to select and crop away unnecessary parts of your image. Once you're finished, move on to the next section. Take a look at figure 10.15 to see how my final image looks once it's sculpted and ready to use.

Part III Advanced Image Techniques

Fig. 10.15
Similar to my original
image, this
photograph is ready to
float onto the Web.

Make sure that white is set as the current background in the Color Palette,
then set the current background color to be transparent. Save your image,
and you are complete.

CAUTION

Don't accidentally save your new image over your original GIF file. Use the
File, Save **As** or File, Save Copy As command to rename your newly created
floating GIF.

Test Your Image

Once you are done creating your "floating" GIF, take a moment to test it
with a WWW browser. Make sure that your background color is properly
identified.

Figure 10.16 below shows my floating image twice—once as it should
appear and once as it looks when the background transparent color isn't
set right. If your image doesn't display as it should, it's likely that the
color selected to be transparent was incorrect.

Fig. 10.16
The Floating GIF looks
slick when added to a
Web page.

11

Moving Graphics: GIF Animation

Normally, an image is loaded on your Web page and becomes a static part of the screen. These standard Web images are useful, and Paint Shop Pro has a lot of great tools for making them. But wouldn't it be nice if you could just "snap together" three or four GIF images to make a simple animated graphic, without having to deal with extra software components and complexity?

Fortunately, you can combine multiple images into one file. This feature, called GIF animation, lets your browser flip through many images saved within a single file, creating an animation effect. Not only are GIF animations easy to create, but they usually have reasonable file sizes— a cool animated icon can be 20KB or smaller.

Paint Shop Pro 5 makes it easy to create GIF animation files because it comes with its own GIF animator, Animation Shop. This special PSP add-on provides all the tools and wizards necessary to build efficient and effective GIF animations. In this chapter, you'll learn how to create GIF animations and how to optimize them for the fastest possible display using Animation Shop.

▶ **Building a GIF Animation**
Learn to quickly assemble multiple images into an animation file that you can place on your Web pages just like any other GIF.

▶ **Using Layers to Make a GIF Animation**
Learn to use layers in PSP to easily make the component images for an animation.

▶ **Optimizing GIF Animations**
Learn to use the Optimization Wizard to reduce the size of your GIF animation files—sometimes by as much as half the original size.

▶ **Deciding When to Use GIF Animations**
Take into consideration when including GIF animations on your Web pages is useful— and when it's not.

Part III Advanced Image Techniques

Understanding GIF Animation

GIF animation isn't exactly new technology. In fact, multi-frame animation was built into the GIF file format way back in 1989. But that functionality wasn't exposed until Web browsers became popular a few years ago. Now animation has become a very popular and easy way to enhance your Web site.

Basically, GIF animations work like flip-books, where you see an animation as you flip through a book. Each frame originally started out as a separate file. Then using a special tool and optimization process, these multiple files were combined into a single GIF file. If you've never created an animation of any kind before, you may not realize that the illusion of animation is achieved by showing several still images (called "frames") in rapid succession.

Web browsers simply download the animated GIF as they would any other graphic on your Web page and show it as part of the page. You can include this animation in a Web page with the <IMG> tag, exactly as if the animation were an "ordinary" GIF.

GIF Animations can have as many frames as you'd like, but keep in mind that each frame increases the overall file size. Often, you'll want to include a handful of frames for your animation and then have the browser continuously loop through your animation, so you can get the effect of many frames without the extra download time.

TIP

Besides using GIF animation, you can add movement to a Web page in several other ways. You can hire a programmer or spend some time learning Java or JavaScript. You can use a pre-built applet or OLE component to play some sort of video or interactive media file. Or you can ask all the visitors to your Web site to get a helper application or plug-in program to play your favorite media file format. All these solutions may be excellent in many situations, but every one involves an investment of time and resources before you even start to produce animation.

To learn more about building interactive Java animations, visit **http://www. gamelan.com**, the center of all Java applets online. Similarly, a great JavaScript site is **http://www.javascripts.com**.

Building a GIF Animation

To create animated GIFs, you must have a special tool that understands how to efficiently combine multiple images into a single GIF. Included with Paint Shop Pro 5 is Jasc's Animation Shop, an easy-to-use program for assembling animated GIFs.

The first step in building a GIF animation is to create a series of images to be displayed one after the other. Just save your images as GIFs for later assembly in Animation Shop. Figure 11.1 shows a simple set of two images that I'll use in this section to create an animation.

Fig. 11.1
The original GIFs in PSP before the animation is made.

NOTE
The fastest way to create a simple GIF animation with Animation Shop is to select File, Animation Wizard from the menu bar. This will start an "interview" that leads you through all the steps discussed below.

You can also automatically create scrolling text and a number of transition effects with the Effects, Image Transitions and Effects, Text Transitions commands. These commands provide an easy way to add some quick animation effects to simple single-file images.

In this chapter, I'll show you how to create animations using the Animation Wizard. I encourage you to also experiment on your own with the automatic effects.

Part III Advanced Image Techniques

The following numbered steps show you how to make a simple GIF animation. This animation will flip back and forth between the two artistic renderings of the word "NEW" shown in figure 11.1.

1. Before you start to assemble the animation with Animation Shop, start Paint Shop Pro and open the images you'd like to include in the animation. That way, you can touch up and finalize your image frames for the animation.

TIP

You'll find it easier to build and modify animations if you give the component images for each animation similar names. You might name the images for a dog animation dog1.gif, dog2.gif, dog3.gif, and so on. The two images in this example are named new1.gif and new2.gif.

2. Now open up Animation Shop. Animation Shop can be run directly from the Windows 95 Start button (Start, Program Files, Paint Shop Pro 5, Animation Shop) or by selecting **F**ile, Run Animation Shop from the PSP 5 menu bar.

3. To create a new animation, select **F**ile, **A**nimation Wizard or click on the Animation Wizard button on the Toolbar. You'll then see the first dialog box for the Animation Wizard (figure 11.2), which asks for the dimensions of your animation. Select "Same size as the first image frame" and then click Next.

Fig. 11.2
Step One in the Animation Wizard: Choosing a Pixel dimension for the animation.

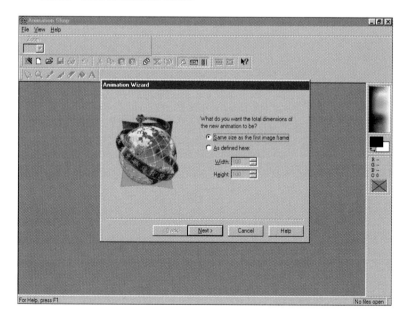

4. You're then asked to set the default canvas color for your frames (figure 11.3), which can be either transparent or opaque. For this example, I selected Opaque and chose white. When you've selected the canvas color, click Next.

Fig. 11.3
Step Two: Picking a background color

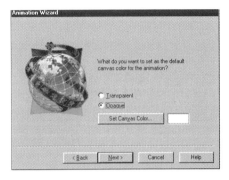

5. The next dialog box (figure 11.4) asks how to position images in the frames and how to fill in any areas of a frame that aren't filled by an image you add to your animation. For image sets like the two in this example, all the components are the same size and each entirely fills its frame. Click Next to accept the defaults and continue.

Fig. 11.4
Step Three: Filling in extra space

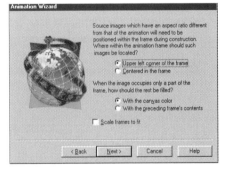

6. The next dialog box in the Animation Wizard asks how you want your animation to loop (figure 11.5). You can have the animation loop indefinitely or loop only a specific number of times. I chose to repeat indefinitely.

NOTE
You can change the looping setting later on, after your animation is built, by selecting Edit, Properties, Animation Properties.

Part III Advanced Image Techniques

7. You can also set the Display Time in this dialog box. The default display time is 10/100 second. Here I chose 30/100 second. The display time is the length of time between the point at which a frame in an animation is first displayed and the point at which the next frame in the animation is displayed.

    When you've made your setting selections here, click Next.

Fig. 11.5
Step Four: Play the animation once, or have it loop through?

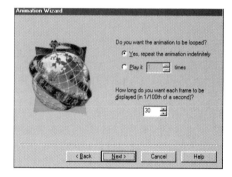

8. The next dialog box (shown in figure 11.6) is where you add the component images to your animation.

    Add the first graphic by clicking the **A**dd Image button, then select and open the file from the selection list. Repeat this step for each component file.

    If you accidentally insert an incorrect file, just select that file and click the Remove Image button. You can select multiple files by holding down your Shift or Ctrl button when clicking on file names. When you've added all your component files, click Next and then click Finish.

Fig. 11.6
Step Five: Adding frames to your animation

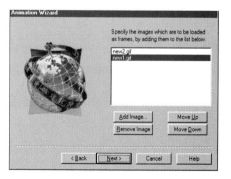

You'll then see a new "filmstrip," the workspace for creating your animated GIF. As shown in figure 11.7, the filmstrip will contain each of the frames for your animation. Each frame has a label that indicates its frame number and display time.

Fig. 11.7
The filmstrip provides a workspace for you to build your animated GIF.

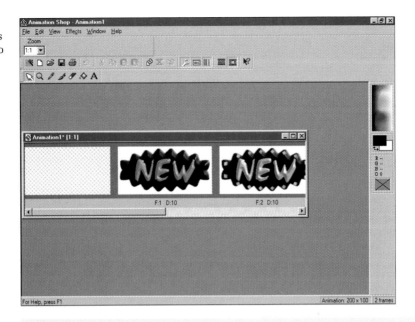

TIP

If at any point you decide you'd like to change the display time for any frame, right-click in the appropriate frame and choose Properties. Go to the Display Time tab and reset the display time.

If you decide that you'd like to add other frames to your animation, right-click on an existing frame and select Add, From File to bring up the Insert Frames from Files dialog box (figure 11.8).

Fig. 11.8
It's easy to add new frames to your animation.

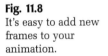

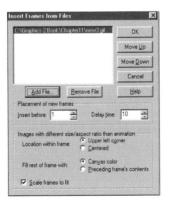

You can then select the image (or series of images) that you want to add, much as you did earlier with the Animation Wizard. Set the Insert Before option to the frame number of the frame that should follow the newly inserted one. If you want your new frame to be the last frame in the animation, set this number to one more than the frame number of the current final frame. Set the Display Time as you like. For now, ignore the other settings and just press **OK**.

If you decide to delete any frames, simply right-click on the frame and select Delete.

9. Save your animation as a GIF using Save As and choosing CompuServe Graphics Interchange (*.gif). When you give your animation a name and click Save, the Animation Optimization Wizard will be invoked (figure 11.9). For now, accept the default settings for the Optimization Wizard by clicking on the Next button.

Fig. 11.9
Animation quality versus file size is an important question to grapple with.

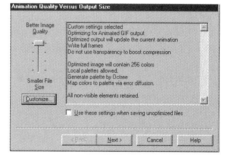

The Optimization Wizard shows you the results of your efforts, including the final file size and estimated download time for this animation. Figure 11.10 shows the Optimization Results for this simple GIF animation.

Fig. 11.10
12K is not too bad a file size for this moving image.

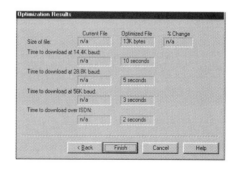

Using your favorite Web page editor, make an HTML document with an <IMG> tag referring to the .gif file you just saved as the SRC (for example, for my "NEW" logo I might use <IMG SRC="new-ani.gif">). To see the results, load the document in your Web browser. Figure 11.11 shows the results of my animation efforts.

Fig. 11.11
See the animation moving for real by visiting the book's home page.

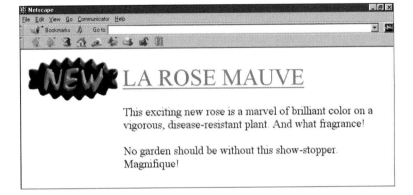

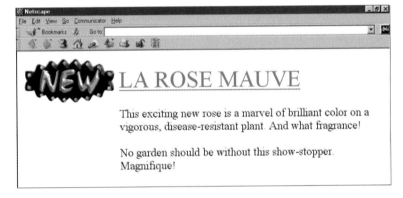

TIP
You can preview the animation within Animation Shop at any time during the construction process by clicking on the View Animation button or by choosing **View, Animation**.

Part III Advanced Image Techniques

Using Layers to Make GIF Animations

I could have created each component image of the "NEW" animation in PSP as separate files, but what I did instead was create the files using PSP's layers. Layering allows you to keep various parts of an image on their own separate layers, where you can modify each independently. This makes drawing simple animations a breeze.

By way of example, let me explain how I created the "NEW" logo, which has text and highlights that blink on a static button background. To start, I made the button as my background layer. Then I made one version of the text for the Dark layer, then copied and edited that text layer to make the Light layer. Figures 11.12a and 11.12b show these two layers displayed separately, on top of the Button layer.

Fig. 11.12a
The layered image with the Button and Dark layers visible

Fig. 11.12b
The layered image with the Button and Light layers visible

To make the two component images for my animation, I selectively hid each of the two text layers, one at a time. With the Button and the Dark layers visible, I used Save As to save these two visible layers as NEW1.GIF. Then I hid the Dark layer and made the Light layer visible and used Save As to save the combined Button and Light layers as NEW2.GIF. The original file is saved in the PSP format as NEW.PSP, with all layering information.

To make your own component GIFs with PSP's layers, you can try one of two approaches.

One approach is to use one layer to draw your basic animated image and drag this layer to the New Layer icon in the Layers palette. Repeat as many times as you like to create multiple copies of the image. Adjust the details for each component image on each layer. Then, for the first component image, hide the layers you don't need and save what's visible. Do the same for each subsequent component image. You're then ready to assemble your component images in Animation Shop.

The second approach is much like the first, except that here you draw the unchanging parts of your animation as the "lowest" layer, then draw only the changing parts on their own separate layers, one layer for each stage of movement. Figures 11.13a and 11.13b show two views of an image that makes use of this alternative approach.

Fig. 11.13a
One view of FOX.PSP, a layered animation source made in Paint Shop Pro.

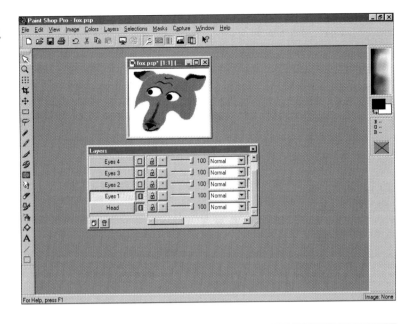

Fig. 11.13b
Another view of the same layered fox image.

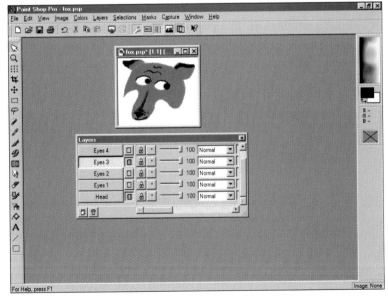

For each component file for this animation, I hid all but one of the multiple layers for the image's eyes and saved that view as a GIF. When I had GIFs saved for each, I assembled them in Animation Wizard.

For more information on layers and how they work, see Chapter 7, "Using PSP Layers."

Part III Advanced Image Techniques

Optimizing GIF Animations

When you save your animation as a GIF in Animation Shop, your animation will be optimized via the Optimization Wizard (or behind the scenes, if you've set optimization defaults in a previous Optimization Wizard session). The Optimization Wizard walks you through a set of dialog boxes in which you select settings to decrease animation file size. By default, the Optimization Wizard performs minimal optimization, but you can use the advanced options to control how and how much your animated GIF is optimized.

One way to reduce the size of your animated GIFs is to reduce the number of colors used in the component images. Optimization Wizard makes it easy for you to reduce the number of colors and choose the color palette for your animations.

Another way to reduce animation file size is to make transparent any part of the image that doesn't change. This reduces the size of the file because a solid region of transparency will compress much more efficiently than the same region filled with complex image data. You can readily accomplish this by setting Optimization Wizard to save only the part of the image that actually changes from one frame to the next, using only this smaller part instead of replacing the whole image in each frame.

You'll learn more about color reduction techniques and transparency in the next chapter, Chapter 12, "Making Your Graphics Lean."

NOTE

The entire image will show up in each frame of the filmstrip, even if you choose to replace unchanging parts with transparency.

Adjusting the Color Palette

When I created the component images for the "NEW" logo, I saved the files as GIFs, which by default have 256 colors. Animation Shop, used as its palette, the full 256 colors of the first component image when the "NEW" animation was saved. But this animation doesn't actually require 256 colors. So I decided to try reducing the number of colors using Animation Wizard.

I opened NEW-ANI.GIF in Animation Shop and chose **File, Optimization Wizard**, which opens up a dialog box that asks whether you want to save your animation as a GIF or a MNG (Multiple-image Network Graphic) and whether you want to replace the current version of your animation or create a new, optimized file.

When you click the Next button, you're shown the Animation Quality Versus Output Size dialog box (see figure 11.14).

Fig. 11.14
The Animation Wizard Animation Quality versus the Output Size window

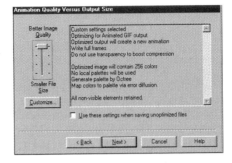

TIP

The MNG (Multiple-image Network Graphic) file format can be very useful for saving intermediate stages of your animation, before you decide to save the final version as a GIF. Based on the PNG image format, MNG animations are just becoming supported in popular Web browsers. This is especially true if your component images are 16-million-color PNGs, since MNG—like PNG—can save all 16 million colors. Waiting until you are finished to save your animation as a GIF can help preserve image quality of animations that include many gradations of color.

You can reduce the number of colors for your animation simply by pulling the Quality/Size Slider down, but I wanted to choose the specific number of colors by hand. So I clicked on the Customize button and went to the Colors tab instead (see figure 11.15).

Fig. 11.15
Tell Animation Shop how to manage colors in your final animation.

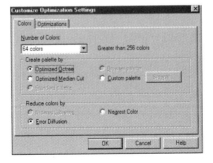

From the **N**umber of Colors list, you select the number of colors you want to use in the color palette for your animation. First check in PSP to see how many colors the component images actually used. If you only use a handful of different colors, you can easily reduce the amount that are saved in the GIF animation.

Part III Advanced Image Techniques

For this example, I decided that the image quality of the animation wouldn't suffer to any noticeable degree if I chose 64 colors.

TIP

Also in the Customize Optimization Settings dialog box are settings for method of palette creation and for method of color reduction. For 256-color GIFs that will be displayed on your Web pages, it's usually a good idea to choose as your palette Browser—the Netscape browser-safe palette. Since I was using fewer than 256 colors, the Browser option wasn't available to me. What I chose instead was Optimized Octree, a good general-purpose method for creating an optimized palette. Because I wanted to avoid dithering, I chose Error Diffusion for the color reduction method.

An animation that includes subtle gradations of color in its component images will look a lot better when dithered, although dithering creates slightly larger file sizes. For complex animations with lots of colors, try the Error Diffusion method to get approximations of all the colors, even when you use the browser-safe palette.

For most situations, though, you should use Animation Shop's nearest color algorithm to change all component images in the animation to solid, rather than dithered, colors. The colors might not look quite as pretty, but the resulting animated GIFs often come out a lot smaller and faster.

When I finished making adjustments to the color optimization settings, I clicked **OK** to return to the Animation Quality Versus Output Size dialog box. Clicking Next then brings up the Optimization Progress window. When the optimization finishes, you click Next to see what effect the optimization had on file size.

For the "NEW" logo, which started out as a 13KB file, this optimization produced a 3.5KB reduction in file size. That may not seem dramatic at first, but keep in mind that this is a 25% reduction in size for this image. That kind of result could translate into considerable savings with larger, more complex animations.

Mapping Identical Pixels to Transparent

Sometimes the most dramatic reduction in an animation's file size can be achieved by saving the unchanging parts of the animation once, then only rewriting pixels that change from frame to frame.

In many GIF animators, to take advantage of this file-size savings you must do all the cutting into pieces and positioning of the pieces by hand. Animation Shop makes things easy for you by doing all the work itself. All you have to do is simply provide all the full-frame versions of your component images and then make one selection in Optimization Wizard.

Here's an example. Suppose you have a multi-framed animation of a cartoon character who does nothing except roll his eyes. A portion of such an animation, made from the layered PSP file we saw earlier in this chapter, is shown in figure 11.16.

Fig. 11.16
A multi-framed cartoon with a large unchanging area.

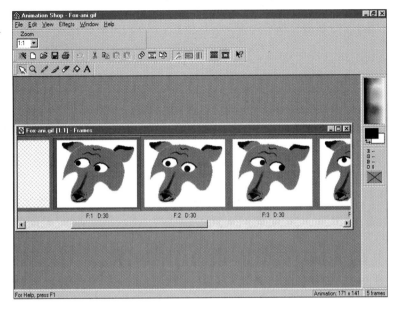

To optimize this animation, fire up the Optimization Wizard, press the Customize button in the Animation Quality Versus Output Size dialog box, and click the Optimizations tab, shown in figure 11.17.

Fig. 11.17
The Optimizations tab of the Animation Wizard's Customize Optimization Settings window.

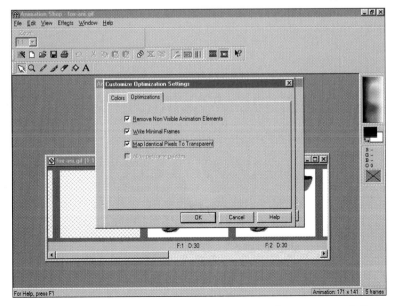

Part III Advanced Image Techniques

Then make sure that Map Identical Pixels to Transparent is selected. Make any other setting adjustments here or at the Colors, and run the optimization. That's all you need to do!

For this particular animation, FOX-ANI.GIF, the file size went from 20KB to about 16KB, a savings of about 21%. And when I also reduced the number of colors to 64, the file size dropped to 9KB—less than half the original file size. Don't be surprised if this technique provides you with similar—or even better—savings in file size.

Looping

Looping isn't directly relevant to optimization, but you should know one thing about looped animations that can affect both the quality and file size of your animated GIFs. Because of the way some browsers process and display multi-image GIF files, you will often find that the first frame of a looping animation is skipped or only half displayed, making a noticeable jerk or some other subtle-but-annoying effect.

The way to avoid this is to repeat the first image at the end of the animation. This way, the "jerk" becomes invisible because it occurs between two identical images. For example, an animation that has seven frames might contain only six different images, with the seventh being a repeat of the first.

Repeating the first image does increase the size of the GIF file, so you may be willing to tolerate a little jerkiness to keep the size down. Also, in some animations such as the "NEW" logo example, you never notice or care about the jerk anyway. So, it's a good idea to try the animation without the first image repeat to see whether you're happy with the results. If you are already pleased, the only reason you might consider repeating the first image is to ensure compatibility and less jerkiness with a few older browsers.

Special Animation Shop Techniques

Besides building GIF animations with layers and separate images, the Jasc Animation Shop has three other innovative ways to create cool animations for your Web site – Image Transitions, Text Transitions, and Video to Animation.

These three techniques are all built into Animation Shop and make it easy for you to build powerful GIF animations with little time or expertise.

Image Transitions

Animation Shop comes with the ability to build twenty-eight different cool ways to affect the way an image loads in the Web browser. By starting with an original image, you can tell PSP to build an animation that shakes, zooms, splits, blurs, explodes, dissolves, or more to an image. Generally, you start with one or two images and then tell Animation Shop which image transition you want to apply. Animation Shop builds all the necessary frames to achieve any of these twenty-eight cool effects.

Highly recommended and a very cool way to jazz up any site in a matter of moments, open any image, click your right mouse button and select Image Transition from the popup box that appears.

Figure 11.18 shows the Add Image Transition dialog box that appears. This box shows the Clock transition being applied. Notice how Animation Shop shows the images I am starting with and ending with and builds a set of frames in between them. For the Clock transition, Animation Shop paints the new image on top of the first image as if a clock hand were sweeping away the original image.

Fig. 11.18
Image Transitions are powerful and very simple to use.

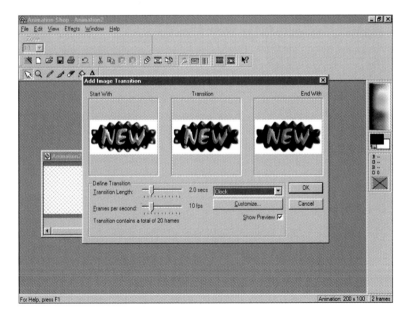

Animation Shop even shows you a live preview of the transition occurring on your image within the dialog box shown in figure 11.18. All of the Image Transitions can be configured by clicking on the button labeled **C**ustomize. You'll want to experiment with and explore this powerful feature.

Part III Advanced Image Techniques

Text Transitions

Similar to Image Transitions, Text Transitions are quick ways to build text only animations for Web sites. Text Transitions don't require you to start with an original image, instead you can just build an animation from a specific word or phrase.

Create a new file within Animation Shop and click the right mouse button within your empty frame. Choose Text Transition from the popup box that appears and you'll see the Add Text Transition dialog box, as shown in figure 11.19.

Fig. 11.19
Text Transitions are great ways to build simple animations.

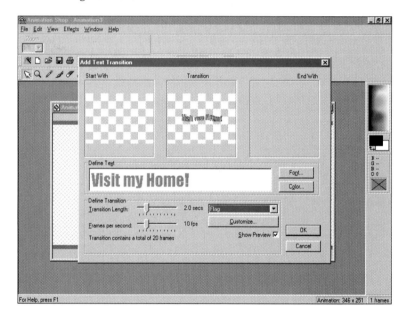

There are six different Text Transitions you can create, including a marquee banner, lighted text, bouncing text, and a waving flag-like effect. Like Image Transitions, all the Text Transitions can be customized or selected from the drop-down menu box.

Type in the text you want to add and set the font and color. Then define the transition variables and click on the OK button. Animation Shop will build all the frames for you to save as a GIF animation image and add them to your Web site.

Video to Animation

The final cool effect that Animation Shop lets you easily accomplish is converting a video clip into a GIF animation. You can open any .AVI file with Animation Shop and it will automatically be converted into GIF animation format. Visitors who stop by your Web site will see only a cool looking GIF file instead of a special video clip that sometimes requires extra software to view, depending on the Web browser they are using.

To convert .AVI files into animations, simply choose **File**, **O**pen from the Animation Shop menu bar. Then select an .AVI file to open and Animation shop brings up the AVI Import Options dialog box (figure 11.20)

AVI files are the standard Video for Windows file format and are commonly used by personal video cameras that connect to your computer. Once they are converted, you can save them as animated GIFs and use them on your Web page. Be careful, converted AVI clips can often be relatively large because they tend to require a lot of individual frames to appear properly as a GIF animation.

Deciding When to Use GIF Animations

You should consider two factors when deciding whether or not to include GIF animations on your Web pages.

▶ Will the animations have a significant effect on the download time for your page?

▶ Will the animation or group of animations add to or detract from the usability and aesthetics of your page?

Animated GIFs almost always have relatively large file sizes compared to similar static Web images. So keep an eye on the file size of your animations, and make liberal use of the optimization techniques discussed in this chapter.

As for usability and aesthetics, your animated GIFs should add to the users' enjoyment of your site, not be something that drives them away. Unless the point of your site is to make users' heads spin, you'll want to keep your animations reasonably tame and the number of different animations on a page fairly small. A subtle animated logo or a few small animated attention-getters that point out new additions to your page might be a nice touch that even repeat visitors will appreciate. And a tasteful advertising banner might be fine. But a dozen harsh, clashing buttons, icons, and banners might send your visitors dashing off to someplace more serene. Visit some sites that include GIF animations and see for yourself what works and what doesn't.

Part III Advanced Image Techniques

To get some ideas for making your own GIF animations, you might also want to visit sites that have animation collections available for download. A place to start is AGAG (**http://www.agag.com**), home of the Animated GIF Artists Guild (figure 11.21). The AGAG site has not only links to animated GIF collections, but also tutorials and tips on making your own animated GIFs.

Fig. 11.21
Learn everything about building and using great animated GIFs at the AGAG site.

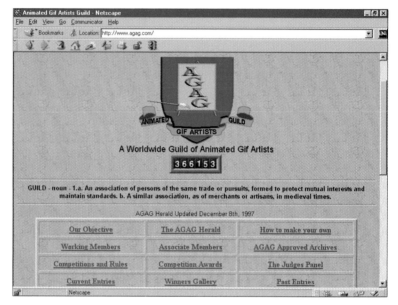

12

Making Your Graphics Lean

As you read the first eleven chapters of this book, you learned how to make and edit all sorts of images for your Web pages. Whether you created a new image from scratch, used Paint Shop Pro's advanced graphics capabilities, or scanned a photograph or logo, you focused on creating and saving your images in an electronic format. Learning how to create and edit good images is the important first step in adding graphics to your Web pages.

There's almost always one important rule to keep in mind when producing Web graphics: the quicker they download, the better your site. Since download time directly correlates to file size, it's crucial that you understand how to squeeze image file sizes as small as possible.

In this chapter you'll learn several techniques for making sure your images are small, are efficient, and take advantage of important file compression possibilities. Since visitors must download each image file before they can see your Web page in its entirety, your site will be much quicker to explore and, consequently, more valuable when you keep your Web graphics small and efficient. Nobody wants to wait too long when visiting a Web site.

▶ **Understand How File Size Equates to Performance**
In general, size, quality, and image format directly affect how long an image takes to download from the WWW and be displayed on your computer. Learn how these different features correlate with one another.

▶ **Changing Image Pixel Sizing Saves Time**
By resizing, thumbnailing, and cropping your Web graphics, you can achieve significant savings in Web page download time. See how you can employ these three strategies to make your graphics more effective and efficient.

Part III   Advanced Image Techniques

▶ **Count the Number of Colors You Use**
Image size is highly dependent on the number of different colors used in the particular image. Learn how to control the number of colors you use in your graphics to see a dramatic difference in file size.

▶ **Understand JPEG Compression**
Like GIFs, the JPEG file format offers special limits to control overall file size. By using JPEG compression, you can change the final file size of an image significantly without losing much image detail.

▶ **Interlaced and Progressive Images**
One popular way to make images appear more quickly on a Web page is by creating interlaced GIFs or Progressive JPEGs. Learn how these special file options allow visitors to explore Web pages immediately.

Why Use Lean Files?

A major obstacle facing Web users today is the time required to browse through WWW pages across the Internet. When you visit a Web page, you must wait for all the text and images to be electronically transferred, or *downloaded*, from the Internet onto your personal computer. The time required for downloading to occur depends on the type and speed of the Internet connection you maintain for your personal computer. The majority of individuals use a modem to browse through the WWW, while many businesses have faster, more direct connections to the Internet.

Modem speed governs the rate at which graphics can be downloaded. Popular modem speeds range from 14.4 to 28.8 thousand bits-per-second (baud), but some people use faster—or slower—modems. In fact, new compression techniques can drastically increase your modem throughput and speed. The higher the baud, the faster the graphics can be downloaded for viewing by visitors. Table 12.1 shows a comparison between several common modem speeds and the amount of data that can be downloaded at each speed.

Table 12.1
Download time comparison

Baud	Amount of data per minute
9,600	60K
14,400	90K
28,800	180K
33,200	210K

As you can see, even at the fastest baud rate, visitors will have to wait several seconds to download and see images on a large Web page. Therefore, a critical task you will face when creating Web graphics is minimizing the overall file size of each image on your page. By reducing the download time, you'll have better response to your Web site from visitors who stop by, and they'll be more likely to return for another visit.

Even people who access the Internet directly from school or work worry about image size and download times. Even though their connections are usually much faster than modem connections, downloading large images can still cause a bottleneck as they browse the Web.

Everyone expects a few moments' wait when visiting a Web site, but nobody wants to wait 30 seconds for each page to load, just to click on a hyperlink to move to another page. Visitors want to quickly see a particular page, read through it, and decide where to go next. The longer people have to wait to observe a particular page, the more likely they will click on the Stop or Back button in the WWW browser and never even see your site.

For example, let's say your home page takes about sixty seconds to download and view. If ninety people visit your Web site every day, one and a half hours are spent downloading your single Web page. By finding some way to reduce the download time to twenty seconds—maybe by reducing the size or quality of an image—you can save your visitors, individually and collectively, a lot of time.

Keeping your graphics small and efficient is not only imperative but extremely challenging. Paint Shop Pro includes several methods you can use to help make your graphics small and lean.

NOTE

A new type of modem technology recently introduced could revolutionize home access to the Internet. Known as Digital Subscriber Line (DSL for short), this new technology lets you get speeds up to ten times faster than 56K modems. Continual innovations like this enable us all to benefit from faster download times and make browsing the Web easier. By the time you read this, DSL modems and enhancements will have been released in many areas around the world.

Part III Advanced Image Techniques

Cropping, Resizing, and Thumbnailing Images

One popular way to reduce the total download time of a Web page is to reduce the actual area in pixels of the image being downloaded. You can save significant time by cropping or resizing an image so that a much smaller image is sent instead of the larger original one. Visitors can then click on a hypertext link if they want to see the larger, full-size version of the image.

This section outlines two excellent ways to reduce the size of images on your Web page. You will use these methods primarily when dealing with photographs and pictures on your Web site.

Resizing an Image

Perhaps the most common mistake Web developers make is using an image that is simply too large and unwieldy. In figure 12.1, I created a Web page for a kitten named Cary. This picture-perfect JPG is over 50K in file size. Visitors have to wait nearly 30 seconds just to see this single picture if they are using a 28.8-baud modem (the most common speed).

NOTE

Another method of controlling an image size is with special HTML tags—HEIGHT and WIDTH. See "Height and Width HTML tags" in Chapter 15, "HTML Tips for Web Images," for more information on the possibilities and drawbacks of using these two tags to control image size and appearance.

Fig. 12.1
Cary is no ordinary
feline; he is part of a
family of five.

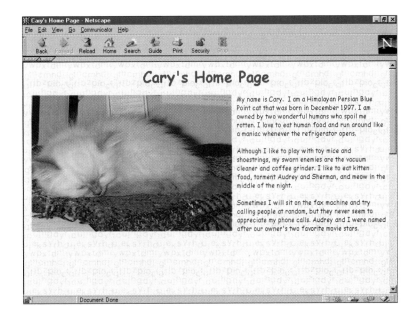

CAUTION

One major mistake that could cause even slower download time is picking
the wrong image format. Figure 12.1 shows a photograph that is saved in
the JPG file format. Although 51K is large, the *identical* image is over 100K
when saved as a GIF instead. The big difference is due to the different
compression techniques I described way back in Chapter 1.

Similarly, if this image were a simple icon or headline, saving it in the JPG
format can make it unnecessarily larger because GIFs are optimized for that
type of image. Make sure you always pick the proper image format, the one
that's optimized for your type of Web graphic. Remember that photo and
photo-like images are usually better saved as JPGs since that format
supports 16.7 million colors.

Although the image looks fine on this Web page, downloading takes too
long. One way to overcome this problem is to resize the image using
Paint Shop Pro. By resizing the image, you make the JPG file size smaller
because the new file will contain fewer pixel coordinates.

Part III Advanced Image Techniques

Originally, this image was 425 pixels wide and 284 pixels tall. I'm going to resize it to half its original size on the screen. The first step in resizing an image is loading the original in Paint Shop Pro. Choose File, Open from the menu bar and select the image you want to work with. To resize images in Paint Shop Pro, choose Image, Resize from the menu bar to bring up the PSP Resize dialog box (figure 12.2).

Fig. 12.2
Your new image can be changed to a variety of sizes.

You can now choose between entering exact size coordinates, or resizing the image as a percentage of the original. For this example, I am going to resize my image as 50% of the original. The resize dialog box, which is very useful, is described in more depth in Chapter 4, "Editing Images and Photos."

CAUTION
Make sure you don't overwrite your original image by mistake. Instead, save to a new file using the File, Save As or File, Save Copy As commands. Rename your image with a similar but distinguishing descriptive name so you can easily tell the difference between the two files. For my example, I used **carycatbig.jpg** and **carycatsmall.jpg**.

You can resize your graphics to nearly any size imaginable. It's helpful to evaluate several different sizes before you select the right one for your Web page.

As you can imagine, the newly resized image has a significantly smaller file size. At 213 x 142 pixels, the new file size is only 11K, quite a difference from the original! At 11K, this image can be viewed comfortably because visitors will see it on your Web page in just about one-fifth the time they required to see the original 51K image.

Figure 12.3 shows the newly redesigned Web page. I added a table, changed the way text flowed around the image, and more. You can tell that the most significant and best change comes from the resized image.

Fig. 12.3
Creative use of HTML tags make this page much more attractive.

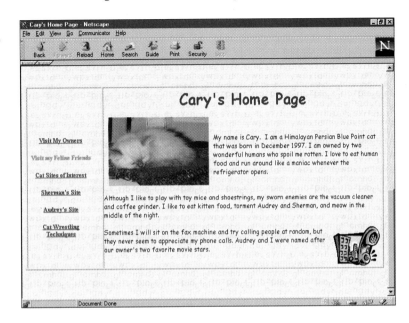

Making Thumbnails

When you resize the graphics on your Web page, you significantly reduce the time it takes visitors to browse your site. Unfortunately, resizing to a smaller image sometimes makes your graphic more difficult to see and less enjoyable for people who really want to see the full-size image. Since the photograph is physically smaller, your visitors have to scrutinize over it more closely to notice smaller, more obscure details.

Imagine that the resized image in figure 12.3 is still too large, and needs further resizing to make it even smaller. Of course, Paint Shop Pro will resize the image for you, but your visitors won't ever get to enjoy the full-size original.

To compensate for this potential problem, many Web sites use a process called *thumbnailing*, which gives visitors the opportunity to see both the large and small versions of a photograph, if they so choose. Thumbnailing is a process by which you display the smaller image on your Web page but add a hyperlink to the larger, full-size graphic. This enables visitors to see the photograph in its original, larger size and form—but only when they choose to.

Thumbnailing is easy. First create and edit the full-sized image. Then, according to the steps outlined in the previous section, make and save a resized version. For this example, I have two files—VERYBIGCAT.JPG and VERYSMALLCAT.JPG. Notice how I named the files accordingly. There is no doubt about which file represents the full-size image of the cat and which is the smaller, or thumbnail-size, version.

Normally, when adding an image to your Web page, you would use the following line of HTML:

```
<IMG SRC="VERYSMALLCAT.JPG">
```

However, when thumbnailing, you want to link your smaller picture to the full-size one. To accomplish this, add the <A HREF> and </A> tags *around* the original image tag:

```
<A HREF="VERYBIGCAT.JPG"><IMG SRC="VERYSMALLCAT.JPG"></A>
```

This line of HTML not only tells your WWW browser to display VERYSMALLCAT.JPG as part of the Web page, but it also tells visitors they can click on that image to download and display VERYBIGCAT.JPG. Your Web browser adds a blue border around the image to indicate that the smaller image links to an additional photograph. Also, your mouse pointer transforms into a hand when placed over the linked image. Figure 12.4 shows the linked image in a browser.

Fig. 12.4
The small cat image is now linked to the larger cat.

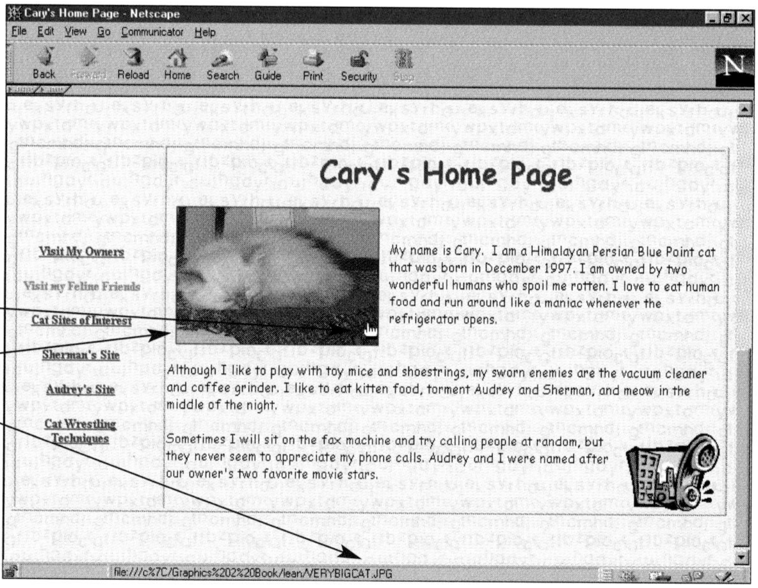

The mouse pointer

blue border

link to image

Cropping

Another way to reduce the size of your Web graphic is to crop it and display a small section of the original image. Image cropping has long been a tool of desktop publishers, newspaper editors, and graphic designers. Often an image includes extra, unnecessary parts that can be cut away. The resulting image is smaller and contains only the useful material.

Here's another example image continuing with the same feline trend. Figure 12.5 shows another image of Cary the kitten. This is another good photo, but we don't need the entire image since only part of it contains the cat. Instead, we want to crop out the non-related material. By cropping to just Cary, we get a smaller image that is much more relevant to the Web site we are creating.

Fig. 12.5
Here's an image that really needs to be cropped.

Part III Advanced Image Techniques

Paint Shop Pro has excellent built-in cropping capabilities. Using your mouse, you can simply indicate which part of the image should be saved and the extraneous parts will be discarded. To crop an image, follow these steps:

1. Load your original image in Paint Shop Pro using the **File, Open** command.

2. Click the Crop icon from the Tool Palette. This permits you to select a rectangular area of your image to crop and save. Make sure the Control Palette is showing and you are in the Tool Controls tab.

3. Using your mouse, select the part of the image you want to crop. Figure 12.6 shows an area being selected within Paint Shop Pro.

Fig. 12.6
I only need the cat from this photo.

The Selected Area to Crop

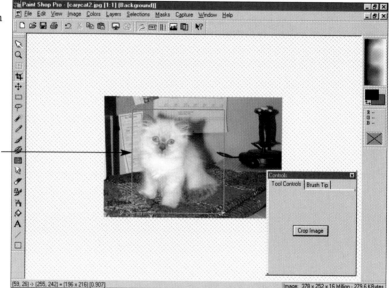

4. Double-click on the cropped area with your left mouse button or click on the Crop Image button on the Control Palette. Paint Shop Pro will keep the selected area and discard the rest of the original image. Figure 12.7 shows the newly cropped area.

Fig. 12.7
Where'd the rest of the
image go?

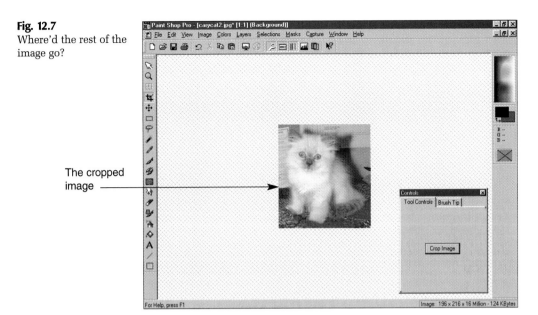

The cropped
image

5. Save your newly cropped image with the **F**ile, Save **A**s command so
    you don't overwrite the original graphic.

For this example, the resultant cropped JPG is only 7K, significantly
smaller than the original, which was around 50K. Since we cropped the
picture instead of resizing it, visitors won't have to squint to see the
image because it is the original size and detail of the photograph.

As with resized images, many Web developers also link the cropped
image to the full-size one. This enables your cropped image to serve as a
thumbnail so that visitors have the option of seeing the entire photo.

Consider cropping images when using them on your Web page. Had I
decided not to crop my cat picture, my visitors would have been forced
to download a large image that included a lot of pointless background
material.

Cropping by Selection

Instead of using the cropping tool, oftentimes you can achieve a similar
effect using the Selection tool. This tool is nice because you can select
rectangular or circular areas of an image, letting you create an odd-shaped
final image. When you use the Selection tool, you have to copy and paste
your selected area as a new image, instead of cropping around the section
you select. Although the technique is different, the results are similar to
what you get when simply using the Crop button.

Part III Advanced Image Techniques

For example, if I wanted to crop an elliptical area around Cary instead of a square, I'd click on the Selection tool. Then Choose **Ellipse** as the Selection type in the Control Palette. Using your Selection tool, you can then draw an elliptical area around the part of the image you want to crop (figure 12.8).

Fig. 12.8
This is how you create an odd-shaped cropped image.

Then choose I**mage**, **C**rop to Selection from the PSP menu bar. Paint Shop Pro crops away all of the unselected area and leaves one with rounded edges. Figure 12.9 shows this image effectively used on Cary's Web page.

Fig. 12.9
The rounded image adds a little personality to this page.

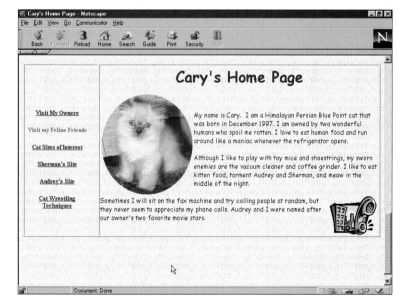

How Many Colors Are Right for a GIF Image?

The number one way to decrease the file size of GIF images is to reduce the number of colors being used in the image. In GIF files, the number of different colors used has a direct correlation to the size of the file. The fewer the colors used, the smaller the file size. The GIF file structure is different from the one JPEG images use, where the file format depends less on the number of colors used, and more on the compression level chosen. You'll learn how to shrink your JPEG images in "JPEG Compression" later in this chapter.

In this section, you'll learn how changing the number of colors can affect the appearance and file size of your image. Reducing the number of colors in a Web graphic offers the highest level of file compression for enhancing performance, but you can lose significant detail from your original full-color image.

How Colors Affect GIF File Size

Actually, the file size isn't as dependent on the *number* of colors used as you might think. The *placement* of colors in an image also affects the GIF file size, as I explain below.

According to the specifications of the GIF format, an image is saved as a series of horizontal lines that go across the screen from left to right. Starting with the first pixel on the left-hand side of the screen, the image records the specifications for that particular color—let's say it's blue. Continuing to the right, one pixel at a time, the GIF assumes that it should continue using the exact same color until a different one is specified. So, if the whole line is a single shade of blue, only one color definition is needed for the whole line of that image. Often a single line of an image contains several different colors. Each time a different color needs to be displayed, that information is saved into the GIF file. Once the right-hand side of the image is reached, the GIF starts over, like a typewriter, and starts defining the next line (pixel by pixel) of colors in the image.

It's easy to see that when the whole image only requires one color, the file is likely to be small because there are no color changes. The more color changes, from left to right, the larger an image. Therefore, a single-color Web graphic that is 300 x 300 pixels is only 1K. However, an image of the same pixel dimensions will have a dramatic increase in file size if it has several different color changes on each line.

Figure 12.10 shows two 300 x 300 images with strikingly different file sizes due to the number of colors and color changes in each one. The image on the left is only 1K, while the image on the right is around 8K. Only fourteen different colors are used in the second example, but there are a lot of different switches back and forth from one color to another.

Fig. 12.10
Same image height and width but completely different file size.

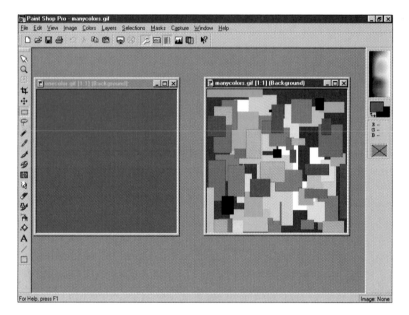

Unfortunately, this strategy only works for GIF images. JPEG files always have 16.7 million colors available and use a file structure and compression scheme different from that used for GIFs. As a result, a large GIF file that uses lots of colors will often significantly improve when converted into the JPEG file type. You'll notice this benefit particularly when working with scanned photographs for your Web page, which always use lots of colors and require a significant number of color changes.

JPEG Compression is not dependent on the number of colors. Instead, JPEG files use a different form of compression that can sometimes lose detail. See Chapter 3, "Creating Simple Graphics," for an in-depth look at the GIF and JPEG file formats.

Usually, you'll want to save your Web graphics in both GIF and JPEG format to see which represents the best file size. Remember that file size isn't the only metric in creating Web graphics. Special features, such as transparency, interlacing, and animation, all have bearing over what file format you choose.

Reducing Colors

Now that you understand the correlation between the number of color changes and the resulting GIF file size, here's how and when colors can be manipulated to reduce your file size. By reducing the number of colors and color changes in an image, you can shrink your image's file size by as much as 75%!

The most popular color-reduction strategy is to take an existing 256-color GIF and transform it into a 16-color image. Paint Shop Pro does all the color mapping and switching for you. This strategy must be used carefully. Sometimes reducing the number of colors degrades your image's appearance to the point where it is not usable on a Web page. You'll have to transform each GIF image individually and evaluate the results yourself.

When you reduce the number of colors, instruct Paint Shop Pro to transform your 256-color image into one that uses only 16 separate and unique colors. Paint Shop Pro tries to match each of the original 256 with one of the 16 remaining. If a close match can't be found, then it alternates the pixels of two similar colors, fooling your eyes. For example, if Paint Shop Pro needs to put a green section on the image, but doesn't have a matching green in its 16-color palette, PSP might mix yellow and blue pixels together. When your eye looks at the image, you'll see the green instead of individual colors.

The first step is to get an idea of how many colors are currently being used in your GIF image. Load your GIF in Paint Shop Pro and choose **C**olors, Co**u**nt Colors Used from the menu bar. A small dialog box will appear (figure 12.11) that will show you the unique number of colors in this image. For this example, my image has 244 different colors. Click on the **OK** button to remove this dialog box.

Part III Advanced Image Techniques

Fig. 12.11
244 colors of the 256 maximum allowed are in use.

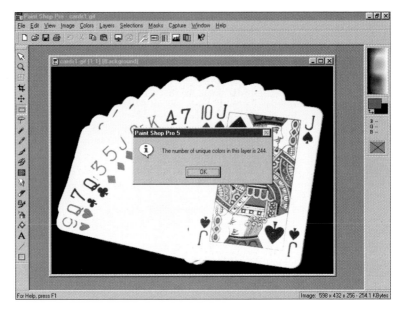

To reduce the number of colors in a GIF, choose **Colors**, **D**ecrease Color Depth, **16** Colors (4 bit) to bring up the Decrease Color Depth dialog box (figure 12.12). This dialog box lets you specify exactly how you want Paint Shop Pro to mix and match hues it doesn't have in its 16-color palette.

Fig. 12.12
The Nearest Color reduction method is often best for most images.

This dialog box has many options available to you, including Palette and Reduction Method, which are explained in the next section. Click **OK** to continue. Paint Shop Pro automatically interpolates your current image and displays the resulting new one to you.

By reducing the number of colors from 256 to 16, you get a wide variety of results, depending on what your original image looked like. For example, figures 12.13a and 12.13b shows an example of a great transformation from a 256-color GIF to a 16-color GIF—you simply cannot tell the difference between the two images. The file results are excellent. The original GIF was 67K, which is too large for most Web pages. After the transformation with Paint Shop Pro, the new GIF is only 29K.

Fig. 12.13a
The original image at
256 colors.

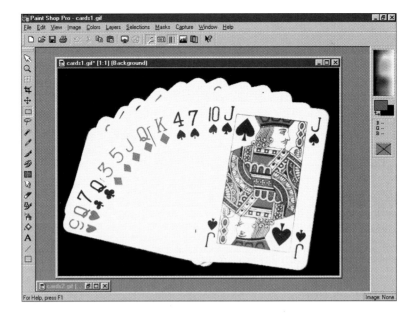

Fig. 12.13b
For substantial
savings, you might as
well use only 16
colors here.

Part III   Advanced Image Techniques

TIP

This is an excellent example of when resizing the image would help. By shrinking the image to half the original size, you don't lose any of the original image's effect—you still see a hand of cards. By shrinking the image and reducing the number of colors to 16, my new image is now only 12K.

Palette

The Palette selections of the Decrease Color dialog box let you tell Paint Shop Pro which set of 16 colors you want to use in the new image.

▶ **Optimized Median Cut**

This option lets Paint Shop Pro automatically select the most appropriate set of 16 colors. So if you are working with an image of a face, it might pick 16 flesh-tone colors, while an image of an ocean might have many blues in the 16-color palette.

▶ **Optimized Octree**

This option uses a standard set of 16 colors that is common across many images in the world. Since this palette isn't optimized for your image, the quality isn't usually as good as Optimized Median Cut Palettes.

▶ **Windows**

The Microsoft Windows specifications name sixteen standard colors that must be supported by color monitors. Choosing this selection optimizes images for Windows machines, but you can lose a lot of quality because of poor dithering.

Almost always, you'll use Optimized Median Cut, which allows Paint Shop Pro to analyze each image individually and find a palette that works best for each situation. But it is often worth testing the other methods to see if the resulting image quality and file size are significantly improved.

Reduction Method

In the Decrease Color dialog box, you can also select a Reduction method for your images:

▶ **Nearest Color**
   This option replaces the original colors with the closest match from the 16 new colors.

▶ **Ordered Dither**
   This option only works with the **Windows'** palette and is optimized for graphics that you are going to print.

▶ **Error Diffusion**
   This option practices the dithering concept so that your image blends together nicely.

Usually you'll use either Nearest Color or Error Diffusion, both of which work well for reducing the number of colors in your images. In fact, you might want to save your original and reduce the number of colors twice, using each Reduction method, to see which one yields the better quality image and which the smaller file size.

Other Color Reduction Examples

Reducing the number of colors you use in your image isn't always a perfect solution. Sometimes you lose significant detail and precision from the original image. This happens primarily when a vast range of different colors is used within a single image. Matching 256 colors to a 16-color set becomes a difficult task. Paint Shop Pro does the best job it can, but as figures 12.14a and b show, sometimes image deformations occur.

In this example, however, we reduced a 150K GIF down to a manageable 40K—just by reducing the number of colors. Although we lose some quality, the performance gains may be worth it for your particular Web site.

Part III Advanced Image Techniques

Fig. 12.14a
The 256 Color GIF

Fig. 12.14b
The poorer 16 color GIF.

Sometimes, of course, reducing the number of colors deforms your original image so much that the results aren't even worth the reduction in file size. Although the above car example lost some detail, the resulting image was still usable. Figures 12.15a and b, below, shows an example where reducing the number of colors just doesn't work.

This picture of an apple branch offers 75% compression when reduced from 243 colors to only 16 colors (101K down to 26K), but nobody would recognize the newly created image if it were added to a Web site. Visitors would certainly not think the site designer put care and time into building Web graphics.

Fig. 12.15a
A decent 256 Color GIF, but at 101 K it's too big for the Web.

Fig. 12.15b
You'll never want this 16-color GIF on your Web site, the quality is too poor.

As you can observe, reducing the number of colors used in a GIF image yields wildly different results, depending on what the original image looked like. The performance results may be marvelous, but you often pay a price in quality and detail. Test your Web images by reducing the number of colors and evaluating the results.

Part III Advanced Image Techniques

JPEG Compression

For GIF images, the best way to reduce file size was to reduce the number of colors in the graphic. As you observed, in some situations you received a huge file savings.

Similarly, the JPEG file format allows you to tweak performance and file-size metrics, but in a different manner. The JPEG file format allows you to specify how much detail/compression should be used when saving a file. The higher the compression setting, the smaller the overall file size. Of course, there's no such thing as a free lunch. By compressing JPEG images, you lose some image quality. This loss isn't usually noticeable—unless you have an extremely high-resolution image with lots of details, or until the compression level is very high.

In Paint Shop Pro, JPEG image compression is selected when you are saving your graphics. Open any JPEG image and choose **File**, Save **As** to bring up the PSP Save As dialog box. Select the JPG file format and click on the **O**ptions button to bring up the Save Options dialog box (figure 12.16).

Fig. 12.16
JPEG Compression is controlled here.

You'll find a bar in this dialog box with which you can set the JPEG compression level. The default compression level is 15, which is optimal for JPEG file size and image quality. You can drag the bar right and left to increase or decrease JPEG compression levels. Alternatively, you can type in a compression level with your keyboard.

Compression levels range from 1 to 99. The higher the number, the better compression your JPEG will use and, consequently, the smaller the resulting file size will be. When the image is saved, the compression level is also saved with the image. Click **OK** to return to the Save As dialog box. From here you can specify a file name for your JPEG image.

Let's look at an example of how JPEG compression affects the way images appear on a Web page. Figure 12.17 shows the same JPG image displayed in six different compression levels ranging from 01 to 99. Each image is labeled with the compression level used and the file size of the image when saved at that level. Unless you have tremendous eyes, you probably can't detect much difference between the images using compression levels 1, 15, 40, and 60. However, the images using 80 and 99 compression settings are of noticeably lower quality and are probably not worth the file savings because of the image degradation.

Fig. 12.17
Four of these six images are virtually interchangeable.

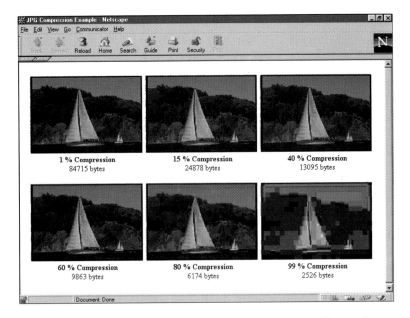

In general, compression levels above 75 provide so much interference that your image becomes unusable. Since my original image was 25K at a compression level of 15, and only 9K at compression level 60, it's easy to see how effective JPEG compression can be.

Much like reducing the number of colors used in GIF images, saving your JPEG at several different compression levels is a great idea. Doing so gives you the opportunity to compare the files and choose the level that has the smallest file size yet retains quality. This example alone provided nearly a 70% reduction in file size with no significant reduction in image quality.

Part III   Advanced Image Techniques

Using Interlaced and Progressive Images

Back in Chapter 3, "Creating Simple Graphics," you learned about interlaced GIFs and progressive JPEG graphics. You learned that interlaced GIFs display themselves in several passes, with each pass becoming more detailed and clearer.

Interlaced GIFs are nice when downloading a gigantic GIF, because you can get a general idea of what the image looks like as it is downloading—a nice feature for visitors using a slower modem. The JPEG file format allows similar functionality when saving an image in the Progressive JPEG format.

Saving an image in either an interlaced or progressive format is simple. After creating your image, choose **F**ile, Save **A**s to bring up the Save As dialog box. Interlaced and Progressive settings are both selected by clicking on the **O**ptions button after you have selected the file format you want to use for your graphic.

Figure 12.18 shows the GIF image options. When saving a GIF, you can choose between Interlaced and Noninterlaced image formats. Click on the proper radio button then click **OK.**

Fig. 12.18
Interlaced images are the way to go for larger Web graphics.

Similarly, figure 12.19 shows the Save Options dialog box for JPEG images. With JPEGs, you can use Standard or Progressive Encoding.

Fig. 12.19
Progressively encoded JPEGs work like interlaced GIFs.

As a general rule, saving your images in Interlaced or Progressive format is only useful when dealing with images that are 10K or larger. For smaller icons, buttons, and bars, don't worry about Interlaced or Progressive formats; such images are so small that they download almost instantaneously.

Saving in Interlaced or Progressive format makes your image file around 10% larger than the original file, but the benefit is well worth the increased file size when you are saving larger images. Allowing visitors to see a rough outline of an image as it downloads increases usability for a Web page because visitors can start reading information on that page before the whole image is completely downloaded. Figures 12.20 and 12.21 show an interlaced image being downloaded from the WWW.

Fig. 12.20
This interlaced image has just finished its first pass.

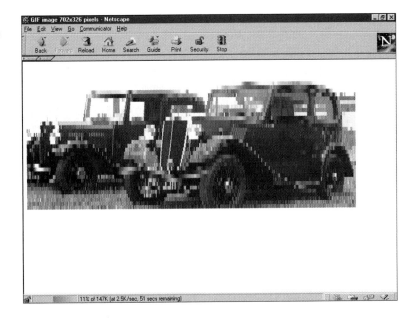

Fig. 12.21
Now the interlaced image has become completely clear.

Part III Advanced Image Techniques

Part IV

Practical Use of Images on Your Web Pages

13

Web Graphics as Image Maps

Normally, images appear on your Web page as decoration, to make your site more colorful, fun, and enjoyable. In Chapter 6, "Picture Tubes and Web Graphics," you learned how PSP can be used to make many different types of effective images on your Web page. Much of this book is geared toward using PSP to build images from scratch. In this chapter, I'll show you how to take your images one step further and put them to work for you.

These enhanced Web graphics, called *image maps,* are easy to use and have become a popular tool among Web creators all over the world. Using image maps, you can link different areas of a single image to different HTML files, or URLs. This lets visitors to your Web page navigate from page to page by using their mouse to select different areas of an image.

In this chapter, I'll show you how image maps work, explain what kinds of images do and do not work as image maps, and introduce you to the necessary tools for creating your own image map.

▶ **Understand How Image Maps Work**
Clickable image maps are easy to use and add a useful dimension to Web pages, as long as you understand exactly how they work when visitors stop by.

▶ **Build a Simple Image Map for Your Web Page**
Nothing demonstrates how easy image maps are to create as does making one on your own—with the right tools.

▶ **Link Sections of Images to Other HTML Files on the Web**
Learn how the mechanics of the HTML tags actually link different sections of a picture to separate HTML files.

How Do Image Maps Work?

You are already familiar with adding graphics inline to Web pages. By embedding the <IMG> tag inside a Hypertext reference, you can create links from images, just as you would from text. Look at the following HTML example:

```
<A HREF="ROME.HTML"> <IMG SRC="ROME.GIF"> </A>
```

Shown in figure 13.1, this example adds an image of the Coliseum in Rome to my Web page. When visitors click the image, the browser automatically loads the file ROME.HTML.

Fig. 13.1
Linking an image to
an HTML page is easy.

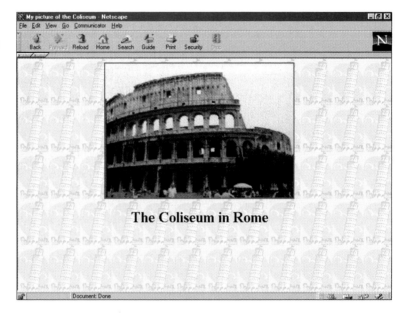

No matter where on the picture you click, you always link to ROME.HTML. This is where an image map could come into play. Using an image map, you can link different areas of an image to different HTML files, based on what section of the image is clicked.

This is an extremely useful technique because it lets visitors who see this Web page get accustomed to a single image, and lets them navigate from page to page by clicking different sections of that image.

Part IV   Practical Use of Images

Look at the L.L. Bean home page **(http://www.llbean.com)** for an excellent example of an image map (see figure 13.2). Here, the developers have included a picture of a skier and then three different "buttons" at the bottom of the image. This is really just one image, different parts of which are linked to different pages. There is never any doubt where you'll go when you click somewhere in this well-designed site.

Fig. 13.2
L.L. Bean bundles up
its Web site nicely!

There are many good uses for image maps. For example, Italy might place a virtual map online. Using your mouse, you would click whichever region or city of Italy you wanted to learn more about. Clicking Rome might bring up the Coliseum, and Pisa could link to the famous leaning tower. Or Boeing might place a picture of its gigantic 777 plane on the WWW. Visitors could click different parts of the cockpit to learn how the plane operates.

Virtually any image can become an image map—and they're easy to create. With the right tools, image maps can easily be designed and incorporated into a Web site within minutes.

Image Maps Are Not New Technology

Clickable image maps have been around for a long time. If you knew the right steps to follow, you have always been able to add one to your Web page. With the release of Netscape 2.0, though, adding image maps to your Web page has become significantly less complicated.

Previously, to add a clickable image map to your Web page, you were dependent on your Web server software. Called *server-side image maps*, your Web server software controlled all access to image maps at a particular Internet site. To add an image map to your page, you had to find the right image, decide how each part of the image would link to a different HTML file, and then set up and customize your server properly. This was quite a hassle, even for people who understood every step—and some Web servers don't permit image maps to run on them. Therefore, using server-side image maps on Web pages was essentially limited to professional Web developers and larger companies; few individuals used them on personal Web pages.

Today, creating image maps is much easier. A new development called *client-side image maps* makes it easier for individual Web page developers—like you—to add clickable image maps to a Web page. More image maps are being created every day because they are now relatively easy to set up.

Client-side image maps (called CSIM for short) are significantly simpler, easier to use, and more efficient when they interact with Web servers. As far as users can tell, the same image appears on-screen, but what happens when they click the image is different. Web browsers automatically know which HTML file to link to—and take you there automatically when you click on an image. Each region in the image has its pixel coordinates defined within the same HTML file as the rest of the Web page, so you can link to another page of HTML just as if it were using a normal <u><A HREF></u> tag.

Creating an Image Map

Since client-side image maps are easy to create, maintain, and use, server-side image maps are rarely created nowadays. Although many exist on the WWW today, server-side image maps are older technology and will eventually be out of use completely. It's time to learn how to build a client-side image map on a Web page.

Finding a Good Image

When creating image maps, the first step is to select a good image to use. Make sure that it will be clear to visitors who see the image that they can select from several different areas on the picture to link to different items. Select definitive images with different regions that are easily delineated on-screen and make sense to visitors.

Figure 13.3 shows a sample image that will make for an excellent Client-Side Image Map for the ACME Block Company. Of course, this is a contrived example, but you can easily see how each box will take you to a different Web site.

Fig. 13.3
The big blocks make it easy for users to identify the different regions of the image map.

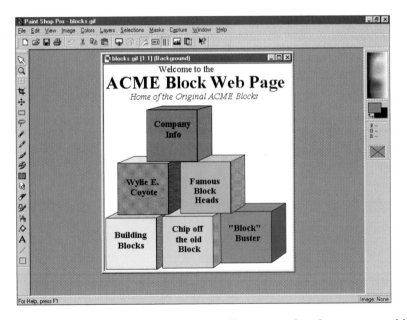

Image maps can be created from virtually any graphic that you can add to your Web page. Icons, buttons, bars, pictures, and images of all types can be sectioned out and presented as an image map for visitors. Not all images, however, make sense for use as image maps.

In general, pictures become difficult image maps because they often lack clearly defined areas for the user to click. Recall the picture of the Coliseum earlier in the chapter (see figure 13.1)—this image wouldn't be a good image map because it doesn't include well-defined areas within the large image of the Coliseum. But you can easily create good candidates with Paint Shop Pro. For example, figure 13.4 shows an alternative Italian image that might make a good image map.

Fig. 13.4
Each city represents a new link for this image.

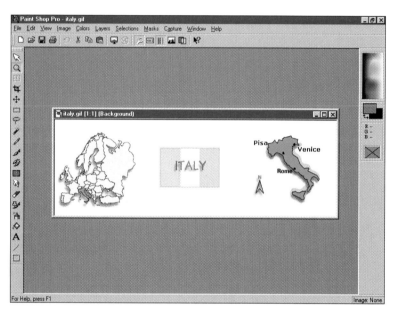

TIP

Maps often work well as image maps because they offer clear delimiters and borders. The maps and flag from figure 13.4 were found at **http://www.graphicmaps.com**, a free encyclopedia containing hundreds of different maps you can use when developing your Web site.

Planning the Map

Once you've selected an image, the next step is to logically divide it into different regions and define how you want the image map to work.

For this sample block graphic, each individual block should be linked to a separate Web page (see figure 13.5).

Fig. 13.5
Planning each link from
your image map is an
important step.

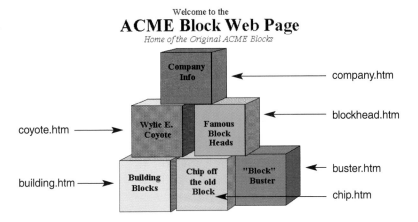

Welcome to the
ACME Block Web Page
Home of the Original ACME Blocks

company.htm

blockhead.htm

coyote.htm

buster.htm

building.htm

chip.htm

Once you have a good idea of how to divide your image map, you're
ready to take the next step: adding the necessary HTML tags to your
Web page.

When you create an image map, it is important to realize that you are
now working with multiple Web pages. You are creating a path that
visitors can use to explore the different aspects of your site.

For more information on creating a set of themed images for your entire
site, check out Chapter 6, "Picture Tubes and Web Graphics."

CAUTION
Make sure that each HTML file your image links to actually exists. It's easy to
forget to create one or more of the HTML files when you create your image
map before completing all your files.

Finding the Right Tools

Once you've created/selected the image to use, the difficult part is
finished. Now it's time to start building the Image map. Image maps are
part of the HTML language, and require several advanced and
complicated tags in order to work properly. Basically, you need to define
each region on the image graphically and point that region to another
Web page.

Think of each image as a large piece of graph paper, on which you have
to identify the exact X and Y coordinates for each section that links to an
HTML file. For images, coordinates are measured in pixels (the dot
resolution of your computer monitor). You have to specify the pixel
dimensions of each section so it will properly link to an HTML file.

Fortunately, several handy tools exist that make specifying each distinct section for the image map easy. One of the best, LiveImage, has become the standard in the Image Map arena. LiveImage lets you graphically draw the different coordinates on your image and map each section to a different URL without learning any complex codes or HTML tags.

LiveImage is shareware software, meaning you can download and use it for 14 days before deciding whether you want to register it for $29.99 or not. You can download LiveImage from **http://www.mediatec.com**. Once you download the latest version, install it by double-clicking on the downloaded file from the Windows Explorer. LiveImage will take you through a simple installation routine that will have you up and running in short time. Figure 13.6 shows the home page of Mediatec, the maker of LiveImage.

Fig. 13.6
Find the latest version of LiveImage here.

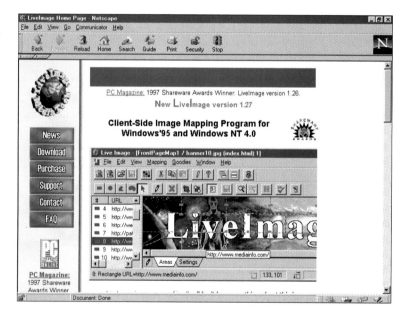

NOTE

Literally dozens of different programs can take care of Image mapping for you automatically. In fact, many HTML editors such as Microsoft FrontPage, Hotdog, or HoTMetaL Pro come with this functionality built in so you won't have to buy a separate program.

This chapter shows you how LiveImage, the best image map–only program out there, works. You can also choose to create your image maps using one of many other software programs, all of which follow a very similar procedure.

Using the LiveImage Wizard

This section takes you through creating a complete image map from scratch using LiveImage.

1. Once you've downloaded and installed LiveImage, run it from your Windows Start button. If you haven't registered it yet, LiveImage tells you how many days you have left before the program will stop working. The Welcome to LiveImage dialog box appears (figure 13.7).

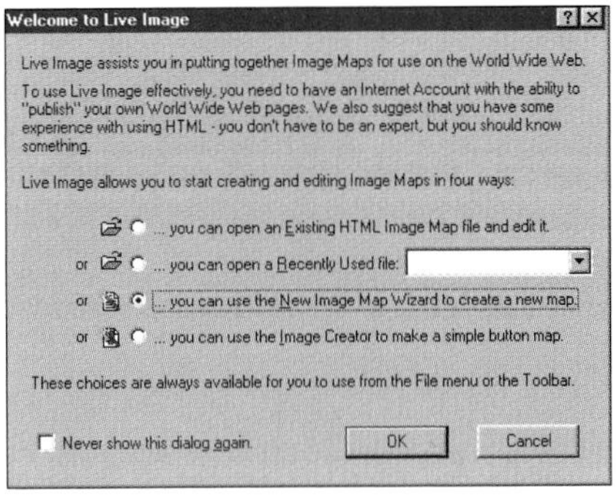

Fig. 13.7
LiveImage has several "wizards" built in to make building and editing image maps very easy.

2. LiveImage lets you edit previously existing image maps or create your own. For this example, I will select **New Image Map Wizard to create a new map** and click on the OK button. Figure 13.8 shows the New Image map dialog box that appears.

Fig. 13.8
Either add to an existing or create a new HTML file with the Image Map Wizard.

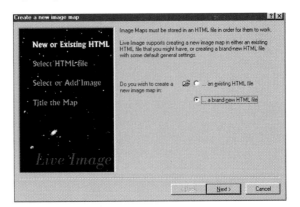

3. You can choose to add your image map to an existing file, or create a new HTML file from scratch. I'll choose to create a new HTML file for this example. Click on the Next button to continue.

4. LiveImage next wants to create and name your HTML file. Choose the proper folder on your system to place the new HTML file and click on the Next button.

5. Next, LiveImage asks for the GIF or JPG file to use as the image map. Again, find the graphic on your computer and then click on the NEXT button. Figure 13.9 shows me pointing to blocks.gif for this example.

Fig. 13.9
You're almost
finished!

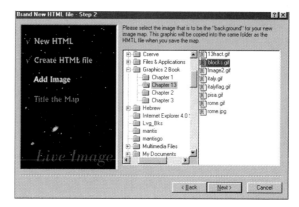

6. The final step in this wizard lets you name your image map. The name is important because multiple image maps can occur within a single Web page, and this is how the browser knows which set of coordinates to use with each image. Name the image (figure 13.10) and click on the **Finish** button.

Fig. 13.10
Always use a
descriptive name for
each image map to
make future editing
easier.

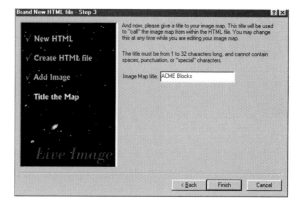

Mapping Each Section

Once you've completed the LiveImage Wizard for setting up the HTML and graphics files you want to use, you are ready to start associating each section of your image with another Web URL.

You can create three types of image map sections—rectangles, circles, and polygons. To create any of these area types, simply select the proper LiveImage tool button then draw the shape on your image. Figure 13.11 shows the LiveImage window with callouts to all three shapes you can draw.

Fig. 13.11
From here, you can
map the image with
your mouse.

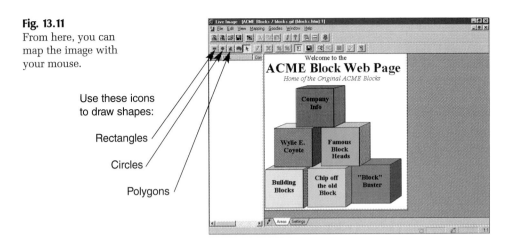

Use these icons
to draw shapes:

Rectangles

Circles

Polygons

For example, to draw a rectangle on the screen, click on the rectangle
icon. Then you need to point out the top left and bottom right corners for
the rectangle on your image. Simply hold down your mouse button, and
LiveImage draws your rectangle automatically. Once you let go of the
mouse button, LiveImage prompts you with an Area Settings dialog box,
where you set the URL for this region (figure 13.12).

Fig. 13.12
Point the region of the
image map to the
proper HTML file.

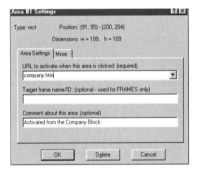

LiveImage shows each region in a list on the left-hand side of the screen
and places a slight grid over your image. This grid doesn't actually appear
on your graphic; it is intended to let you know which parts of your image
are and which parts are not linked.

Now, repeat this step as many times as you'd like, drawing rectangles,
circles, or polygons on your image. Each time you create a new region,
LiveImage will prompt you for the URL of the page to which you want
the region to link.

Figure 13.13 shows the block image with six different regions filled out.

Fig. 13.13
This Image Map is
ready to go!

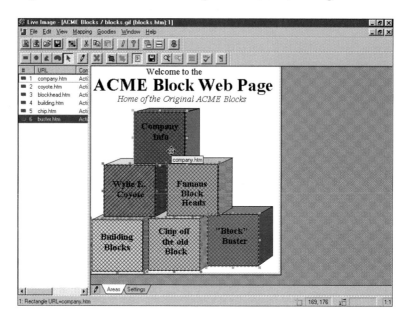

TIP

When you are entering the URL of the file to which you want the region to
link, remember that you have the option of typing in a full URL like the
following:

```
http://www.muskalipman.com/graphics/ACME/company.html
```

or a relative URL and filename such as:

```
ACME/company.html
```

or simply a filename if the file is in the same directory as the image map file:

```
company.html
```

Make sure that you correctly type the full path for the HTML file you want
linked to this region.

CAUTION

The Shareware version of LiveImage only lets you have six different regions on
your image map. Once you register your software, you can have an unlimited
number of different shapes and regions for each image on your page.

Once all your regions have been defined, choose File, Save from the
menu bar, and LiveImage will add the proper set of codes to the HTML
file you set up in the Image Map Wizard.

Now you are ready to load this page into your favorite Web browser. LiveImage created all the complex codes and tags for you. Just for your reference, here is the HTML that was generated for this example:

```
<!— Image tags modified by LiveImage for Client Side Image Map
    insertion —>
<IMG SRC="blocks.gif" USEMAP="#ACME Blocks" BORDER=0 WIDTH=400
    HEIGHT=430></P>
<!— Start of Client Side Image Map information —>
<MAP NAME="ACME Blocks">
<!— #$-:Created by LiveImage available at
    http://www.mediatec.com —>
<!— #$-:Unregistered copy (Andy Shafran) —>
<!— #$VERSION:1.27b —>
<!— #$DATE:Wed Feb 04 21:35:11 1998 —>
<!— #$GIF:blocks.gif —>
<AREA SHAPE=RECT COORDS="91,95,200,204" HREF="company.htm">
<AREA SHAPE=RECT COORDS="28,206,137,315" HREF="coyote.htm">
<AREA SHAPE=RECT COORDS="161,203,270,312"
    HREF="blockhead.htm">
<AREA SHAPE=RECT COORDS="2,319,111,428" HREF="building.htm">
<AREA SHAPE=RECT COORDS="122,317,231,426" HREF="chip.htm">
<AREA SHAPE=RECT COORDS="247,308,356,417" HREF="buster.htm">
</MAP>
<!— End of Client Side Image Map information —>
```

You wouldn't want to have to create that from hand!

Figure 13.14 shows what this sample image map looks like in a browser. Notice how the status bar at the bottom of the screen shows the URL which this block links to.

Fig. 13.14
Here's the finished product—the ACME Block image map.

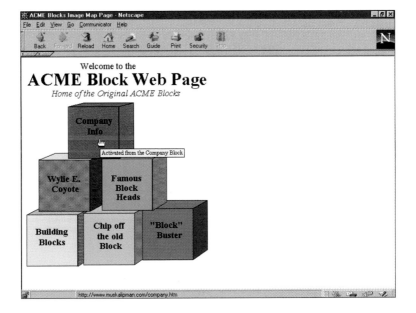

Test the Image Map with Browsers

Once you're finished creating the image map, make sure you test it thoroughly with Netscape or Internet Explorer (or both). Test every region, one at a time, to make sure that your links have been created properly.

Many people overlook this step, assuming that they didn't make any mistakes as long as they followed the above steps exactly; however, typos, incorrect filenames, and other mistakes can easily create flaws in your image map.

Providing a Textual Alternative

Although virtually all new Web browsers support client-side image maps, it's always a good idea to provide some sort of textual alternative. This accommodates visitors to your page who are using a browser that doesn't read client-side image maps, or who don't want to wait for the entire image to download before selecting a region on the image map.

Figure 13.15 shows how the ACME Block home page is updated to have textual links as well as graphical ones. Using a two-column table with the left-hand column displaying the main image map, and the right-hand column showing a simple list of links, this page balances Web graphics and text well.

Fig. 13.15
This simple table provides an alternative to using my image map.

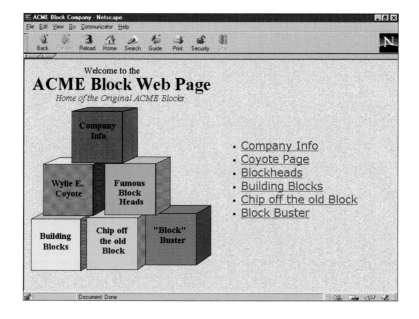

Image Map Design Tips

This section consolidates several important tips you should keep in mind when you begin using client-side image maps in your Web pages. Some of them repeat information presented throughout this chapter, others provide additional information. Basically, this is a last-minute checklist for you to run through before you let everyone on the Web have access to your image maps:

▶ **Be careful of file size.** Images that are mapped tend to have larger file sizes because they usually appear larger on-screen. Make sure that your image's file size isn't outrageous (for instance, above 100K); otherwise, visitors to your Web page will become impatient. Chapter 12, "Making Your Graphics Lean" contains many tips for keeping images small and to the point.

▶ **Use interlaced images.** *Interlaced images* are those that load in multiple levels, starting out fuzzy and slowly becoming more detailed. Interlaced images are ideal for image maps because, as soon as visitors recognize which area they want to click, they don't have to wait for the whole image to appear.

▶ **Define mapped areas clearly.** Make sure that you use an image that makes it easy for visitors to know which sections are mapped to other HTML files. It's easy for visitors to overlook small areas (or illogical areas) on an image map.

▶ **Test your image map at least twice.** I can't stress this enough. I've seen too many image maps that haven't been tested thoroughly. Usually, some regions link properly to files, but other regions don't. Nobody enjoys using an untested image map.

14

Background Graphics and Colors

Web page backgrounds are much like art gallery or museum backdrops on which graphics, images, and text are displayed. Backgrounds can be made from any digital image or can simply be any solid color. Because backgrounds often set the mood of a page, you should give some serious thought to your background choice before making a final decision. The background is often the first thing a viewer sees, is a major factor in defining the style and mood of your page, and can greatly add to or detract from the content and the design. It has the potential to grab visitors so they want to stay and see more or to cause viewers to go somewhere else. The background, therefore, should contribute to the style of the page, help set its mood, and invite viewers to stay.

This chapter shows you how to create and use many different types of backgrounds on your Web pages. Specifically, in this chapter you'll learn about:

▶ **Understanding How Backgrounds Work**
Backgrounds load behind the rest of a Web page. You'll see how they work and how to add them to your site.

▶ **Creating Backgrounds Using Paint Shop Pro 5**
You will create two very different backgrounds in Paint Shop Pro 5 using step-by-step tutorials.

▶ **Customizing More Advanced Backgrounds**
You'll make backgrounds with depth using text, images, and logos that don't distract from the content of your page and are customized to your needs.

Understanding How Backgrounds Work

Browsers display Web page backgrounds by reading the HTML code written by the designer. Other objects (text, images, tables, and forms) are displayed on top of the background. Solid-colored backgrounds are added by sending the browser the color you want to use, while images are created in PSP then downloaded by the browser along with your Web page.

Figure 14.1 shows a simple small image in Paint Shop Pro. When this image is used, the browser loads the background image and "tiles" it across and down the page. The tiled image will repeat various times, depending upon the size of the image and the screen size (see figure 14.2). Consider the way each image or graphic tiles, and visually test it at various screen sizes to be sure it tiles well.

Fig. 14.1
A simple pink dot background image is created easily in Paint Shop Pro 5.

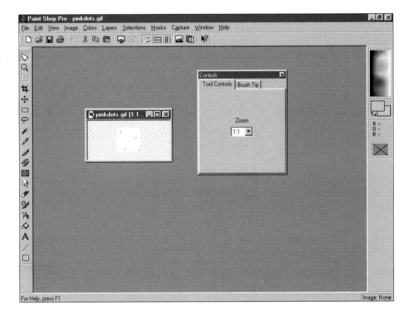

Fig. 14.2
Here the pink dot
background image is
tiled by the browser
across and down the
screen.

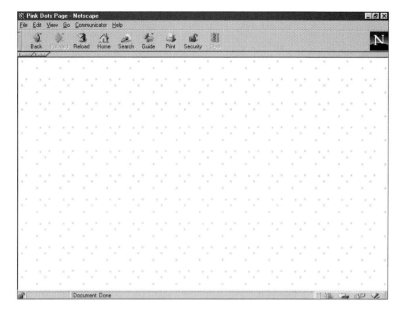

In this chapter we will discuss what kinds of backgrounds suit your
pages and how to create unique ones using Paint Shop Pro 5.

TIP

In general, the texture or images on the background should be subtle and
add depth to the page; backgrounds should never be so distracting that
viewers can't read the text.

Backgrounds come in two main types:

Solid Color — Any plain, flat solid color can be added as a
background using only HTML code. No image is required for this. All
you need to know is the name (or number) of the color.

Images — Any GIF or JPG image can be used as a background. The
image will be tiled across and down the screen by the browser. (refer
to figure 14.2 again).

The type of background you choose depends on what mood or style you
are trying to create, as well as how many images you already plan to use
on your page. Solid single-color backgrounds are the easiest to add, and
they display very quickly. Graphic or image backgrounds can add a
unique flavor of their own but take more time to load.

Using Solid Color Backgrounds

A solid-color background can be used as a stand-alone background or in conjunction with a graphics background. By simply adding a solid color background to a Web page, the designer can add mood, enhance the images on a page and keep page-loading time to an absolute minimum. Some images look best when presented on a flat, solid-color background rather than a textured or multi-colored background. Figure 14.3 shows the All About Dogs Hotlinks page:
http://www.ptialaska.net/~pkalbaug/hotlinks.html.

Fig. 14.3
This site is designed using a solid blue background with colorful graphics displayed on top.

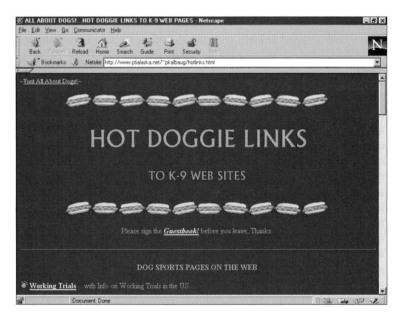

Web designers often use solid-colored backgrounds when testing during the initial design phase of a Web site to determine on which main color background their images display best. Once a main color is chosen, the designer will find or create a background graphic that approximates that color.

Advantages of using a solid-color background include:

▶ The page loads quickly, especially if you have other large graphics on the page.

▶ Creates mood and enhances the style of the page.

▶ The page designer, not the viewer, controls the color.

▶ Text will be readable if the viewer has images turned off, especially if some text on the page is light.

▶ Unless the color is poorly chosen, the background color won't detract from other images on the page.

Using the Sixteen Named Colors

The easiest way to add a solid background color to a Web page is by using one of the standard sixteen named colors within the HTML BODY tag:

```
<BODY BGCOLOR="TEAL">
```

This code, added to your HTML file, loads a teal background on your Web page.

Currently, sixteen different named colors are accepted by the W3C, a group of interested parties that sets the HTML standards for the World Wide Web. Because the sixteen standard colors developed by the W3C should display similarly in all browsers, I advise you to stick with them.

The sixteen colors supported by the W3C HTML Standard are shown in table 14.1 below:

Table 14.1
The sixteen named colors and their HEX code equivalents

Named Color	HEX Code	Color Swatch
Aqua	00FFFF	
Black	000000	
Blue	0000FF	
Fuchsia	FF00FF	
Grey	808080	
Green	008000	
Lime	00FF00	
Maroon	800000	
Navy	000080	
Olive	808000	
Purple	800080	
Red	FF0000	
Silver	C0C0C0	
Teal	008080	
White	FFFFFF	
Yellow	FFFF00	

Using named colors gives you the advantage of not having to convert the RGB decimal values to Hex codes. You are, however, limited in the number of colors from which you can choose; the full gamut of 16.7 million colors is not available via specific color names. Some older browsers may not support all named colors, although this is becoming less of a concern today.

NOTE

Netscape, Microsoft, and Web TV have expanded the standard 16-color selection to include 256 named colors. To see what colors Netscape, Microsoft, and Web TV currently support, go to:

http://www.htmlcompendium.org/colors.htm

Be careful when you use nonstandard named colors developed by Microsoft, Netscape, and Web TV, as they may not display the same in all browsers.

Using Hexadecimal Colors

Many times you'll want to use colors other than the standard 16 or 256 named ones provided. Like any good artist, you want to use the whole spectrum available. Instead of using a named color in your HTML tag, you can use its hexadecimal equivalent:

```
<BODY BGCOLOR="#EE8ZEE">
```

The tag above would set your Web page background to Violet.

All 16.7 million colors available are indicated by a special six-digit hexadecimal code. Hexadecimal digits range from 0–9 and A–F and are made up of three pairs of two digits that tell browsers how to mix different shades of red, green, and blue to make all the possible colors in the spectrum.

Actually, Hexadecimal colors aren't special colors at all. They are computer codes used for designating RGB colors in Web pages. The RGB color space uniquely identifies millions of different colors by using three separate numbers from 0–255 for each component color (red, green, and blue). The first number expresses how much red is in a particular color, the second how much green, and the third how much blue, hence RGB.

At one end of the spectrum, pure black is expressed in **Decimal** format as R=0, G=0, B=0 or 0,0,0; at the other end of the spectrum, pure white is expressed in decimal format as 255,255,255. Pure red (red with no green or blue added) is expressed as 255,0,0; pure green is 0,255,0; and pure blue is 0,0,255.

Part IV   Practical Use of Images

Unfortunately, browsers can't simply say they want color 255,212,081—they have to translate those numbers into Hexadecimal, which is a Base 16 counting system.

NOTE

Counting in hexadecimal is easy, once you understand how it works. Here are the numbers 0–19 in Hexadecimal format:

00 01 02 03 04 05 06 07 08 09 0A 0B 0C 0D 0E 0F 11 12 13 14

So the number 10 actually equals #0A in hexadecimal. Counting all the way up to 255 in hexadecimal yields #FF in this alternative counting language.

This counting is important to you because, when you see the hexadecimal color #0AFF13, you can now get a rough idea of what that color will look like (probably greenish because of the high green value).

Don't worry if hexadecimal counting seems confusing to you, because you don't have to translate between it very often. Usually, PSP tells you the hexadecimal equivalent of a color you want to use without any hassle.

Now that you roughly understand what a hexadecimal color is, and how it relates to RGB, let's explain why this is important to Paint Shop Pro. In PSP, every color you paint with is assigned an RGB and hexadecimal value, which shows up by default within the Color Picker. Figure 14.4 shows the default PSP Color dialog box, which gives you both color translation values of your colors.

Fig. 14.4
All colors have RGB and Hexadecimal values.

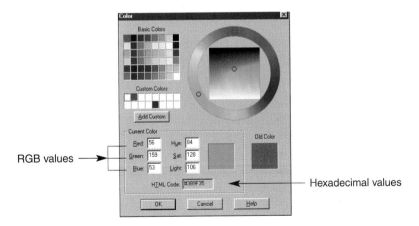

RGB values

Hexadecimal values

Remember that any of the named colors can be used if you type their hexadecimal equivalent. So to use the greenish background in figure 14.4, you'd use the following HTML tag:

```
<BODY BGCOLOR="#389F35">
```

Using Images as Backgrounds

Besides using a single color, you can also create a unique background with a graphic or image. This happens when you add a slightly different attribute to the existing <BODY> tag and upload the graphic to the server along with the revised HTML code. The graphic or image must be in GIF or JPG format.

TIP

You can find many ready-made background graphics in graphic libraries on the Web, or you may create your own. Creating your own background graphics ensures that your page will have a one-of-a-kind setting. Plus it's fun! Appendix A, "Graphical Resources on the Web" suggests several sites with backgrounds you can use. One of my favorites is Realm Graphics located at **http://www.ender-design.com/rg/.**

When graphics or images are used as backgrounds, the browser tiles the image across and down the screen (figure 14.2). Choose an image that you think might work well on your page. Remember that any pattern on the background will repeat itself across and down the page. Some backgrounds that look nice as a stand-alone 100 x 100 pixel graphic may not work well when tiled or may be too distracting for users to read the text from the page.

Save the image to the same directory as the HTML file and add the following attribute to the <BODY> tag of your HTML file:

```
<BODY BACKGROUND="mybg.gif">
```

Remember, keep the image small—in both dimension and file size. Smaller images load faster and tile more efficiently. Large graphics take a long time to download, do not tile well, and may look unusual at various screen sizes. As a rule of thumb, a background graphic should have dimensions no larger than 100 x 100 pixels and a file size under 10KB—the smaller, the better.

Using a Solid Color and Image Together

Many Web designers will use both a solid background and a graphic or image background in the BODY tag. When used together, the solid background will pre-load and be visible before and until the graphic background drops into the page. This Web design trick ensures that viewers will be able to read the text until the background loads and makes the transition less shocking when the graphic background finally loads.

When using both attributes, the body tag looks like this:

```
<BODY BGCOLOR="TEAL" BACKGROUND="tealbg.gif">
```

Adding a BGCOLOR attribute (alone or in conjunction with the BACKGROUND attribute) has the advantage of putting the Web designer in control of the background color, even when viewers have changed their default background color settings or are browsing with their images turned off.

Creating Simple Backgrounds

Now that you understand all about using images in the background of your Web pages, it is time to use Paint Shop Pro to make some for you.

The first background I will create is the "Pink Dots" example that was shown in figures 14.1 and 14.2.

Create a new 50 x 50 image with a white background.

Click on the Paint Brushes icon. Open up the Control Palette, click on the Brush Tip tab and change your settings so you have a small round brush (size = 6). Click on the Tool Controls tab and make sure that Paper Texture is set to 'None'.

Choose a light color (I chose a dusty rose color #FFADAD or 255, 178, 178).

Dab some dots on the image with the paint brush (figure 14.5).

Fig. 14.5
This Pink Dot background image was created in Paint Shop Pro.

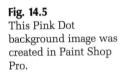

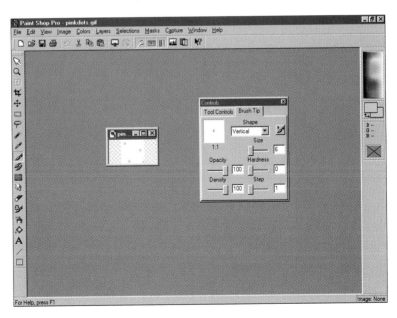

Save your image into the same directory as your HTML files, then add it to the background of your Web page.

Tile the image using the BACKGROUND attribute and visually test it in an HTML document with some text added (figure 14.6). Notice how your browser automatically tiles the image across and down the screen.

Fig. 14.6
Testing the new background in a browser.

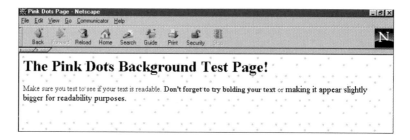

Making Cool Textured Backgrounds

With that simple Background graphic under our belt, let's move to a graphic with some texture!

Open a new image—size 75 x 75 pixels, white background color, 16.7 million colors.

Set your foreground color to 255, 128, 0 (or #FF8000) and the background color to white: 255, 255, 255 (or #FFFFFF).

Choose the airbrush tool. Then go to the Tool Controls tab of the Control Palette. From the 'Paper Texture' drop-down box, choose 'Fruit Peel.' Set the brush options under the Brush Tip tab in the Control Palette dialog box to the following (see figure 14.7):

> Shape=Round
>
> Brush Options=Normal
>
> Size=110
>
> Opacity=32
>
> Hardness=100
>
> Density=11
>
> Step=1

Fig. 14.7
Airbrush settings for
creating orange peel
texture

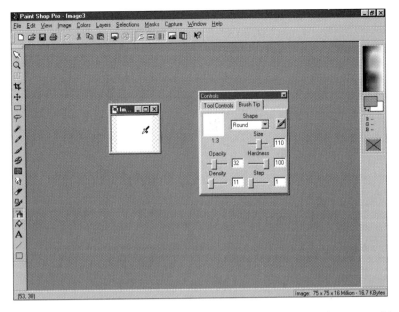

With the airbrush tool, click and drag the mouse quickly but smoothly across the center of the image from left to right to apply color once or possibly twice, depending upon how much color you want to add (see figure 14.7 again).

If you're happy with your image, save it as a GIF file. Figure 14.8 shows my resulting image.

Fig. 14.8
My Orange Peel
graphic.

Then, visually test it as potential background by tiling the image on-screen in an HTML file with text and images over it. Some images, such as this goldfish, work fine on this background; but even black text is somewhat hard to read (figure 14.9).

Fig. 14.9
This image makes a decent background, but could use improvement for tiling and text readability.

Experiment with other brushes and settings. Check out other paper textures as well as other tools and colors. Have fun and let your creativity blossom!

Achieving the Seamless Effect

I'm sure you have seen many backgrounds on the Web that could benefit from Paint Shop Pro's seamless option. The orange peel texture from figure 14.9 is a perfect example!

What is a seamless background?

A seamless background is one that doesn't show lines, or seams, between the tiles. If you look closely at the orange peel background, you can still see seams along the edge of the image (see fig 14.9 again).

Use seamless images for your background graphics to hide abrupt color changes or visible lines that distract when viewed or tiled in a browser.

TIP

Paint Shop Pro's seamless tool works best when you want to tile only a fairly small portion of an image or graphic.

If you want to select a larger portion of an image, and Paint Shop Pro tells you you're too close to the border to do a seamless selection, you may be able to cheat a little by enlarging the canvas (**Image**, **C**anvas Size] or by pasting the image into a larger new image. You may have to do a little touchup with the retouch tool around the edges to get the exact effect you want.

How to make a seamless tile with PSP 5

Let's fix the orange peel background by making it seamless.

Open the image you wish to make into a seamless tile. In this case, we'll use the saved Orange Peel graphic.

NOTE

If you're working with a GIF file, you have to Increase the color depth (Color, Increase Color Depth, 16 Million Colors) to make the Seamless option available. Paint Shop Pro will reduce the final number of colors down to 256 when you re-save your GIF.

With the rectangle selection tool, select an area you'd like to make seamless (figure 14.10).

Fig. 14.10
Using the Rectangular Selection Tool to pick an area to convert into seamless background

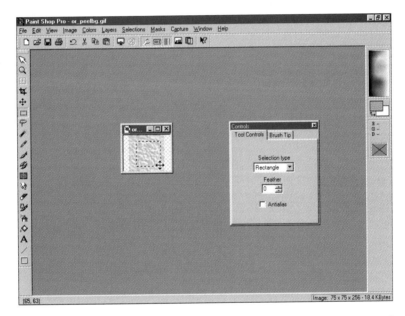

Choose **S**election, **C**onvert To Seamless Pattern from the PSP menu bar. Paint Shop Pro creates a new copy of the selected area with seamless edges.

Save the new image as a GIF, then test it in an HTML file. When PSP asks whether it should decrease to 256 colors to save as a GIF file, click Yes. Figure 14.11 shows the improved orange peel background.

Fig. 14.11
The orange peel background looks much better with seams removed!

Using One Large Image

Besides using a small image that tiles on your page, you can also use larger images that appear only once inside your Web browser. You might think using one large image as your Web page background is a great idea; and, at first glance, it may look really nice (figure 14.12). There are, however, a couple of major drawbacks to using a large image as a background.

Fig. 14.12
This example shows a large image background in Netscape at 640 x 480 desktop screen size.

The most obvious drawback of a large image is, of course, increased file size and increased download time. A prevalent theme in this book is decreasing an image's dimensions in order to decrease file size, which ultimately decreases the download time. It is extremely difficult, if not impossible, to get a 640 x 480–pixel image down to a reasonable file size no matter what file type or compression ratio you use. The Sawyer Glacier image weighs in at a hefty 178 KB! That is definitely too large for use in the background. The other problem is that the designer has no control over what size desktop area each visitor sets up for his or her monitor. Some people prefer a 640 x 480–pixel desktop area, while others opt for a 800 x 600 display. Nowadays, some visitors even use 1024 x 768 or higher resolution.

If you size a background image for 640 x 480, it will tile extremely inefficiently on a larger desktop area. Now our beautiful image of the Sawyer Glacier has tiled itself for the viewer with an 800 x 600 screen resolution (figure 14.13).

Fig. 14.13
The Sawyer Glacier background image doesn't tile well.

So why not just design it for the larger desktop area to cover the smaller screen? If you do that, what happens to your beautiful image? It now has the bottom and the right side cut off. Plus the image file size will necessarily be larger due to the increased dimension of the image. Usually, you just can't win when using large images as backgrounds on the Web.

My recommendation is to avoid using a large image as a background. If you want to use a large image on your Web site, compress the file as much as possible to keep the download time to a minimum, re-size the image proportionally to fit the smallest screen width (no more than 600 pixels wide), and display it on top of a solid-colored background. An even better idea is to use a thumbnail image and let the viewer decide whether he or she wants to download the larger image.

NOTE

A thumbnail image is a significantly re-sized version of a Web graphic that is placed on a Web page, but links to the larger version of the image. This enables visitors to see a preview of the graphic and decide whether they want to download the entire graphic.

Backgrounds with Margins

For the more advanced HTML enthusiast who knows how to lay out text and images using HTML tables, a refreshing alternative is to design a background in which the left margin is a different color or texture than the main body of the background. The left margin is generally used for menu buttons or navigation information, with the body of the text to the right of the margin. The result looks much like a page designed with frames, but it is laid out with tables instead.

An example of page using this type of background is Timberwolf Gifts located at **http://www.timberwolfalaska.com** and shown in figure 14.14.

Fig. 14.14
This Web site uses a left margin background that matches the company's logo.

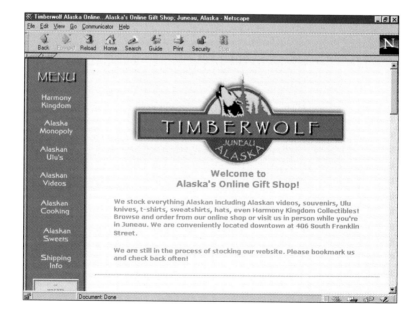

Creating these backgrounds is more easily accomplished than you might think, but doing the HTML layout of the page can still be tricky. Be sure to visually test the finished page at various desktop screen resolutions, and in multiple Web browsers and versions if possible, since each will look a bit different for your visitors.

This type of background usually includes very long bars that wrap off to the right of the browser. Since they are wider than most people's desktops are set to, when they tile, they get placed on top of each other, creating an illusion of an entire column of color on the left-hand side of the screen.

Figure 14.15 shows the Timberwolf image loaded into PSP. This image is 1025 pixels wide (to accommodate those visitors who have their desktops set for 1024 pixels wide), and contains two colors—light green and dark green. The first 135 pixels are sectioned off and filled with dark green, while the designer used the Flood Fill tool and a light green color for the rest of the image. Notice that the image is only 30 pixels tall. This particular image's height dimension could actually be decreased to only one pixel because there is no texture or pattern; then the image would load even more rapidly!

Fig. 14.15
Here is the background image from the Timberwolf Web site.

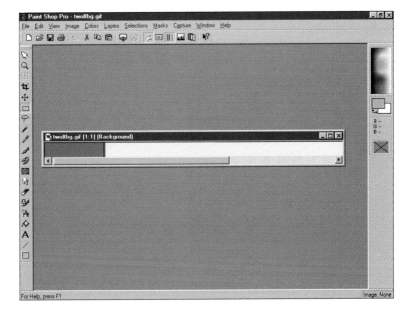

Backgrounds That Incorporate Text or Logos

Another more advanced background that can add a 3-D depth effect is one in which a faint logo or text shows behind the body of the text or images.

For example, visit the Fairbanks Beginning Experience Homepage at **http://www.siriusweb.com/BeginningExperience/,** as shown in figure 14.16.

Fig. 14.16
This example displays a logo in the background.

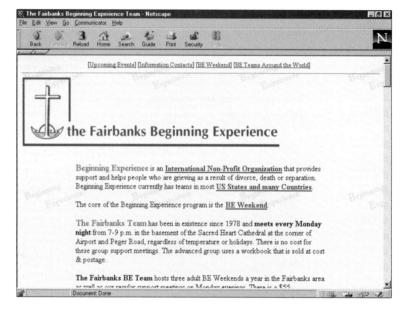

Be very careful when adding text or a logo to the background because it tends to take over the page. You might select a color that blends into the existing background color, play with the Luminance settings located in PSP under **C**olor, **A**djust H**u**e/Saturation/Luminance, or try other options in layers such as "Opacity" and the Layer Blend modes. Figure 14.17 shows a very light company name that can be used as a background image.

Fig. 14.17
Light, faint text works well for background images, as long as you don't overdo it.

15

HTML Tips
for Web Images

Throughout this book, you've learned a great deal about making cool graphics for your Web pages. You've seen how to draw unique shapes, create neat buttons and icons, scan photos directly into Paint Shop Pro, and even make spectacular special effects such as GIF animation. By this point, you should be an expert in image creation and understand the ins and outs of building efficient graphics for the Internet.

While all these details are important when it comes to *creating* your Web graphics, there's another important piece of the puzzle to learn when *using* your graphics on Web sites. All Web pages are built with HTML, Hypertext Markup Language. HTML has many important features that affect how graphics appear on your site.

This chapter introduces you to many advanced HTML tips and Web techniques that'll come in handy when you create Web sites. You'll see that understanding the features of Paint Shop Pro is only one part of creating effective graphics for your site. You'll find these HTML features extremely useful for controlling exactly how your images will appear on a Web site, including their size and placement.

▶ **Define Your Image Size**
HTML lets you control the exact height and width in which your image should appear (in pixels). Learn how to take advantage of the significant flexibility in your image's appearance, without resizing or editing the actual file.

▶ **Use Tables and Frames with Graphics**
Two common HTML structures Web developers use are tables and frames. Learn how you can integrate Web graphics with these two features to create an effective Web site.

▶ **Successfully Find Your Images**
One common problem designers encounter when adding images to Web sites results from pointing to an incorrect image file. See how you can build the correct and complete file path to your Web graphics.

▶ **Get Familiar with Page Layout Tips**
Graphics designers have been creating effective, good-looking flyers, newspapers, and books for years. Take advantage of some of their easy-to-use secrets when you put together your complete Web page.

Controlling Your Image Appearance

By now you should be able to create all sorts of fantastic and impressive graphics for your Web site. Whether you scanned in a photo, built a set of home-page buttons and icons, or created your own dazzling background images, you've spent countless hours producing just the right images for your site.

When it comes to adding these graphics to your Web page, most Web developers simply use the <IMG> tag, as described in Chapter 1, "A Web Crawler's Beginning." With a basic understanding of HTML, you can add an image to your Web page and control the alignment on which it is placed. Fortunately, you have many more exciting tags and ways to use images on Web pages than the standard <IMG> tag. Learning just a few more HTML details can really enhance the way your page will appear to visitors.

In this section, you'll read about some more advanced HTML concepts that will likely enhance the way images can be used at your site. You'll learn new HTML keywords and tags and how to integrate images with other HTML elements such as tables and frames.

Height and Width HTML Tags

In Chapter 12, "Making Your Graphics Lean," you learned how to resize and crop your image within Paint Shop Pro. Resizing your image allows you to reduce the overall file size and make an image fit slightly better on a Web page.

Besides using Paint Shop Pro, you can also directly control the size and appearance of your image with special HTML keywords. PSP allows you to make changes to your actual GIF or JPEG file, saving the image with its new pixel sizes. Using HTML sizing techniques, you only affect the way the image appears on a Web page without making physical changes to your graphic.

You can control the size your image appears with the HEIGHT and WIDTH keywords that work within the <IMG> tag. Both HEIGHT and WIDTH can be assigned pixel values that subsequently control the sizing of an image on a page. For example, to see an image 200 pixels tall and 400 pixels wide, I'd use the following line of HTML:

```
<IMG SRC="BENCH.JPG" HEIGHT=200 WIDTH=400>
```

You can resize an image to almost any set of coordinates. Figure 15.1 shows an image in several different sizes. The original size of this image is 668 pixels wide and 298 pixels tall.

Fig. 15.1
Here's the same image in several different sizes.

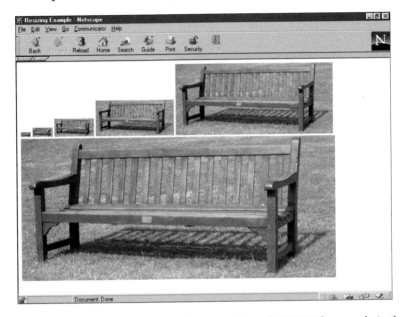

One great advantage to using the HEIGHT and WIDTH keywords is that this method allows you to use the same image multiple times on the same Web page to get different results. A button or bar can be stretched and sized in different ways to fit on a particular Web page. The real benefit, however, comes when visitors only have to download the image once, thus they save a lot of time. Your Web browser displays the image from the computer's cache, or memory, instead of downloading the image again.

Without a small buffer, headlines and graphics may run together, or two images placed side by side may be indistinguishable. To counter this problem, use the HSPACE and VSPACE keywords in your <IMG> tag. HSPACE affects the horizontal buffer space to the left and right of the image and VSPACE refers to the buffer size above and below the image.

Much like HEIGHT and WIDTH, described in the last section, HSPACE and VSPACE require you to type in the number of pixels you want to use as a buffer around your image. To fix the example in figure 15.2, I simply added a 20-pixel buffer area to the sides of the image and a small 10-pixel buffer on the vertical axis (figure 15.3):

```
<IMG SRC="DEER.JPG" HSPACE=20 VSPACE=10>
```

Fig. 15.3
This page looks much better because of the slight buffer change around the image.

CAUTION

Using the HEIGHT and WIDTH keywords doesn't change the amount of time required to download and view a Web graphic. Even if you display an image using very small HEIGHT and WIDTH coordinates, visitors still have to wait the same amount of time as they would to observe the full-size version. However, the rest of the Web page will load quicker because your Web browser knows exactly how large the image will be. This technique allows the browser to place text and other images on your Web page immediately without waiting for the image to be downloaded. If you want to use HEIGHT and WIDTH to get additional performance benefits on a Web page, your best bet is to create smaller, resized versions of your graphics and embed the new versions on your site.

The large bench image used in figure 15.1 is 86K in size, so resizing it, instead of just using the Height and Width keywords, would make a lot of sense.

Buffering Your Image

Another important way to control your image's appearance is to set the horizontal and vertical buffer space that appears around each graphic. Often, you'll find that your WWW browser will place images and text closer together than you prefer, as is shown in figure 15.2.

Fig. 15.2
A little buffer space around the image would be nice.

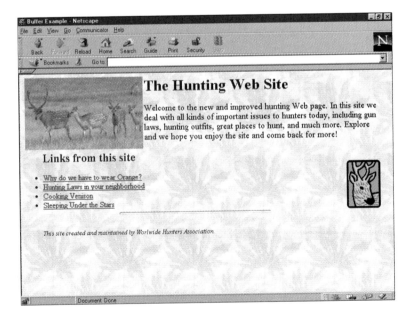

Using Tables with Graphics

Tables are an important feature of HTML that allow Web developers to organize information on their pages in a column and row format. Often, tables are used to compare and contrast information or are used in the design of a Web page.

When displaying Web graphics, tables can sometimes be used in a special way to organize and set off important images on a page. Working with tables is easy—you simply need to learn a handful of tags, including <TABLE>, <TD>, and <TR>. You organize a table by designating information to appear in each cell of data for each row within the table. For example, to create the simple two-row by two-column table shown in figure 15.4, use the following HTML:

```
<TABLE BORDER=1>
     <TR>
            <TD>Row 1 - Column 1</TD>
            <TD>Row 1 - Column 2</RD>
     </TR>
     <TR>
            <TD>Row 2 - Column 1</TD>
            <TD>Row 2 - Column 2</RD>
     </TR>
</TABLE>
```

Fig. 15.4
Here's a very simple table.

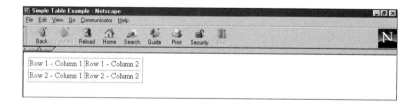

Tables are very flexible to work with when you are building a Web page with graphics. Below, I've listed a few situations in which you may want to consider using tables on your Web site.

▶ **Image Grid**—When you want to display many different images on a single page, try using a table to control the appearance on screen. Figure 15.5 shows a well-designed Web page that mixes tables and images for good layout.

Fig. 15.5
The Ziff-Davis
University Web page
(http://www.zdu.com)
uses HTML tables
nicely.

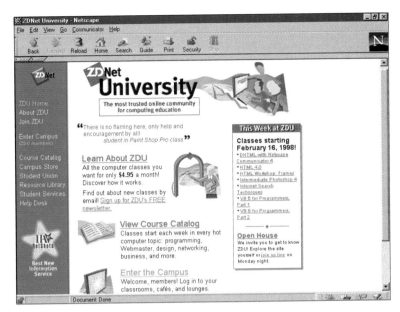

▶ **Attention Grabber**—Sometimes you will want to draw extra attention
to an image—perhaps one that serves as a large headline at the top of
the page. These images are usually as important as the other textual
headlines themselves. Figure 15.6 shows a single image within a
single-cell table that uses a black background color for the cell.
Notice how it really draws attention to the image.

Fig. 15.6
You can't miss this
image when browsing
the Web!

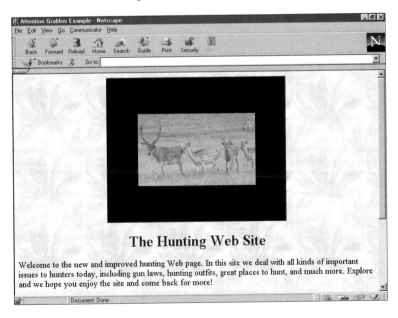

In this small section, I barely touched the tip of the iceberg in describing how tables can be used. There are many more keywords and table-related tags you can use to improve the effectiveness of your images and Web page. For a more complete reference of using tables effectively on your Web site, check out *Creating Your Own Web Pages, 2nd Edition*, published by Que.

Introducing Frames

Another method frequently used to structure Web pages is using frames. Frames allow you to split up the browser window into multiple areas, each displaying a separate HTML file. Frames have many different uses and possibilities for site designers working with Web graphics.

Probably the most popular use of frames is to keep a standard header or footer on the screen for visitors exploring a Web site. Figure 15.7 shows an example of the L.L. Bean Web page that uses a footer at the bottom. This footer contains several images that stay at the bottom of the screen. As you surf the Web, you will find many other sites that use frames to keep their logo or main headline ever present.

Fig. 15.7
Frames keep a logo always visible at a Web site.

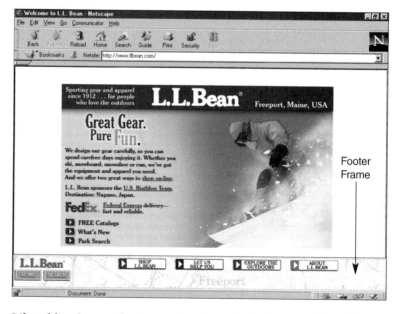

Footer Frame

Like tables, frames also have virtually unlimited use and flexibility on Web sites. The HTML behind frames isn't complicated, but it can be tricky. Basically, each frame is a separate page of HTML that loads a set of images or text. Then you need another HTML to tie the entire site together.

To learn how to use and build frames, check out any comprehensive manual or book on HTML.

Finding the Right Image Path

The most basic way to add an image to a Web page is to use the <IMG> tag and simply specify which GIF or JPG file you want to display. For example, to display a file named **ANDYLIZ.GIF** on a Web page, I'd build the following line of HTML:

```
<IMG SRC="ANDYLIZ.GIF">
```

By just listing the file name in the <IMG> tag, you are telling your WWW Browser to look in the same subdirectory as the HTML file for **ANDYLIZ.GIF**.

Often, you'll want to reference an image that is saved in a different subdirectory from your HTML file. To do that, you must understand how to properly build the link to another subdirectory, or even to a different drive on your computer.

Link to a Subdirectory

For example, let's say **ANDYLIZ.GIF** is instead saved in a subdirectory called **PICTURES**. In this case, your tag would be:

```
<IMG SRC="PICTURES/ANDYLIZ.GIF">
```

Remember that the path to your Web graphic depends on where your HTML file is stored. The path concept works the same way even when your image is saved in a subdirectory of a subdirectory. For example, if **ANDYLIZ.GIF** were saved in a subdirectory called **PICTURES**, which is in a subdirectory called **WWW**, your tag would be:

```
<IMG SRC="WWW/PICTURES/ANDYLIZ.GIF">
```

One Directory Above

Similarly, sometimes your images might be saved in a directory one level above where your HTML file is located. In this case you'd use the <IMG> tag like this:

```
<IMG SRC="../ANDYLIZ.GIF">
```

Link to a Different Drive

Sometimes you'll want to add an HTML reference to an image that is stored on a different drive from your current HTML file. In this case, finding the proper path is a little bit more complicated. For example, if my file was saved on the **D:** drive, I'd use the following tag (Notice how my slashes are reversed when pointing to a local drive):

```
<IMG SRC="FILE:///D:\ANDYLIZ.GIF">
```

Of course, you can even point to a file saved in a subdirectory of a
different drive:

```
<IMG SRC="FILE:///D:\PICTURES\ANDYLIZ.GIF">
```

NOTE

Linking to images on a different drive is only useful when building Web
pages on your personal computer. Internet Service Providers (ISPs) usually
require that your entire collection of files for your Web site are in one system
of directories and subdirectories without access to other drives.

Images elsewhere on the WWW

Another useful technique is available; you can display an image that is
saved at a completely different Web site. This powerful trick allows you
to use images that are saved anywhere in the world just by listing the
correct URL in the <IMG> tag.

Let's say you wanted to use a button from a friend's Web site. Instead of
copying the image through Netscape, simply use the actual file that your
friend uses on his or her site. To use this button on your Web page, you'd
add the following line of HTML:

```
<IMG SRC="http://www.shafran.com/links.jpg">
```

This line of HTML tells your WWW browser that, when loading your
page, it should go to **www.shafran.com** and download **links.jpg**. Your
Web Browser (such as Internet Explorer or Netscape) makes pointing to
an image at a different file location very easy. If you're browsing the Web
with Netscape and find an image you want to use, simply click your right
mouse button on top of the image (figure 15.8) and choose Co**p**y Image
Location. Netscape copies the full URL of your image into your
computer's clipboard so you can simply paste it into your HTML file!
Internet Explorer doesn't allow you to copy the URL into your clipboard,
but you can create an Internet Shortcut to the image and save it on your
personal computer.

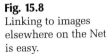

Fig. 15.8
Linking to images
elsewhere on the Net
is easy.

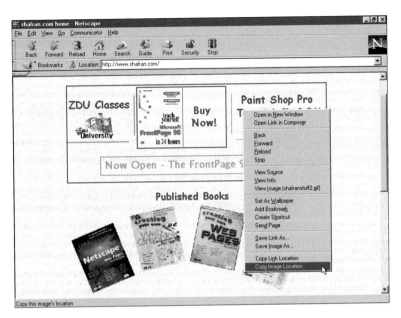

Part IV   Practical Use of Images

Using images from other Web sites has its advantages and disadvantages. Many personal developers like to use this technique when they don't have room on their server for lots of images, or when the image they point to is updated regularly.

Linking to images elsewhere on the WWW has several drawbacks as well. Below, I outline each of them so you are aware of possible problems that may occur.

▶ **Performance**—When you link to an image at another site, visitors who stop by your site must first download your entire page of HTML and graphics, then wait for the Web browser to connect to the other site and download the images stored there. Often, this creates a real bottleneck that can significantly increase the time it takes visitors to view your Web page.

▶ **Files Change**—Every so often, Web sites are updated and changed by replacing old graphics and files with new ones. When you link to another site, you are at the mercy of that Web developer to maintain the particular image you are using. If the image changes or is deleted, it no longer appears on your Web page—a real bummer!

▶ **Server Consideration**—When linking to an image at another site, you place an increased workload on the second WWW server. Although it isn't a big deal when a few people link to the image on my site, imagine if thousands of people had Web pages that used my images! My poor Web server would be swamped!

▶ **Legal Issues**—A hot topic among Web developers nowadays is the issue of copyright. Images that are on another page are not automatically yours for the picking. They have been painstakingly drawn, scanned, and created by someone else and may be copyrighted. On the Internet, copyright laws have not set clear precedents yet; but, if you don't have the creator's permission, using images from other sites may cause problems for your Web site.

Sometimes, you will have no choice but to link to an image at another site. For example, I have a built-in graphical Web counter on my home page as shown in figure 15.9.

Fig. 15.9
Created and maintained on another Web site, all I did was add a single <IMG> tag.

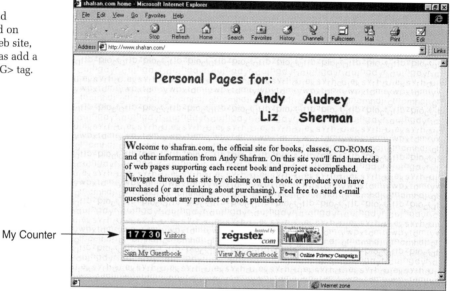

My Counter

This counter is created and incremented by a WWW server elsewhere on the Internet. Every time someone stops by my home page, their WWW Browser goes out and explores **http://www.digits.com** and downloads a simple GIF that displays the visitor number from that site.

Besides linking to images on another site, browsers make it easy to download, or "borrow," images from other Web sites. Downloading images from other people's Web sites without their permission then using them yourself could definitely create legal problems. While linking to images on another site lies in a legal grey area, representing other images as your own is as clear as black and white: illegal.

In general, if you want to use an image from another Web site, it's best to e-mail the designer, asking for permission to use the images. Many individuals don't mind sharing their graphics, but large companies often do. Once you obtain permission, simply save the image to your personal Web site and use it like any standard GIF or JPEG.

TIP

Although downloading and using images from another site is against the law, experimenting and using those images to learn how to use Paint Shop Pro better is not a problem. Often, when I explore the Web and find a cool graphic, I will download it and open it up inside PSP.

Then I might experiment with a variety of different techniques—but I never use these graphics on my Web page, or for any other purpose.

Fixing a Broken Image Pointer

If you are confused as to how the many file references work, relax; you're in good company. Using an incorrect path when attempting to add images to their Web pages is among the most common problems experienced by Web developers for all sites, large and small.

When you point to the wrong place for an image file, Web browsers display a simple "broken image" icon on the page where the correct image would have appeared. Figure 15.10 shows how the "broken image" icon appears in Netscape.

Fig. 15.10
The broken image icon tells visitors the file can't be found by the Web browser.

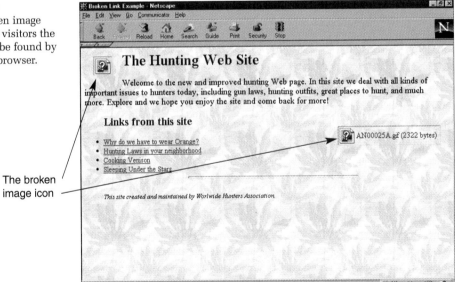

The broken image icon

When you see this icon on your Web page, you know that either the WWW browser simply couldn't find and download the image or that the Web Server didn't send the image to your computer within the allotted time. Most likely, there is a typo in the image's file name or the HTML file has mistakenly set the image's path to the wrong location. If you see this icon while browsing the Web, try reloading that particular page to see whether it is a server problem or an incorrect image path.

Don't let all the hard work you put into creating great Web graphics go to waste. If you see this icon on your pages, track down the problem immediately so visitors can experience all the glory of your Web graphics.

Image Design Suggestions

So far in this chapter, you've become aware of several technical specifications that will be useful when you incorporate your graphics into a Web page. In this section, I'll switch gears and demonstrate how several important design considerations can affect your Web page's appearance, no matter how great your images are.

Don't worry if you forget to use some of these techniques; they are offered only as guidelines. I've included them so you can be aware of how professional Web developers evaluate their sites and make small, but significant, improvements that most people might not consciously notice.

Image Visioning

Borrowed from the newspaper industry, image visioning helps control the direction of a viewer's eye on the page. Image visioning to a Web designer is the technique of correctly placing graphics on a Web page so that visitors' eyes will naturally flow into, instead of away from, the meat of the page.

You'll see this practiced all the time in your local newspaper. Image visioning helps editors decide on which side of the paper to place photographs and drawings. Figure 15.11 illustrates what I mean with a simple Web page. Notice how I placed the image on the left side of the screen, with the headline and text on the right side. That's because the image points toward the right. When you look at this image, your eyes automatically follow the line of vision provided by the cow image and you are naturally drawn into the text and headline.

Fig. 15.11
This picture draws
your eyes toward the
text on the right.

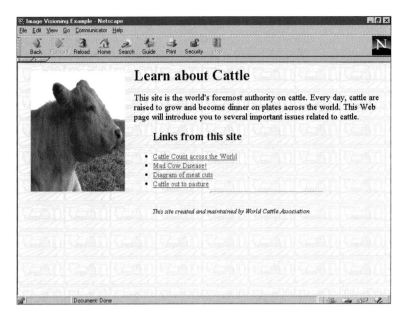

Now, look at this Web page with the same image on the right-hand side of
the screen (figure 15.12). It just doesn't have the same effect. Most people
don't even notice this subtle placement of the image unless they compare
two example pages, as in this situation.

Fig. 15.12
Not quite the same
effect, is it?

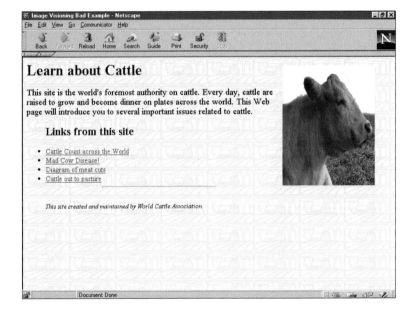

You want to draw visitors *into* your Web page. That helps ensure that they'll read the page instead of leave it quickly. Image visioning ensures that visitors will follow the line of vision in a graphic.

Site Consistency

Another detail to remember when using Web graphics on a page is the importance of maintaining a consistent look throughout your site. Consistency allows visitors to become familiar with your set of pages. For example, Chapter 6, "Picture Tubes and Web Graphics," taught you how to create all sorts of different icons for your site. You also learned that icons are important navigational aids that let visitors meander through your set of pages. If you have navigational icons on one page, it's a good idea to use them on all pages. That way visitors will recognize the icons and know how to maneuver through your set of pages.

Maintaining consistency is also important when you create a set of pages on a related topic. My Web site **(http://www.shafran.com)** includes a set of support pages for each published book, a half dozen different pages that are all related. I want each page to look like part of the same collection.

I therefore use the same format on each page—a headline at the top next to the book cover, a sub-headline, and then the full page of information over the same background image. I use the same standard links on each page, always on the left side, so visitors will know how to get through the site. Figures 15.13 and 15.14 show two sample pages.

Fig. 15.13
Here's a page from my Web site.

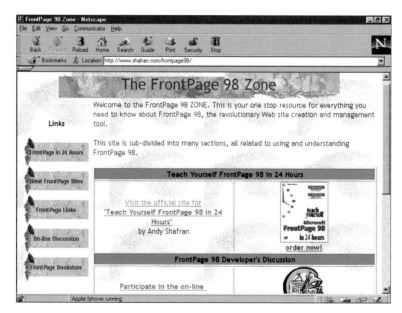

Fig. 15.14
This is a different
page, but the
appearance is
consistent.

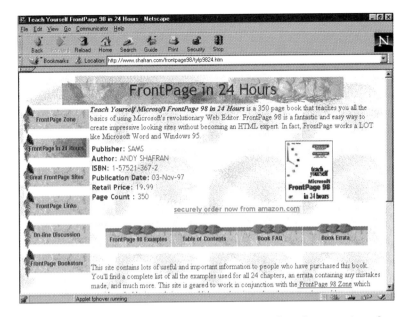

Consistency is important when you create graphics because it makes your pages fit with one another. Imagine serving dinner at your home with each guest drinking from a different type of glass. One uses a mug, another a flute, yet another a plastic cup. Sure, everyone gets to drink, but using a set of the same glasses would look much better. Apply the same concept to your Web site. Creating pages that look similar will enable visitors to enjoy your site more.

Color Coordination

Every day, you wake up and get ready for work. Along the way, you must make conscious decisions about what clothing to wear. When you put on light blue pants, surely the orange-striped shirt stays in the closet. Most people are capable of matching and color-coordinating clothes; we make such easy and quick decisions daily.

The same concept works on the WWW. When creating cool graphics and images of all colors, it's a good idea to match the color of text on your page so that it fits with your style or theme. For example, if you create a Web page about the Ohio State Buckeyes, you might want to use Scarlet and Grey text, while Florida fans would stick with orange and blue.

Coordinating text color on your page is an important and very effective aesthetic touch. Figure 15.15 shows a simple home page on the Web **(http://www.flower.com/).** At this site, the developer has a light red color (rose) background topped by an image of an actual rose. With such coordination, you know this page is about flowers and roses. Without the matching colors, this page might be less exciting.

Fig. 15.15
This rosy site really scores on the color coordination scale.

Changing your text color to match your graphics is easy. You simply surround the specific text with the <FONT COLOR=> tag. So, to mark a sentence as red, I'd use this tag:

```
<FONT COLOR=RED>This is red text</FONT>
```

Your Web browser recognizes sixteen different colors that you can specify by name, such as the Red used above. Chapter 14, "Background Graphics and Colors," discusses the use of named and unnamed colors in significant detail.

16

Cool PSP Techniques

This chapter will discuss briefly how to use simple tools of Paint Shop Pro to generate some neat effects that look difficult to create. I won't spend a lot of time describing tools because this has been done earlier in the book. However, I will present some cool tricks you can use not only to give your own graphics some sizzle, but to give you a solid launching ramp toward unlocking the true power of Paint Shop Pro.

Gradient Backgrounds

Several of the easiest effects already built into Paint Shop Pro are the fill tool options. Let's create a gradient background for a Web page, like the one in figure 16.1.

Fig. 16.1
This linear gradient background with tan text isn't as difficult to create as it looks.

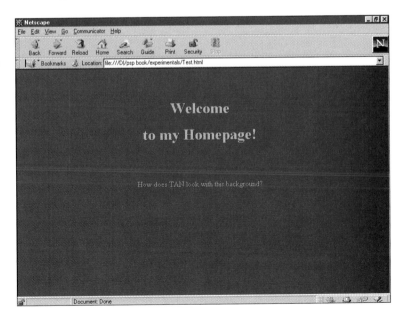

This background image looks big, but it isn't–and it is quite easy to create. Instead of creating a gigantic image, you are creating a very small one that repeats over and over again behind the text on your Web page. This makes the image very small and quick to download.

To create this gradient background, follow these steps:

1. Choose **File, New** from the PSP menu bar to bring up the New Image dialog box (figure 16.2). Make sure to use 16.7 million colors and set the background color to White. For the gradient background, be sure to have an image that will go all the way across the screen without being repeated or tiled in the visitors' Web browser. So, set the Height of this new image at 3 pixels, and the Width at 1024.

Fig. 16.2
These are the New Image settings for the gradient background.

TIP

Most of the time, 1024 pixels wide will do the trick. I've used 3 pixels high here, but you could make the image taller. In the case of a texture or sidebar background, you will need to consider how the image fits together on the top and bottom to get a seamless effect. For more on creating textured and seamless backgrounds, check out Chapter 14, "Background Graphics and Colors."

2. Once you have your new image window open, select your colors. I've used black for the background and blue for the foreground color. When you use the linear gradient option of the fill tool, you fill from the foreground color to the background color or vice versa. Therefore, you need to pick your colors with some caution to be sure they work well together and do not clash on the page. Background colors that compete with the text or other features of your page are not effective.

3. Next, select the fill tool from the PSP Tool Bar.

4. In the Control Palette, you have several options that affect the way the flood fill tool operates. You can select fill style, fill match mode, tolerance and opacity of the area you are filling. In addition, there are several advanced settings available by clicking on the Options button. Figure 16.3 shows the Flood Fill Options dialog box. This example uses a 90-degree linear gradient flood fill. Choose **Linear Gradient** from the drop-down Flood Fill box (in this dialog box or the Control Palette). Then set the degree of fill to be 90 degrees. You can either type in **90**, or turn the direction bar 90 degrees with your mouse. Notice how the preview box changes as you modify these settings.

Fig. 16.3
Getting ready to fill.

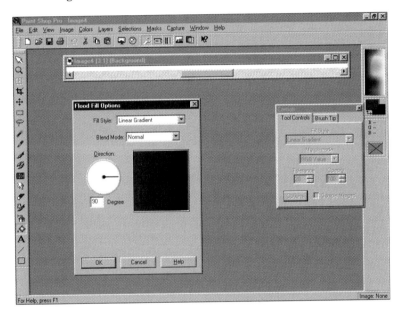

5. Once the fill options are set, zoom in on your image to make it much easier to see and work with. Choose View, Zoom In from the PSP menu bar. For this example, we are going to zoom in 7:1.

CAUTION
Check in the Tool Controls tab of the Control Palette to be sure that you have the opacity set to 100%. Otherwise, the Flood Fill colors may look washed out.

6. At this point, go ahead and click your left mouse button in the blank image window. This causes you to flood fill the entire image. Since you are zoomed in so much, you won't be able to fully appreciate the gradient fill of the image. Zoom back out to 2:1 or 1:1, and you can see how the blue gets darker from left to right.

TIP

You can switch the order of the fill in PSP by using the right or left mouse button. The left button will fill from the foreground to the background, and the right button does the opposite. In our case of filling horizontally, the left mouse button will start filling with the foreground color (blue here) on the left of the image.

7. Now that the image is filled with the linear gradient, it's time to save your file. Since GIF files are only capable of 256 colors, save this Web graphic in the JPG format. The gradient fill uses thousands of different blues in this one image.

8. Now you can use it as a background image on your Web page. Use the <BODY BACKGROUND="BLUE.JPG"> HTML tag. You get a page that looks like figure 16.1, shown earlier.

Text for Headers

With HTML, adding headline text to your Web page can result in boring and rather bland-looking text. The default header text is black and in a standard font. You can control the color of text, but changing the font is dangerous because not everyone has the same fonts on their computer as you have.

As a result, Paint Shop Pro lets you create great-looking graphics that serve as headers on your Web pages. Although the headers are still usually text-based, PSP lets you use many neat effects, such as shadows or unique fonts, as you build your graphics.

Figure 16.4 shows an example headline graphic created in PSP. It uses shadowing, and each letter is filled with a pattern instead of plain color.

Fig. 16.4
This example shows a
header that will jazz
up a Web page.

You can produce all sorts of headline images for your Web page that use
different fonts and colors. Below is the step-by-step procedure used to
create the graphic in figure 16.4. Feel free to follow along and use your
own text and fonts.

Creating a Texture

The first step is to create the texture you will use to fill in your text. This
process is very similar to the one described in Chapter 14, "Background
Colors and Images," except that this example is optimized to work well
with text instead of Web page backgrounds.

1. We must first create a texture to use on the header, as shown in figure
    16.4. Paint Shop Pro has many useful techniques for creating textures
    and patterns.

2. Create a new image that sets Height at 150 pixels, Width at 500
    pixels, color at 16.7 million, and background color to Blue.

3. Next, choose your foreground color. For this example, I selected a
    light aqua since it will coordinate with the blue background nicely.

4. Select the airbrush tool. From the Control Palette, choose a paper
    texture with which to paint. This example uses the Marble, but you
    can use virtually any paper texture to achieve an effective graphic.

5. Next, switch to the Brush Tip tab of the Control Palette. Set your
    brush size to be something greater than 75 to ensure that you get an
    even and smooth effect when using the airbrush. For this example, I
    used 100.

6. Now you are ready to paint! Airbrush the paper texture onto your
    blue graphic. Don't worry if you don't cover every nook and cranny
    of the image; we are only going to select part of the graphic to use as
    a texture for the headline image. Figure 16.5 shows the resulting
    image after airbrushing.

Fig. 16.5
Creating a texture to
use on our header.

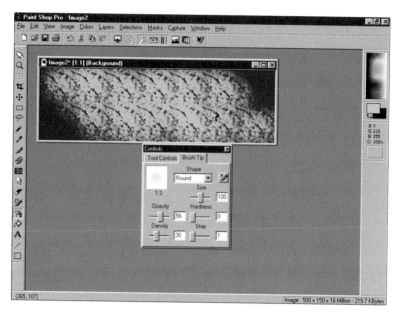

7. Now you will select a portion of the image that you'll use to paint your letters. Click on the Selection tool and select a small area of your image that has a fairly even-looking pattern. I would not select anything larger than about 75 pixels (or 1") in size. Let your image pattern and texture guide your selection so it will go together well at the seams.

8. After you have your selection marked, choose Image, Crop to Selection to crop to the area you've selected.

9. Save this textured image for use in this set of steps and in the future.

Creating the Textured Headline

Once you have finished the texture, you are ready to create the actual headline for your Web page.

1. Create another new image with the Height set to 150 pixels, Width set to 500, and background color set to white.

2. Select the text tool and click in your graphic to bring up the Add Text dialog box. Type in the headline for your Web page and select the font, size, and attributes you want to use. When you have your text ready to go, click **OK** to apply it to the image. Move the text around until it is centered on your image, but don't click the right mouse button to place it yet!

3. With the Text still selected, choose the fill tool. Click on the Options button in the Control Palette, and you again see the Flood Fill Options dialog box. This time, choose **Pattern** as the fill style.

Once you choose **Pattern**, then you can select the **New Pattern Source** as well. From that drop-down list, make sure you pick the texture that you created in the previous set of steps. Paint Shop Pro shows you a preview of the pattern you choose to fill with. Figure 16.6 shows the Flood Fill Options dialog box with the proper options selected and the aqua-blue-marble background previewed.

Fig. 16.6
Settings for our pattern fill.

4.   We are going to use a pattern-fill technique for getting our texture onto the text. Make sure that you use a relatively high value for the tolerance in the Control Palette. For this example, I used 120.

NOTE

The reason we chose a high-contrast color for the text initially is so that we can use a high-tolerance setting here. This lets the fill tool include most of the blending pixels that are on the edge of text where it begins to blend into the background. To understand better, zoom an image in to 10:1 or higher until you can see the actual pixel make-up at the edge of the color. What you will discover is that some pixels are not the true text color or the true background color, but they are a different color somewhere in between. By using the high tolerance setting it will allow us to include them in the fill.

The tolerance setting affects how you deal with these in-between colors. A zero tolerance setting tells the fill tool to ignore *all* variation of color and fill only the actual color you click upon, while 200 is complete tolerance to all other colors. Filling with a 200 setting would overflow your entire image because the fill tool is tolerant of all the other colors and will overwrite them. As an example, let's say we have the tolerance set at 50. This tells us that in the RGB color spectrum, any color that falls within 50 either way of the target pixel will be included in the fill. Once you understand this, the rest is easy. Simply set the tolerance as high as you can (or need to in most cases), but not so high as to let the fill bleed out to other colors that are adjoining your target color. The whole purpose is to make a clean, even fill all the way to the edges of the text—without having extra dots around the edges.

5. With the text still selected, fill the letters with the pattern by clicking in the selected area. Figure 16.7 shows the fill process underway.

Fig. 16.7
Fill the text with your
pattern.

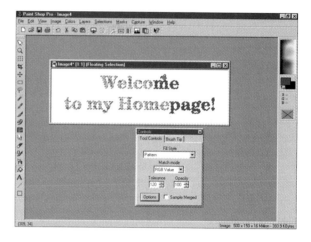

Adding a Shadow

Now that we have the text filled with our texture, the final step in this technique is to add a 3D/Shadow effect to the text. To create this impression, we will use the cutout feature in PSP.

With the text still selected, choose **I**mage, Effects, **Cu**tout to open the Cutout dialog box, as shown in figure 16.8. Apply the default settings by clicking on the **OK** button, leaving the text selected for the final step.

Fig. 16.8
This figure shows the
settings I used in the
example heading.

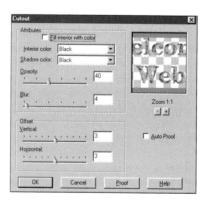

TIP

The Cutout effect is a very useful and powerful technique. Check out Chapter 5, "Images and Special Effects," for a more detailed description and set of examples.

Finally, we will apply a drop shadow to the image to complete the 3D effect. With the text still selected, choose Image, Effects, Drop Shadow from the menu bar to bring up the Drop Shadow dialog box. Here are the settings I've used: Shadow color is black, Blur is 5, Opacity is 40, and the Vertical and Horizontal Offsets are both –3.

Now, all you need to do is save the image as a transparent GIF and add it to your Web page. Figure 16.9 shows the final image inside of PSP.

Fig. 16.9
This is the final image before saving it as a transparent GIF for use on the Web.

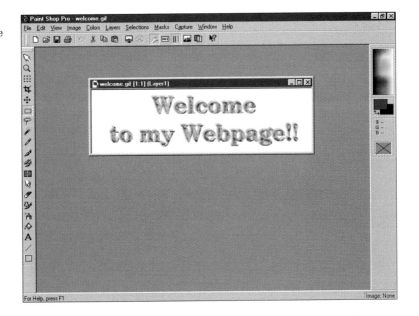

Effectively Using Drop Shadows

Here are two classy effects that use the drop-shadow technique of Paint Shop Pro. I've nicknamed them "haloing" and "charging" because of the overall effect they have when placed on a Web page. Both techniques are similar and use PSP drop shadows.

Creating a Haloed Image

The basic concept for Haloing is to create a shadow of some text that is the same color as the background of your image, so that only the shadow is visible. This leaves only a shadow, which spells out a word or phrase—a very cool-looking technique. While difficult to describe in words, you can see the effects in figure 16.10.

Fig. 16.10
Haloing effectively uses the drop-shadow effect within PSP.

Haloing is a term that has been coined to describe this effect since it leaves a halo from the drop shadow around the text. To create a "haloed"image, follow the steps below.

Open a new image with a white background, then add your text and make sure to leave it selected.

Choose Image, Effects, Drop Shadow to bring up the Drop Shadow dialog box (figure 16.11). Set the Horizontal and Vertical Offsets to 0, then experiment with the Opacity and Blur until you get the effect that you want. I used 40 Opacity for the Haloing, and Blur is set to 20 for this example.

Fig. 16.11
Shadows can be made and customized here.

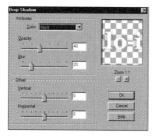

I am using white text on a white background. Since I am setting the shadow color to blue, and it is included in the drop-down list for the Color, I do not need to worry about foreground and background colors with this image.

Haloing is an impressive technique that can be used to dress up professional pages without overdoing them. The process is also quick to evaluate and implement—only a single command. Figure 16.12 shows the haloing technique used unobtrusively as a navigational button. The only difference between the images in figures 16.12 and 16.10 is the smaller text in figure 16.12, which made Edge Enhancing the image necessary. Choose Image, Edge, Enhance from the menu bar to initiate this process.

Fig. 16.12
Here is an example of an image used as a navigation tool for a page.

Charging an Image

Charging is descriptive of the neat effect I use to make an image or name look like it's been struck by lightning or is 'charged' with energy to give it emphasis. By using the same drop shadow technique described above, only with a bright color such as yellow with light opacity (which decreased the amount of color used), you can use this technique to spice up plain text. Figure 16.13 shows a "charged" image.

Fig. 16.13
This image is charged up with a PSP Drop Shadow! I also use Charging when I want slight emphasis on the text to pull it out of the background slightly.

CAUTION

One word of caution: Drop Shadows seem to work best on white backgrounds. You can, of course, apply them to any background color you choose; but you're likely to encounter problems when using the GIF transparency settings. For instance, when you save an image such as those in this section, you will likely save it as a transparent GIF file with white being the transparent color.

Problems occur when you look at the way a GIF saves transparency information. As you remember from Chapter 10, "Creating Transparent GIFs," you can only have one transparent color from the 256 colors available in a GIF. The problem occurs where the edge of the drop shadow meets the background. At that spot, the color is a mixture of many different color shades, not a single color. Thus the transparent effect doesn't look complete.

Fixing a Picture

Another common technique is touching up or fixing a photograph to look good on your Web pages. For example, figure 16.14 shows a picture of a balloon taken after a piece of fuzz fell into the camera when the film was being loaded. Normally, you'd pick a different image to use, but with PSP you can touch up your photographs so that nobody would notice the fuzz. With a bit of airbrushing, this photo, which would otherwise have been unusable, can be used for any electronic purpose.

Fig. 16.14
A good balloon picture except for the fuzz in the corner.

the fuzz

The best way to touch up this photo involves using the Paint Shop Pro Airbrush. The airbrush lets you blend and mix colors together without acting like a true paint brush. By spraying colors over the fuzz, you integrate that mistake into the rest of the photo. Remember that the PSP Airbrush emulates a real airbrush, which resembles a detail-oriented can of spray paint.

A similar way to do this type of touch-up work would be to use the Clone tool. In this image though, there is too much deviation in color from left to right and top to bottom to make this my preferred choice. We need to blend the original colors back into the blemished area.

TIP

Working with the airbrush can make it tough to create great detail. One tip to keep in mind is that the viewer's mind will fill in details for you, freeing you from fixing every tedious pixel.

For example, when you look at a painting on the wall, you see the whole picture. Have you ever gotten up close and looked at that same picture? Chances are you might notice all the chunks and lumps of paint, the blatant brush and knife marks. You may not be as impressed with your analysis of a small section of the painting; but stepping back a few feet, the painting usually looks great.

Take a lesson from the great painters of the world, and focus on how the complete image looks. Missing a pixel here and there isn't as critical as looking at the overall image.

Use the Dropper tool here to match the colors of the airbrush with the sky around the fuzz. We must be careful as the shade of the sky changes drastically from one side of the blemish to the other. You'll switch colors regularly, and the dropper helps you mix and match shades of blue.

Select the airbrush tool, then open up the Control Palette and use the following Brush Tip settings:

Size to 10

Opacity to 30

Density to 30

Round brush

These settings help you optimize the way your airbrush will work when painting. Zoom in to 5:1 to see the minute changes in color. This example also uses the Fog paper texture, set in the Tool Controls tab of the Control Palette.

Slowly begin matching the colors around the blemish and painting in a little at a time, as seen in figure 16.15. Occasionally I will use the PSP Color Picker to lighten or darken a color rather than picking a new color from the photo. Keep a close eye on the surrounding sky to be sure that it matches as closely as possible. When doing this, be careful you avoid doing too much retouching at once, or you could shift the color of the area too much.

Fig. 16.15
Paint over the blemish using the airbrush, blending the colors as you go.

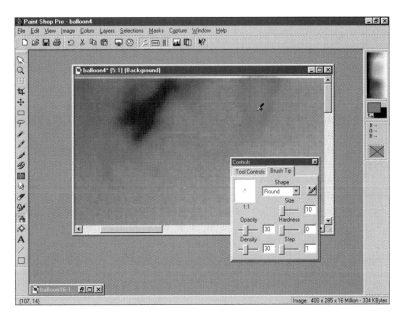

After some work gradually painting the colors, I have the image mostly fixed—except for a final general blending of the colors as you can see in figure 16.16. Small fast strokes are preferred to match the graininess of the original photo. You will also need to continually look at the normal size image to check your progress. Reduce the image zoom to 2:1 or 1:1 to regularly check out how the complete snapshot appears.

Fig. 16.16
Ready to blend the colors.

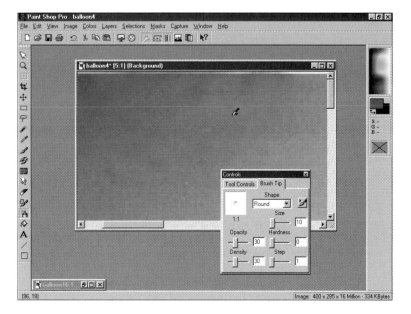

To blend the colors, I'll increase the brush size to 60, reduce the opacity to 15, and make long, fast strokes with the airbrush so only a small amount of color is laid onto the image. I will continue to select the colors as before. Notice that the color runs in a semicircle centered in the upper-left corner of the photo. When we blend the colors, we will want to match this line as closely as possible.

When the image is almost finished, you may have to experiment with brush size, opacity, and density in order to make the colors blend properly for your final touch-ups. The last step was to crop the image to remove any unnecessary empty space. Figure 16.17 shows the final improved image.

Fig. 16.17
The finished photo with the final brush blending.

Working with Clip Art

The next technique shows you how to easily resize and reshape clip art to achieve complex results. In figure 16.18, you will see an image that I created with clip-art trees. Although the image includes six trees, I used only three different trees to create all six. By using the Resize tool of Paint Shop Pro, I was able to make several versions of each tree.

Fig. 16.18
Image created with resized clip-art trees.

I started with a linear gradient background and added a snowfield with the airbrush. You can also use Paint Shop Pro layers here for the background and snow to make it easy to edit and modify those pieces individually later. Then I added the different sized trees.

Smudging a Shadow

Before I started working with the trees, the first step was creating the background and snow. The snow was easily created with the Airbrush tool, but the shadow effects were slightly more difficult.

First, airbrush some darker streaks on top of the snow. This doesn't integrate well with the image so you need to use the PSP retouch tool. Once you select the Retouch tool, you have many options available in the Control Palette. Select Smudge Image as the Retouch Mode.

Also, you have to set the Brush Tip settings for how you want to Retouch tool to work. Open the Brush Tip tab in the Control Palette to set these options. For the example, I used the following settings:

Size 25
Hardness 20
Step 1
Density 40
Opacity 30

Then, retouching the image, you can smudge the snow and dark streaks together to end up with shadows in the snow. Figure 16.19 shows the before and after effects.

Fig. 16.19
Here's the background and snow complete with dark streaks for shadows.

Before Smudging

After Smudging

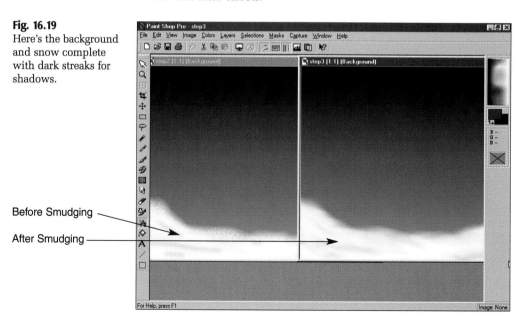

Resizing Your Clipart

Once the snow is finished, the next step is to add the trees. For this example, I found several images of trees from a clip-art CD and opened them from Paint Shop Pro.

PSP lets you resize and change the way the clip art appears without much trouble. Table 16.1 below shows three different original trees and three modified versions.

Table 16.1
Tree Comparison

Original Image #1

The original tree increased by 165% using **Image Resize**. Resized as a Percentage of the Original, maintaining the Aspect Ratio.

Original Image #2

Image increased only in height. Using **Image Resize**, uncheck Maintain Aspect Ratio while increasing the pixel Height of the image.

Original Image #3

Image increased in height and width, but not proportionally. Using **Image Resize**, uncheck Maintain Aspect Ratio while increasing the pixel Height and Width of the image.

Part IV   Practical Use of Images

Building the Forest

Once you have a variety of trees, it's time to place them on the snowy image. Adding the trees to your image can be tricky because you need to be careful not to change the snow/background of the forest. We have to use the selection tolerance features to make sure we get each of the trees, but none (or no more) of the white background behind them than we want.

1. Pick the first tree image to add to your scene, then choose **S**elections, Select **A**ll from the menu bar.

2. Then, choose **S**elections, **M**odify, **T**ransparent color. Choose a transparent color of white for this example, and tolerance ranging from 20 to 75 depending on the amount of white snow to leave on the trees. Click **OK** and notice how the selected area becomes only the tree (figure 16.20).

Fig. 16.20
Notice how only the tree is selected from the white background.

3. Choose **E**dit, **C**opy to copy the tree to your clipboard.

4. Activate the image that you are pasting the tree into—the snowy image in this example by clicking on the title bar.

5. Choose **E**dit, **P**aste, As **T**ransparent Selection. This adds the tree to your image.

6. Position the tree in the image and choose **S**elections, Select **N**one to glue the image down. Figure 16.21 shows the snowy background with a single image.

Fig. 16.21
Here is our image
after the first tree is
pasted in.

You should now have a tree set into your main image. Repeat these steps for each tree you want to add.

You will notice that I left a fair portion of white on the tree images to simulate snow on them. This occurs because of the Tolerance settings selected in step 2 when setting the Selection's transparent color.

To blend the tree images into the picture, I've used the Retouch tool again. Using this tool, I pushed the colors around the base of the trees to give the look of snow depressions around them and also of a slight shadow from the stars.

The final step in creating this image was adding a few evening stars to the graphic. You can use a very small paintbrush to add the stars, or you can select and paste them in as I did here. Once the stars were added, I used the airbrush to make those that are lower in the sky appear a bit darker and more natural. This also helped to integrate them into the image.

You will have to watch carefully and go slowly here. I zoomed the image in to 2:1 while working on the stars. Since the gradient background runs from top to bottom, the similar colors run left to right. It makes sense then, to work horizontally on stars that are at the same height in the image. Gradually reduce the amount of paint-over to allow the stars to shine brighter as you get higher up in the image. Figure 16.22 shows the airbrushing of the stars in progress.

Fig. 16.22
This image shows the airbrushing of the stars blending them into the image.

The 3D Gold Technique

To finish out this chapter, let's add a simple yet amazingly good-looking text technique to the last image to make text appear gold and three-dimensional.

1. Select the Text tool from the PSP tool bar, and make sure that you have white set as the foreground color.

2. Click on you image to bring up the Add Text window and make your style and size selections. Click OK to add the text selection to your image.

3. Position your text on the image and leave it selected.

4. Go to Image, Effects, Cutout. Choose a Shadow Color of black, Opacity set to 40, Blur set to 4, and both Horizontal and Vertical offsets set to 3. The text will now have a grey highlighted look to it. Leave the text selected.

5. Now for some color. Select **C**olors, **C**olorize from the menu bar and select your color by adjusting the Hue and Saturation settings. I have used Hue 30, and Saturation 204 for this gold effect. Remember to leave the text selected.

6. Often I find that using the Sharpen filter helps with the highlights on text. Go to **I**mages, **S**harpen, **S**harpen.

7. That's it! You can now right-click to glue your image in place. This is simply the easiest way to achieve a 3D gold text effect. See the finished image in figure 16.23.

Fig. 16.23
Gold text applied!

Appendixes

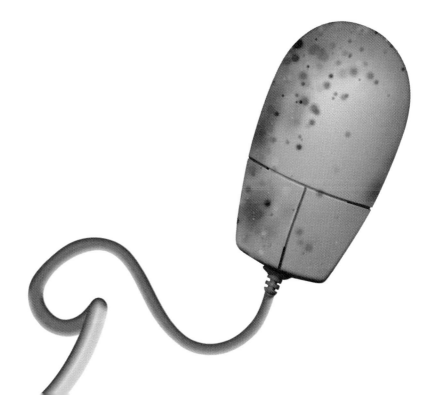

Appendix A
Graphical Resources on the Web

This appendix lists all of URLs covered in this book and many others that are of interest to you as a reader and Paint Shop Pro user.

The most important URL for you to remember is the home page for this book, where I'll always keep an updated set of links, examples, and more of interest to you, the reader.

Here are some of the most important sites mentioned:

http://www.muskalipman.com/graphics
Home Page for *Creating Paint Shop Pro Web Graphics, 2nd Edition*

http://www.jasc.com
Jasc Software Inc. Home Page – download Paint Shop Pro here

http://www.shafran.com
Andy Shafran's Home Page

Cool Sites

Throughout this book, I mentioned many cool sites that use graphics in a creative or innovative fashion. This section lists the companies that I referenced.

Larger Example Sites

http://www.amazon.com
Site where you can purchase books on-line

http://www.yahoo.com
Yahoo!

http://www.cnn.com
CNN On-line

http://www.llbean.com
L.L. Bean

http://www.covergirl.com
Cover Girl Makeup Home Page

Smaller Example Sites

http://www.timberwolfalaska.com
TimberWolf Gifts

http://www.ptialaska.net/~pkalbaug/hotlinks.html
All About Dogs

http://www.siriusweb.com/BeginningExperience/
Beginning Experience Page

http://www.airplane.com
Airplane Home Page

http://www.flower.com/
Flower.com

http://www.zebra.com
Zebra Software

http://www.dalmatians.com/dca
Dalmatian Club of America

http://www.photogs.com/bwworld/index.html
Black and White World magazine

Great Graphics Resources

This section lists many important sites mentioned in the book that are useful when creating cool graphics. You'll find sites for scanners, graphics tools, reference information, and more.

Graphics Reference Information

http://www.cdrom.com/pub/png/
PNG Information Page

http://www.htmlcompendium.org/colors.htm
256 Named Color Proposal

http://www.inso.com/products/retail/qvp-retail/html/qvpretai.htm
Using Other Image Formats

Web Hosting Sites

http://www.forman.com
Forman Interactive

http://www.siteamerica.com
Site America – An Affordable place for Web hosting

http://www.tangodevelopment.com
Tango Development

http://xoom.xoom.com
Xoom.Xoom – Home to 1 Million Web pages

http://www.geocities.com
Geocities – the original spot on the Web for free space.

Cool Development Sites

http://www.websitegarage.com
Web Site Garage

http://www.gamelan.com
Gamelan, home to Java Applets

http://www.javascripts.com
JavaScripts.com – Home of thousands of JavaScipt snippets

http://www.alienskin.com
Alien Skin Software

http://www.agag.com
Animated Gif Artists Guild

http://www.mediatec.com
Media Tec – Download LiveImage here

Useful Sites for Digitizing Images

http://www.hp.com/peripherals/main.html
Home of HP printing and imaging products

http://www.microtekusa.com/
Home of Microtek scanners and accessories

http://www.hsdesign.com/scanning/
Sullivan's On-line Scanning Resources and Tips—great place to learn some advanced scanning techniques

http://www.kodakpicturenetwork.com
KODAK Picture Network

http://www.quickcam.com
QuickCam Web Site

http://www.play.com
Snappy Video Digitizer

Graphics Collections

http://xoom.xoom.com
Xoom. Xoom - Thousands of Free Graphics

http://members.aol.com/minimouze/private/ICONS.html
Free Icon Collection

http://www.graphicmaps.com
Graphic Maps - Great Map Images for Free

http://www.ender-design.com/rg/
Realm Graphics Library

http://www.geocities.com/Heartland/1448/
Iconz Library

http://www.meat.com/textures/
Texture Land for Background Graphics

http://infinitefish.com/texture.html
Infinite Fish Seamless Textures

Appendix B
Paint Shop Pro 5 Tool Reference

Here's a list of tool and toggle buttons you'll find in PSP 5's friendly user interface. PSP's tools are available in one of its three toolbars: Standard, Tool Palette, and the Color Palette. You can move these toolbars to any area of the screen by clicking and dragging on the grey area around the toolbar's edge. Then you can either dock it against a screen edge or let it float anywhere you choose.

This appendix will cover the default PSP icons and buttons that appear when you open your program for the first time. Once you are familiar with PSP's interface, you may want to customize PSP 5's toolbars to suit your needs.

To add, remove, or change the location of any of PSP's tool buttons, look under File, Preferences, Customize Toolbar. To make many of the tools available (not greyed-out), you must first open a new or existing image in PSP 5 or click on the title bar of an open image.

NOTE

Keep in mind that this appendix is not the definitive source for every command found within Paint Shop Pro. It is intended as a guide that will give you an idea of what each default PSP button does.

Within most commands and settings, you can find additional ways to enhance or change the way the setting operates by using the Control Palette. For a comprehensive reference for how each PSP tool operates, please refer to the help file included in PSP (choose Help, Help Topics from the menu bar) or the PSP 5 User Manual.

In addition, many of these commands are covered in depth elsewhere in this book. Look in the appropriate chapter or the index to find more information about each tool.

Appendixes

The Standard Toolbar

PSP 5's Standard Toolbar includes the following buttons: New File, Open File, Save File, Print, Undo, Cut, Copy, Paste, Full Screen Preview, Normal Viewing, and Help. Also included in the Standard Toolbar are four Palette Toggle buttons and a Histogram Window Toggle Button, which we will discuss in this section.

 NEW FILE: <CONTROL+N> Opens the New File dialog box to create a new image.

 OPEN FILE: <CONTROL+O> Opens the standard Windows 95 Open file dialog box.

 SAVE FILE: <CONTROL+S> Saves the active image.

 PRINT: <CONTROL+P> Prints the active image.

 UNDO: <CONTROL+Z> PSP's Multiple Undo function is an extremely useful feature. It reverses each previous step in order. To see a history of your last few commands, choose **Edit, Un**do History from the menu bar. The Undo option is only available during your current session (before you close PSP 5).

 CUT: <CONTROL+X> The cut option is only available after a selection has been made. When making a cut, the portion of the image that is cut is replaced by the current background color. The cut is also affected by options (such as the feather option) chosen from the Control Palette's Tool Control tab.

 COPY: <CONTROL+C> Copies the active window (if no selection is made) or the current selection to the clipboard. Does not affect the current active image in any way.

 PASTE AS A NEW IMAGE: <CONTROL+V> This button pastes the image or selection from the clipboard into a new image window. To paste into another image or selection, see the **Edit, P**aste options in the PSP menu bar.

FULL SCREEN PREVIEW: <SHIFT+CONTROL+A> Press this button to see the image displayed on a full screen (without any buttons) and with a black background. Press the Escape key to return to normal viewing.

 NORMAL VIEWING: <CONTROL+ALT+N> This is a quick way to return to normal viewing after a zoom. If you've zoomed in or out on an image and wish to return to 1:1 viewing, click this button once.

 HELP: <F1> Provides helpful information about Paint Shop Pro 5 in standard Windows Help format. This index can be browsed or searched.

PSP 5 Palettes

To control important areas of its functions, PSP contains four very useful palettes: Tool Palette, Control Palette, Color Palette, and Layer Palette. You'll find on/off toggle switches for each palette as buttons on your toolbar. If you ever lose any of your palettes, select the appropriate toggle buttons! Additionally, an on/off switch toggles the Histogram Window.

 TOGGLE TOOL PALETTE: This button toggles the Tool Palette on and off. The Image Tool palette contains various PSP tools available for use on images, such as cropping, painting, or adding text. By default, the Tool Palette runs down the left-hand side of the screen.

 TOGGLE CONTROL PALETTE: This button toggles the Control Palette on and off. The Control Palette is a new feature of PSP 5 that replaces the Style Bar from earlier versions. It incorporates PSP's brush options (shape, type, size, hardness, step, opacity, and density), which are located under the 'Brush Tip' tab, with various customized options available for each tool. You'll find these unique options for each command on the Tool Palette under the 'Tool Controls' tab. The Control Palette is dynamic, changing for each different tool that you select.

 TOGGLE COLOR PALETTE: This button toggles the Color Palette on and off. The Color Palette is the color center of PSP 5, showing the current foreground and background colors. You can also pick colors to use in your images from the Color Picker (rainbow display) within the Color Palette. This palette also displays the RGB or HEX value (depending upon how your preferences are set) of the current foreground and background colors.

Appendixes

TOGGLE LAYER PALETTE: This button toggles the layer palette off and on.

 TOGGLE HISTOGRAM WINDOW: This button toggles the Histogram window on and off. The Histogram window shows the levels of red, green, blue, and the luminance of the active image.

PSP's Image Toolbar

At the heart of PSP 5 are various tools used to create or manipulate images and graphics. They include the following tool buttons: Arrow, Zoom, Deform, Crop, Mover, Paint Brush, Clone Brush, Color Replacer, Retouch, Eraser, Picture Tube, Airbrush, Flood Fill, Text, Line, and Shapes, as well as three Selection tools: Freehand, Magic Wand, and Dropper.

Remember that each Tool has its own set of parameters, accessible through the Control Palette.

 ARROW TOOL: The Arrow tool is used much like a cursor is used in other Windows programs. You can use the Arrow tool to drag a window around by the title bar to another location within PSP 5 or to quit another tool. Choose the Arrow tool when you want a neutral cursor that won't make changes to the image.

 ZOOM TOOL: (View, Zoom In, and View, Zoom Out) The Zoom tool is used to zoom in and out of any image file. To zoom in, click on the Zoom tool to activate it, then left-click on an image. To zoom out, click the right mouse button. You can also use the preset drop-down dialog box on the Control Palette when you are within the Zoom tool. The zoom tool doesn't change the actual image size, just the viewing size.

 DEFORM TOOL: The Deform tool rotates, skews, or resizes an image layer or selection. If applying to a nonlayered image, you must first create a selection and then click within the selection to make the Deform tool available for use. If using the tool on a layered image, you need not make a selection or click with the mouse, as the tool should already be available. When using the Deform tool, PSP 5 will automatically select any nontransparent area within the current layer.

 CROP TOOL: Use this tool to crop a selected area. By using this tool rather than the plain rectangular selection marquee to crop an image, you can resize the selection area before you crop.

 MOVER TOOL: Moves a nonfloating selection (right-click and drag) or the uppermost layer and all layers linked to it (left-click and drag) to a different position within the image.

DROPPER TOOL: Allows you to pick an exact color from a pixel in an image, graphic, or from the rainbow color palette in the Color Palette toolbar. To use, select the Dropper tool, and move it over the pixel from the image you want to match. Click the left mouse button to set that color as the foreground color or the right mouse button to set the background color in the Color Palette.

PAINT BRUSH TOOL: Allows you to select a paint brush from a variety of sizes, shapes, and types. Other options include opacity, hardness, density, and step as well as whether to paint with a solid color or a paper texture. All paint brush options are located in the Control Palette.

CLONE BRUSH: Allows you to copy (or clone) part of an image within the same image, or into another image of the same color depth. Select the Clone tool then select a source area by right-clicking on the area of the image you wish to copy. Options for this tool are found in the Control Palette under the 'Tool Controls' tab. This tool is useful to cover up a defect by cloning the background over the defect. The clone brush has two different modes available in the Control Palette – Aligned and Non-Aligned. Aligned Mode is best demonstrated when a point is designated by right clicking in an image to designate the desired cloning point, then left click elsewhere in the image and take note of where the starting point of the source brush is.

COLOR REPLACER: The Color Replacer tool replaces a color within the image with another color. Options for this tool are displayed in the Control Palette under the "Tool Controls" tab, where you can control Color tolerance, Paper Texture, and Brush Tip options. There are many ways to replace colors using this tool. You can replace all of one color in an image with another, or you can select an area (using a selection tool) to apply the color replacement. Choose colors to replace by using the Dropper to select a background and foreground color. You can replace the background color with the foreground color by double-clicking anywhere in the image with the *left* mouse button. You can replace the foreground color with the background color by double-clicking anywhere in the image with the *right* mouse button. Similarly, you can also use a paint brush to replace background with foreground or vice versa (also using the *left* or *right* mouse buttons).

RETOUCH TOOL: The Retouch tool allow you to retouch an image or graphic using various brush sizes and options in various modes: lighten RGB, darken RGB, soften image, soften layer, sharpen, emboss, smudge image, smudge layer. You can also Retouch using PSP Paper Textures.

Appendixes

ERASER TOOL: Erases by painting with the background color on nonlayered images. On layered images with transparent backgrounds, it erases to the transparency. If the layer does not contain any transparency, it erases as in a nonlayered image, using the background color. Options available in the Control Palette are the same as for the Paint Brush tool—Brush Tip and Paper Texture options.

PICTURE TUBE: This fun new PSP tool can only be used on 24-bit color images (16.7 million color) or 256 grey scale images. You can increase the color depth of an image by choosing the following from the menu: **C**olors, **I**ncrease Color Depth, **16** Million Colors (24 bit).

This tool adds various images (cars, coins, pointing fingers, leaves, and such) complete with drop shadows, and scales them to size. Many different options that control the use of these images are linked to this tool. Experiment with Picture Tubes—they're lots of fun!

AIRBRUSH TOOL: The Airbrush tool acts much like a real airbrush spraying paint onto a surface. Paper Textures and Brush Tip options can be set in the Control Palette.

FLOOD FILL: The Flood Fill tool can be used to fill an image or selection with the current foreground or background color. Other options available in the Control Palette include Fill Style, Match Mode, Tolerance, and Opacity. Additionally, on 24-bit color or 8-bit grey scale images, the Flood Fill tool has options (located in the Fill Style drop-down box): to fill with a solid color, a pattern from another image, and four different gradient fills (sunburst, linear, rectangular, and radial gradients). You can also change the gradient's highlight.

TEXT TOOL: The Text Tool adds text to an image using any color, size, font, or attributes you select. To add text, choose the color you want the text to be as the foreground color, click on the Text Tool button then click inside the image to which you wish to add text.

The Add Text dialog box appears. Enter your text in the designated area, choose the font, font style, text effects, and alignment; then click **OK.** If the 'Floating' option has been checked (recommended), the text will appear as a floating selection. You can then move it into any position in the image. When you are satisfied with the position of the text, you can deselect it by using the keyboard shortcut 'Control+D'; by choosing **S**elections, Select **N**one on the menu bar; or by clicking the *right* mouse button.

LINE TOOL: The Line Tool adds various types of lines to the current image. To add a line to an image, click the Line Tool, position the cursor where you want the line to begin, and click and drag the cursor across the image. The options in the Control Palette are width (measured in pixels) of the line, type of line (Normal and Bezier [curved] and Antialias).

The Bezier option adds a curve to the line. To use this option, first create a new line, then click (or click and drag) near the line where you want the apex of the curve to be. The antialias option gives curved lines a smoother, nonpixelated appearance.

 SHAPES TOOL: The Shapes Tool creates various shapes, either filled or outlined. The shape options found in the Control Palette are circles, ellipses, squares, or rectangles. Shapes are outlined or filled with the current foreground color. The user determines the size and placement of the shape.

PSP's Selection Tools

PSP includes three selection tools, each of which can be used to customize selections in various ways. Some PSP 5 tools and options are only available (not greyed out) when a selection has been made. Selections appear as broken lines that move or march around the perimeter of the selected area(s).

With all selection tools, you can add to the selection by holding down the SHIFT key while selecting more area with one of the selection tools; or subtract from a selection by holding down the CONTROL key while selecting the area you wish to remove.

 SELECTION TOOL: This tool will create a plain rectangular, square, elliptical, or circular selection. Options to change the shape of the selection are found within drop-down boxes in the Control Palette.

 FREEHAND TOOL: This tool, which creates a freehand selection, is useful for tracing around portions of an image to make a polygon, or odd-shaped selection.

Appendixes

MAGIC WAND TOOL: This powerful tool allows you to make a selection based on a specific color match or range of colors within an image. The selection, based on a color tolerance value between 0 and 200, is determined by choosing (clicking on) a specific pixel in the image to be matched. After clicking on a specific pixel with the Magic Wand tool, PSP will select all pixels of the same color value or tolerance value within the image or within an area of the image. A zero value (no tolerance) selects only pixels of the exact same color. A 200-tolerance value selects virtually all pixels in the color spectrum. Additionally, you can choose an option in the Control Palette to feather the selection. Feathering means that an additional number of pixels is selected, regardless of how well they match the color tolerance.

Sometimes selecting an area of same or similar colored pixels in an image is necessary, and it would be impossible or impractical to do this with a plain marquee selection or a polygon freehand selection. This is where the Magic Wand selection tool comes into play. To select an area of similar colored pixels, set the tolerance to 0 and click on the pixel you wish to match with the Magic Wand tool. If the selection is what you want, you can stop. If not, increase the tolerance and try again. Try to click on the same pixel you did the first time because this directly affects which pixels are chosen. Check the selection and increase the tolerance again if necessary until your selection is as desired.

Index

Index

Index

MUSKA&LIPMAN

Order Form

Postal Orders:
    Muska & Lipman Publishing
    9525 Kenwood Road, Suite 16-372
    Cincinnati, Ohio 45242

On-Line Orders or for more information visit:
    http://www.muskalipman.com

Please send _____ copies of Creating Paint Shop Pro Web Graphics, Second Edition, by Andy Shafran at $44.99 per copy. My check or money order is enclosed for the total below.

Ship to:

    Company _____

    Name _____

    Address _____

    City _____ State _____ Zip _____ Country _____

_____ (number of books) x $44.99 = _____

Sales Tax   _____
(please add 6% for books shipped to Ohio addresses)

Shipping   _____
($4.00 for the first book, $2.00 each additional book)

TOTAL PAYMENT ENCLOSED   _____

Educational facilities, companies, and organizations interested in multiple copies of this book should contact the publisher for quantity discount information. Training manuals, CD-ROMs, electronic versions, and portions of this book are also available individually or can be tailored for specific needs.

Thank you for your order.